Filmosophy

Filmosophy

DANIEL FRAMPTON

WALLFLOWER PRESS
LONDON & NEW YORK

First published in Great Britain in 2006 by
Wallflower Press
6a Middleton Place, Langham Street, London W1W 7TE
www.wallflowerpress.co.uk

A catalogue for this book is available from the British Library

ISBN 1-904764-84-3 (pbk)
ISBN 1-904764-85-1 (hbk)

Book design by Elsa Mathern

Printed by Replika Press Pvt Ltd., India

contents

For my Mum and Dad
Evelyn and Douglas Frampton

acknowledgements

I'd like to thank, in a somewhat chronological order:

My father's father, Frederick Frampton, for being a photographer and passing on his equipment, eventually, to me.

My mother and father, for fairly obvious reasons, and also for great and ineffable reasons.

My brothers, David and Saul, for inexplicable and unprintable reasons.

Two early teachers from Kettering, the artists Bob Pollak and John Pearson.

Colin MacCabe and John O. Thompson, for inspiring and jumpstarting the whole caboodle.

Birkbeck College and the British Film Institute.

The British Academy; Paul, Malcolm and James at Channel Films; and John Sayers at Firefilms, for their financial assistance.

Laura Mulvey, for shaking some sense into the text.

Giles Frampton and Cynthia Clerk, for putting me up.

Ian Christie and Geoffrey Nowell-Smith, for their critiques.

D. N. Rodowick and Lionel Bently, for their encouragement and advice.

Yoram Allon and the team at Wallflower Press.

And my friends Julie Bush, Alison Fydler, Kate Godman, Nick Makasis and Michael Williams, for keeping me going.

London, UK
September 2006

introduction

In the summer of 1896 Maxim Gorky attended a screening of the Lumière Cinematograph in Nizhi-Novgorod, Russia, and famously recorded his experience of this early silent black and white projection for a local newspaper:

> Last night I was in the Kingdom of Shadows. If you only knew how strange it is to be there. It is a world without sound, without colour. Everything there – the earth, the trees, the people, the water and the air – is dipped in monotonous grey. Grey rays of the sun across the grey sky, grey eyes in grey faces, and the leaves of the trees are ashen grey. It is not life but its shadow, it is not motion but its soundless spectre.[1]

A hundred years later, on the DVD of *Contact*, Jodie Foster offers her own commentary on the making of the film, and at one point talks about a simple conversation scene between her character and her love interest, played by Matthew McConaughey. Foster points out, with not a little shock, the fact that the director, Robert Zemekis, had digitally readjusted her facial expression at one point. Zemekis had removed her eyebrow movement in a way to make her character react differently to McConaughey. Foster seemed obviously annoyed – not only that her original performance was deemed unsuitable, but that her person had almost been violated by a digital effect: 'Stop fooling with my face!' she says.

Both Gorky and Foster are illustrating a simple fact about cinema: that it has never been, and is definitely becoming less and less, a simple and direct reproduction of reality. Cinema is a world of its own – whether a grey soundless shadowy world, or a fluidly manipulatable one. This film-world is a flat, ordered, compressed world; a world that is subtly, almost invisibly organised. A world that is a *cousin* of reality. And the multiplicity of moving-image media in the twenty-first century means that this film-world has become the second world we live in. A second world that feeds and shapes our perception and understanding of reality. So it seems especially important that we get to grips with the moving image, that we come up with a sufficient range of conceptual frameworks by which to understand it. Because before we can confidently argue a sociology of the cinema we must have an adequate range of moving image philosophies. That is, before we can talk confidently about the social *effects* of film we first must study the personal *affects* of film – how film affects us directly, emotionally. And both philosophers and film theorists have been doing this since cinema was invented. They have realised that how we engage with film informs and reflects how we engage with reality – and that the nature of aesthetic experience, as a form of knowledge, is as valid as rational thought. For Immanuel Kant aesthetic judgement is not a conceptual, intellectual judgement: we are necessarily aesthetic beings with a natural aesthetic emotion and a practical appetite, a rational need, for emotions such as wonder and pleasure. The brain is mobilised by the eye; beauty lies in the eye of the beholder; therefore if beauty is removed, we are removed – that is how important aesthetics is to philosophy. We are not aesthetic beings only during some sort of 'contemplation' in front of art works; we are thinking aesthetically all the time – framing our friends, meditating on vistas, even while watching television. And the validity of this aesthetic thinking is being proved ever more important in this visually saturated age.

But forget culture and theories and philosophies for just for a moment, and think of film, just film – think simply of the personal experience of film: what does it present that we find interesting and thoughtful? What kind of world does it show? Why is it both strange and familiar? What does its separateness and its closeness reveal? We all enjoy film fictions – these unmessy, streamlined stories – partly because we live a bad wondering script that seems to take a lifetime to get going (perhaps we all secretly want to live a film-life). And I am quite happy to admit that going to the cinema can be a classic wish for escape – a daydream drug. The expectation as you arrive and take your seat is part of the pleasure: it is an expectation of enjoyment, of gaining knowledge, of aesthetic rejuvenation, of spectacle and forgetting. And the cinema's darkness seems very necessary for the full encounter between film and filmgoer: we lose our bodies and our minds take over, working alone, locked to the film-world.

And when I leave the cinema I personally often feel drained and confused, almost disconnected, if only for a few moments. Reality now appears random, structureless, chaotic. This blinking return from another world is an experience in itself – bearings are found and sustenance is sought (usually at the nearest pub). It takes time for the film to leave my head; and it takes time for reality to become real again – time for my mind and body to re-adjust. But some films have a longer, lingering effect: not always an altering, transfiguration of reality, but a gentle continuing inhabitation of our perceptions. Life outside the cinema is released, illuminated, freed-up. Time is elongated and movements magnified – my perceptions become images: my eyes become cameras, unafraid to lock onto faces or scenes or moments. Film reveals reality, exactly by showing a distorted mirror of it. Film transforms the recognisable (in a small or large way), and this immediate transfiguration provokes the idea that our thinking can transform our world. The feeling when you step out of the cinema can result in a new realisation, a change, 'a little knowledge'. Why do we feel this way? What does film do to create this feeling? It appears that film, in some of its forms, can rejig our encounter with life, and perhaps even heighten our perceptual powers. Cinema allows us to re-see reality, expanding our perceptions, and showing us a new reality. Film challenges our view of reality, forcing a phenomenological realisation about how reality is perceived by our minds.

It is the unique way that film takes and refigures reality that seems to be behind this effect on the filmgoer. But do we always need to start with questions about cinema's 'relationship to reality' in order to understand film? Writers always pose the relationship, but then find they need to stretch it out of all recognition. For example, for the mysterious early French theorist Yhcam, writing in 1912, film presents 'an improbable realism'.[2] Writing six years later, Emile Vuillermoz, a French music critic by profession, noted that cinema seems to produce a 'superreality' which may be 'more intense than the truth'.[3] Just because cinema usually shows us a recognisable world does not mean we have to work out 'why it isn't a copy of reality', but how it is a new reality, *a new world*. The epistemological difference is the key here – and, for a filmmaker like Vsevolod Pudovkin, the key to understanding film as art: 'Between the natural event and its appearance on the screen there is a marked difference. It is exactly this difference that makes the film an art.'[4] In one sense the world 'taken' by film is immediately transfigured, but it might also be argued that it is only a certain cinematic slice of the world that appears, that when the camera is turned-over a certain kind of reality pushes its way to the front, like a star-struck wannabe. This *cinematic reality* was noted by the German theorist Walter Benjamin, who saw that 'a different nature opens itself to the camera than opens to the naked eye'.[5]

In his 1971 book *The World Viewed* the American philosopher Stanley Cavell reminds us that part of the reason we enjoy cinema so much is simply because we have a natural wish to see the world recreated and retold in its own image. For Cavell, cinema is about artists reorganising pictures of reality as best they can: film is a succession of 'automatic world projections' given significance by 'artistic discoveries of form and genre and type and technique'; the film-artist simply masters and deploys these 'automatisms' as creatively as they can.[6] The poetry of film, for Cavell, is 'what it is that happens to figures and objects and places as they are variously moulded and displaced by a motion-picture camera and then projected and screened'.[7] This remoulded world exists beyond us (and perhaps reflects our estrangement from our own world): 'The "sense of reality" provided on film is the sense of *that* reality, one from which we already sense a distance.'[8] Cavell's film-world is a distant copy of reality, a reality that is reorganised by the artist. He continues by asking whether film is a recording of a past performance, or a performance of an always present recording. Are we seeing things that are not 'present'? How can this be if we accept that the film itself is present? Cavell's first conclusion is that the reality in film 'is present to me while I am not present to it; and a world I know, and see, but to which I am nevertheless not present … is a world past.'[9] It is only a hundred or so pages later that he reconsiders this position: 'the world created is neither a world just past nor a world of make-believe. It is a world of an immediate future.'[10] It is in this sense that Cavell seems to find a world existing in passing, a world neither now nor then, but new.

An author with a similar outlook to Cavell is the English film theorist V. F. Perkins. For Perkins, film subtly alters the reality it records, changing time and space relations, yet the end product is a 'solid world which exists in its own right.'[11] But Perkins argues that many early theorists were unable to assign recorded action any artistic worth, and that film can only shape what it first must record. The obvious point to make here is that nowadays it is hard to find a film that *does not* include some images of places or people that were never in front of the camera (digital stand-ins, imaginary backdrops, computer-designed buildings). Film is no longer a question of automatic photography – even without considering the classic artistry of the simple choice of angle, exposure, and so forth – and to *generalise* that the film-world is a simple copy of reality seems limiting. Modern computer-generated imagery not only makes Perkins' statement from 1972 that everything that happens on the screen in a live-action picture 'has happened in front of the camera' historical, but also demands of us a great re-thinking of the cinematic image.[12] It is exactly this possible fluidity of the film image – this new digitally manipulatable film image – that might make us realise that we need (and in fact have always needed) a new conception of film.

Yes film *uses* the real; but it takes it and immediately moulds it and then refigures it and puts it back in front of the filmgoer as interpretation, as re-perception. Film recording technology automatically changes reality, and the filmmaker artistically refigures reality. For a start, film flattens reality, a notion Cavell characterises as 'the ontological equality of objects and human subjects in photographs.'[13] Characters and buildings and vistas and objects are no longer real, no longer part of nature, but part of cinema. Locking all film to reality disenfranchises the possibilities of film poetry by *conceptually* limiting the routes of film style and world. To get the most out of film, we might acknowledge that film is not *of* the world, film *is* a world (a new world). Film is not simply a reproduction of reality, it is its own world with its own intentions and creativities. Cinema is the projection, screening, showing, of *thoughts of the real*.

The argument of this book is premised upon the idea that film presents a unique world, almost a future-world (not least because the film's 'experience' of its people and objects feels 'new'). Film is its own world with its own rules (and philosophy should certainly learn from its fluid re-situating of experience and knowledge). This creation of a new (immaterial, possible) world is even acknowledged by some fictions: *The Usual Suspects*, the film itself, seems to immediately 'think' the precise worlds recounted by the character Verbal.[14] Part of the project of this book is to question the *conceptual* link between cinema and reality (while simultaneously pushing the transfiguring effect cinema can have on our understanding and perception of reality). There is no doubt that most cinema starts with a recording of reality, but the argument here is that the filmgoer would be impoverished by understanding cinema only in relation to the reality it records. It will surely become more and more tiring to continually compare and contrast the increasingly fluid world of cinema to our own reality.

Film might now be understood as creating its *own* world, *free* to bring us any scene or object it wishes. Film becomes less a reproduction of reality than a *new* reality, that merely sometimes looks like our reality (can be different like film noir, or different like the other world of *Star Wars: Episode 1 – The Phantom Menace*). Film is not transparent, but dependent on the film's *beliefs* as regards the things it portrays. The continual comparison to 'the real' has handicapped film studies, has disallowed a radical reconceptualisation of film-being. Contemporary cinema has given us an endlessly animatable film-world that can be whatever it likes, go anywhere, think anything – 'gigantic visions of mankind crushed by the juggernaut of war and then blessed by the angel of peace may arise before our eyes with all their spiritual meaning', as Hugo Münsterberg noted in 1916.[15] This powerful film-world reveals itself in any form – and so the spiritual metaphors can go on: maybe there is a God and she is busily thinking our world. Perhaps our enjoyment of the experience of film stems from our wish to be part of a perfect world, created by an 'absolute mind'? Film's different reality (film's re-thinking of reality-like objects) creates it own (more formal) question of subjectivity and objectivity. For instance, while Münsterberg argued that film is pre-eminently *a medium of subjectivity*, André Bazin understood cinema as 'objectivity in time'.[16] There may be no possible objective view of the real world, but the view of the film-world is the only one available, and thus 'objective' – yet the images of film also often appear to be 'subjective'.

For Münsterberg the film-world is a complete transfiguration of the real world. Film moves away from reality, and towards the mind. It is the mind that creates this transfiguration, recreating the world in its own form. Film should therefore be seen as its own imagination (*even* when it initially looks normal and realistic). Films have a different space, a space that resembles reality, but flat and bordered. The frame of film makes for a rational space – a decided, intended space – with rational and non-rational thinkings. Film is another world, a new world, an organised world, a constructed world, a world thought-out, and as filmgoers we usually enjoy being swamped by this 'artificial intelligence'. Benjamin intuitively understood the difference between life and cinema: 'an unconsciously penetrated space is substituted for a space consciously explored by man'.[17]

Through cinema man was able to control reality. Film can thus be seen as an incredibly unique and therefore important link between man and world: film becomes the *explanation* of our position in the world – film acts out an interaction with a world, which thus becomes a mirror for us to recognise *our* interaction with our world. This acting out is a kind of intention, a kind of thought. The film-world is an ordered and thought-out world – characters meet and move on and love and die and find themselves, all in about two hours flat. The philosopher Gilles Deleuze found that cinema resembled a higher, spiritual life: 'the domain of cold decision, of absolute determination (*entêtement*), of a choice of existence'.[18] The creation of this film-world is set and immovable and thus untouchable, unchangeable – it is unwavering intention, decision, choice, belief: a filmic kind of thought.

***

Filmosophy is a study of film as thinking, and contains a theory of both film-being and film form. The 'filmind' is filmosophy's concept of film-being, the theoretical originator of the images and sounds we experience, and 'film-thinking' is its theory of film form, whereby an action of form is seen as the dramatic thinking of the filmind. In a sense filmosophy can therefore be understood as an extension and integration of theories of both para-narrational 'showing' and mise-en-scène aesthetics. *Filmosophy proposes that seeing film form as thoughtful, as the dramatic decision of the film, helps us understand the many ways film can mean and affect.* There are two aspects to contemporary film that provoked the idea of filmosophy: that both the unreliable narrator and non-subjective 'point of view' shot are becoming more and more common, and that it has become digitally malleable and free to show virtually anything. To *creatively* and *positively* handle these new forms film studies needs a conception of film-world creation, and a descriptive language of film style, that are both adaptable and poetic.

The filmind is not an empirical description of film, but rather a *conceptual* understanding of the origins of film's actions and events. That is, the filmgoer can decide to use it as part of their conceptual apparatus while experiencing a film – they would then see the film *through* this concept. Filmosophy conceptualises film as an organic intelligence: a 'film being' thinking about the characters and subjects in the film. Yet the concepts of the filmind and film-thinking are not intended as replacements for the concepts of 'narrator' and 'narration', but are simply proposals that reflect the limits of the idea of 'the narrator' and the restrictive and literary nature of theories of 'narration' (the former is incapable of accounting for the creation of film-worlds, and the latter is limited in that it traditionally only handles that which cannot be attributed to character-narrators). The filmind is not an 'external' force, nor is it a mystical being or invisible other, it is 'in' the film itself, it is *the film* that is steering its own (dis)course. The filmind is 'the film itself'.

There are two aspects to the filmind: the creation of the basic film-world of recognisable people and objects, and the designing and refiguring this film-world. This re-creational designing and refiguring is here called 'film-thinking'. One particular sentence in Deleuze's *Cinema* is helpful in understanding film-thinking: 'It is the camera, and not a dialogue, which *explains* why the hero of *Rear Window* has a broken leg (photos of the racing car, in his room, broken camera).'[19] The film surveys the tenement courtyard before returning to Jeffries, asleep in his chair, his leg in a cast, at which point it then moves through his apartment to show the photo of a crashing racing car and a smashed camera. Film-thinking is thus the action of film form in dramatising the intention of the filmind. Importantly, filmosophy does not make a direct analogy between human thought and film, because film is simply different to our ways of thinking and perceiving: as we have noted, film seems at once subjective and objective in its actions of form. Rather there is a functional analogy: film's constant, never-ending 'intent' and attitude to its characters and spaces is here conceptualised as a (new kind of) 'thinking'. Phenomenological metaphors of human perception would limit the meaning possibilities of film (the camera would then be 'another character', and any non-human-like actions of the camera would be signs of excessiveness or reflexivity). Film-thinking resembles no one single kind of human thought, but perhaps the functional spine of human thinking – film-thinking seems to be a combination of idea, feeling and emotion.

Filmosophy is designed as an organic philosophy of film. The filmind allows the filmgoer to experience the film as a drama issuing from itself, rather than taking them further outside the experience to the actions of authors, directors or invisible narrators. The concept of the filmind also means that the whole film is intended, making all formal moves important or possibly meaningful, enlarging the experience of film, and helping the filmgoer *relate* to the formal twists and turns of film. And the concept of film-thinking is organic in two further senses: that it binds form to content, and that it also evolves smoothly into a language of describing film that positively affects the experience of the filmgoer. An organic relation of concept to film to language to experience (to philosophy). The concept of film-thinking bonds form to content by making style part of the action: the experience of film becomes in some sense 'organic' because style is tied to the story with natural, thoughtful, humanistic terms of intention that make film forms dramatic rather than technical. In filmosophy form is not an appendix to content, but simply more content itself (just of a different nature).

How a person is 'shot' can now be seen not just as 'relating' to that person in an indirect, metaphorical way, but a *becoming* of that person's character, or perhaps a thinking of the film's idea of that person. When a film frames a person that act of framing creates a way of seeing that person (as central or peripheral or close-up). The filmgoer sees that person via the film's thinking of that person – this thinking is simply the action of form as dramatic intention. This effect is enhanced by the film-goer's understanding of film's actions as emotional thinkings – through this engagement they merge with the film a little more fully, because their natural aesthetic thinking links more directly with the film. The filmgoer experiences film more intuitively, not via technology or external authorship, but directly, as a thinking thing. In making 'style' integral to the film's thinking (and not an addendum to its 'main content work'), filmosophy hopes to widen and deepen the experience of the filmgoer. Film form is always there, and thus necessarily part of the actions and events, and filmosophy simply, holistically, bonds film's actions to dramatically thoughtful motives and intentions. Film style is now seen to be the dramatic intention of the film itself.

The most obvious result of reconceptualising film as thinking is a change in how we talk about film. First of all it does a necessary job of highlighting the worth and importance of image and sound, something simply missing, in direct terms, from a lot of film writing. The concepts of filmosophy advance on this 'match' between film and filmgoer by providing a more 'suitable' rhetoric derived from the concept of film-thinking. One of the heartfelt aims of the book is to popularise the possibilities of film (of all moving sound-images) by reinventing the language of its description. Too little is written about the power and impact of images – the writing on film that reaches the public is almost exclusively led by plot and acting and cultural references. My argument is that reconceptualising film as thinking will hopefully allow a more poetic entry to the intelligence of film. Filmosophy does not just offer a *linking* of thinking to film (not just an interest in making the comparison), but an analysis of film as its own kind of thought. It is not merely a question of resolving the puzzle of what makes film be, because it is just as important how we construct its theory, its *language of image description*, and its role for interpretation.

Perhaps the study of film and philosophy should die in order to be reborn. It is the linking 'and' that not just separates the two disciplines but disfigures the balance. Like literary theorists in the 1970s, philosophers are turning from Socrates to fiddling about with a video player (and probably not getting a picture). And all that many of them really want to do is simply brighten up a lecture by showing a few scenes from a classic movie or two. These philosophers are simply concerned with how some films *contain* stories and characterisations that helpfully *illustrate* well-known philosophical ideas. But cinema is more than a handy catalogue of philosophical problems, and to say that film can only present ideas in terms of story and dialogue is a narrow, literary view of film's possible force and impact. If the starting point for these philosophers is 'what can film do *for philosophy?*', how long will it take for them to realise what film *offers* philosophy?

So much writing within the area of 'film and philosophy' simply ignores cinematics and concentrates on stories and character motivations. It only takes one character to say 'man is not an island' for somebody to jump up and declare the film philosophical (if someone were to recount a moral fable while doing a jig, then that could be claimed to be 'dance as philosophy'). These are writings that rely much too heavily on the set subjects of academic philosophy, adding the two disciplines together like oil and water: film 'plus' philosophy. Much of this writing takes the form of philosophy offering its services to film, that is, taking a paternal, patronising, condescending stance: the film does not realise what philosophical problem lies within it, philosophy shall show the real, hidden worth of film (to help philosophy). Like academic SAS squads they come in to sort out the mess left by film studies. This is an infecting of film by philosophy. These writers are very simply and effectively *using* film to teach philosophy courses – using film to illustrate philosophy's classic problems and questions. Their attention is only on the story of the film (dialogue and plot outlines and character motivations), and the film is then quickly left behind while they elaborate on the problem. These classical problems of dried-up philosophy departments are *forced* onto film stories – they may as well simply make up a story of a friend of a friend instead of making some readers believe they are *actually telling us something about film*. In a sense they encourage yet another wave of film students to ignore the moving sound-image and concentrate on characters and story.

But the survival of a new-born interdisciplinary subject depends on how well it does actually create a *new* type of study (one that can then continue the revolution by being nomadic in *its* future travels). There is no doubt that film offers dramas that can play as putty in the hands of philosophers. Some film stories do play-out well-known philosophical ideas, and it is most probably philosophers that are best suited to understanding them, but films are more than this, and carry more than dialogue and plot. Some of these writers also still use staid, literary terms, borrowed from those 1970s literature departments, and these exterior (non-site-specific) concepts steer analyses away from the forms of film – whereas studying film for its own (site-specific, cinematic) philosophical worth should open interesting future questions. Philosophy needs to work *for* film studies to re-balance the weight of writings that search films for philosophical illustrations. Working *through* film philosophically, rather than applying philosophy to film, reveals film to be much more 'philosophical' than the latter method could ever produce. As Deleuze writes: 'I was able to write on cinema, not by right of reflection, but when philosophical problems led me to seek answers in cinema, which itself then relaunched other problems.' [20]

So part of the argument of this book is that the questions film philosophy has posed – about how film transfigures its subjects, how it communicates ideas, how it resembles memory and dream and poetry, how it beautifully and gracefully mingles with our minds – can find direction and illumination in the work of filmosophy, and its two main concepts: the filmind and film-thinking. With this incursion of film-thinking into the subject of film philosophy we have new forms of philosophical film to discuss. Where before some were content to write about films that 'contained' philosophical musings or problems, now certain films can been understood as 'thinking philosophically'. Then we can ask: how *Ulysses' Gaze* thinks about landscape and humanity; how *Fight Club* thinks about the self and psychosis; how *The Scent of Green Papaya* thinks about love.

Focusing, editing, camera movement, sound, framing – all 'think' a certain relation to the story being told. Of course there are no shapes and colours to *specific* ideas, or else film would be reduced to language. Philosophy produces ideas in the precise sense, and film is a poetical thinking that achieves a different kind of philosophicalness; a languageless thinking that Wittgenstein saw as impossible in everyday talk. And it is we who complete the thoughts of film, who decide, if we so wish, on the ideas to be gained from a film. Filmosophy ultimately aims to release the image from its secondary position in human interaction – by realising the thoughtful capacity of film. In moving towards an understanding of just what can be thoughtfully achieved cinematically, filmosophy attempts to find the *philosophical* in the movements and forms of film. If this is a new kind of thinking, what does it mean for our thinking, and what can film philosophically imagine? What are the philosophical implications of understanding film in this way? How has philosophy attempted to think with images? How might we practically apply film-thinking to current philosophical problems and discussions? How might we utilise this nonconceptual thinking for philosophy? Philosophy should thus make of film a companion in concept-creation. Film possibly contains a whole new system of thought, a new episteme – perhaps the new concepts of philosophy might even find their paradigms in cinema. Philosophy is not just a subject, but a practice, a creative practice, and film provides a philosopher such as Deleuze with as much conceptual creation as science and philosophy itself: 'Cinema is one type of image. Between different types of aesthetic image, scientific functions and philosophical concepts, there are currents of mutual exchange, with no overall primacy of any one field.'[21] We need to recognise that film can add a new kind of thought to philosophy, which can be helped by the full understanding of imagistic thinking. In turn, philosophy then becomes *another kind of film*.

Filmosophy does not aim to be a solution to film studies, but should be used and changed and adapted alongside other perspectives and interpretive schemas – a purely filmosophical reading of a film is only a partial reading, one to be added to other insights and approaches. This book is consciously designed as a provocation, a manifesto almost: hopefully it should create questions, but also possibilities of application. In this sense it aims to open a new conversation (about film as thinking), one to be argued with, and discussed, and extended where necessary. 'Filmosophy' is not a difficult word to arrive at, and echoes the neologisms of the 1920s – as Ricciotto Canudo wrote in 1923: 'Cinegraphy, cineology, cinemania, cinephilia and cinephobia, cinepoetry and cinoedia, cinematurgy, cinechromism – the list goes on. Only time and chance will tell what terminology will stay with us.'[22]

***

Finally, a note on the layout of the following chapters. Part One is a four-chapter investigation into the linking of film and thinking in the twentieth century, beginning with 'Film Minds', which looks at how film has been variously understood as a visualisation of our thoughts, memories or subconscious, and asks whether film is itself a 'subjective' or 'objective' medium, or perhaps even another kind of thought, a future form of thinking. Chapter two surveys the different film-beings explored by writers: film as camera 'I' or virtual creator, as ghostly or absent author, or as some kind of narratological or post-narratological being. Chapter three considers the impact of phenomenology, and discusses Maurice Merleau-Ponty, Vivian Sobchack and the question of the film's 'experience' of the film-world. Chapter four looks at more nuanced theories of film as thinking, such as Antonin Artaud's pure cinema, Jean Epstein's lyrosophy, Roger Gilbert-Lecomte's future cinema, Sergei Eisenstein's theories of montage and Jean Louis Schefer's experimental dummy, but concentrates on Deleuze's concepts of the mental image and the relation-image.

Part Two concerns the ideas and arguments of filmosophy, and starts by setting out the central concepts of the filmind and film-thinking, looking at how the filmind both creates and re-creates the film-world, and how film-thinking intends through film forms in a transsubjective and postphenomenological way. Chapter six then compares and contrasts the activity of the filmind with classic theories of narration, and chapter seven continues the explication of film-thinking through a multitude of film examples, considering various formal categories: image, colour, sound, focus, speed, framing, movement and edit shifts. Chapter eight discusses cognitivist and phenomenological theories of the filmgoer, before outlining the make-up of a filmosophical filmgoer who actively merges with the affective thinking of film. Chapter nine critiques the technicist rhetoric of much film writing, and argues that the concept of film-thinking provides a more poetic and dramatic rhetoric for film interpretation. And the final chapter, 'Filmosophy', considers the movement in philosophy towards the metaphorical imaging of problems and ideas, and argues that film enacts a kind of 'post-metaphysical thinking' that creates pure concepts within a nonphilosophy.

part one

one | **film minds**

The thousands of tiny frames in a moving filmstrip act like the cells of the human brain: the same overwhelming rapidity of perception, the same multiplicity of many-faceted mirrors which effortlessly juxtapose the farthest horizons, suppress distances, abolish the bondage of time and space, embrace all the cardinal points [of the compass] simultaneously, and transport us in a fraction of a second from one extreme point of the universe to another!

– Emile Vuillermoz (1917)[1]

Since its invention film has been compared to the mind, whether through analogy with human perception, dreams or the subconscious. The shock of seeing a world 'freed' by man's imagination caused many early writers to see a profound link between the mind of the filmgoer and the film itself, leading them to understand film as a mirror of mindful intent. In a sense film offers us our first experience of an *other* experience (the experience of the film camera as it were). Film seems to be a double phenomenology, a double intention: our perception of the film, and the film's perception of its world. Thus our understanding of our world can be informed and changed by this other way of experiencing a world, this other view of a similar world. Whether resembling an omniscient mind or our own consciousness, seeing film as thought-like opens the door to new and interesting avenues. The task is to search through the poetic and the radical in order to provoke new philosophies of film style and meaning.

Early reaction to cinema was almost unavoidably philosophical. In a conversation published in 1985 Deleuze noted that 'cinema critics, the greatest critics anyway, became philosophers the moment they set out to formulate an aesthetics of cinema. They weren't trained as philosophers, but that's what they became.'[2] The first writers were philosophers by necessity – a new art demanded new thinking. These early writers put forward the case of film as art by situating film as the direct creation of the mind and imagination, so as to place it alongside music and painting. (The competitiveness of these early writers should also not be forgotten – who can come up with the purest, most poetic theory of cinema, and so forth.)

For example, in 1926 the screenwriter and theorist Gerard Fort Buckle, though mainly concerned with the *effect* of film on the mind, likened film actions (focusing, angles of frame, movement) to the actions our mind and/or body performs. His simple version of a film mind was 'the artificial or changeable angle of conception, that is, the angle of conception which is determined by the mode of expression or, in other words, technique'.³ Technique produces a particular conception: film thinks around and about its subject. There are no limitations to the mode of expression of film. André Bazin, co-founder of the seminal journal *Cahiers du cinéma*, perhaps hints at this kind of thinking: film 'has a thousand ways of acting on the appearance of an object so as to eliminate any equivocation and to make of this outward sign one and only one inner reality'.⁴

These writers who link film with the mind are few, and sparsely scattered through the twentieth century. They all saw ideas of the mind as an ultimate in relation to film. The mind, the brain and consciousness all became the locale of visual flights, without a wire or a safety net. Mindful of the plethora of metaphors that have gone before – film as eye, as writing, as music, as painting or inscribing with light – I intend to show the lasting importance of understanding all the ways in which film can be linked to thinking, whether fictional, human or other. In this chapter, the first of four to consider the history of the linking of film and thinking, I shall look at some of the mindful ways in which writers have conceptualised film: how film might be understood as a recording of the brain (Edward Small, Parker Tyler), a visualisation of our thoughts and memories (Henri Bergson, Germaine Dulac, Pierre Quesnoy), or similar in form to our subconscious (Emile Vuillermoz, Ricciotto Canudo); how film shows the subjectivity of characters' thoughts in film (Antonin Artaud, Bruce Kawin), and whether film is itself a 'subjective' or 'objective' medium (Hugo Münsterberg); and finally how some writers (Roger Gilbert-Lecomte, Béla Balázs) have realised that film perhaps reveals another kind of thought, a future form of thinking.

Visualising thought

The most direct analogy to be made is that between film and the actual workings of the brain, and much of the theorising that posits this link has been inspired by viewings of experimental film, usually by those that actually work within and write about this genre. In 1980 Edward Small did not argue that film merely acts like a mind, but that (non-narrative experimental) film has the ability to show *mental states*.⁵ Small considered what it might be to *correctly* show various mental states in cinema: how it might precisely show vision, imagination, memory, dream (which provokes questions of how we use images in our thinking).[6] Here the mental is only conceived of in relation to avant-garde, experimental, abstract or 'eidetic' cinema. For Small (as for Eisenstein and Artaud, as we shall see later), only some sort of *pure cinema* can 're-produce' the human mind, and he argues that psychologists could learn from film's portrayal of mental states, and filmmakers could also use psychological theories to perfect their representation of those states.

But it seems nonsensical to argue that cinema makes thought visible. The idea of film recording the brain conjures up (in a strange circular sense) abstract blurry images. The road that writers such as Small take appears a dead end – how could one ever exactly reproduce the brain's imagery? Would not such images only make sense in their original form? It would seem more fruitful and more interesting to form a new course of thinking that was designed via *film's* possibilities. Yet in 1972 Parker Tyler wrote with a similar bent to Small:

> The whole film strip and its revolving images are simply an embodiment of the way the mind works … the closest we can come to the world's naked presence through a medium, till perchance a machine be invented to record the image-by-image processes of the brain.[7]

For Tyler film is uniquely able to show how we think with our imagination – the function of film is to become this mental process. Tyler theorises a particularly ontological consciousness as regards his version of the film mind: he imagines how film can literally photograph 'the life of the mind as the mind converts images into ideas'.[8] For Tyler the film work is a portrait of the brain's content – yet, not only does Tyler fail to produce winning examples, but his poetic rhetoric and philosophy of cinema carries him on to theorise film from multiple and faintly contradictory perspectives. Ultimately Tyler holds a strange 'film-thinking' theory, as his 'film' thinks less via camera and montage than through the subjective actions of characters.

In her 1953 essay 'A Note on the Film', Susanne Langer realises that film is free from spatial and temporal restrictions, and quotes approvingly from R. E. Jones' 1941 book *The Dramatic Imagination*:

> Motion pictures are our thoughts made visible and audible. They flow in a swift succession of images, precisely as our thoughts do, and their speed, with their flashbacks – like sudden uprushes of memory – and their abrupt transition from one subject to another, approximates very closely the speed of our thinking. They have the rhythm of the thought-stream and the same uncanny ability to move for-

ward or backward in space or time … They project pure thought, pure dream, pure inner life.[9]

And 19 years later V. F. Perkins also ventures a direct link, a mirror, between film and thinking, finding editing to be freely able to re-enact the dream-like imaginative associations of the mental process. He also assigns value to those moments,

> when narrative, concept and emotion are most completely fused … such moments compose a unity between record, statement and experience … observation, thought and feeling are integrated: film becomes the projection of a mental universe – a mind recorder … where there is no distinction between how and what, content and form.[10]

It is here that Perkins slips from what might be unique, a mental universe, to what would be (if it ever could be) impenetrable: a recording of the mind.

But the most common analogy has been with our conscious thinking – with the perceptions of the mind: our day-to-day thought, our imagination, our memories. For the French film director and theorist Germaine Dulac, writing in 1924, the cinema can match in expression our thinking and emotions: 'What is more mobile than our psychological life with its reactions, its manifold impressions, its sudden movements, its dreams, its memories? The cinema is marvellously *equipped* to express these manifestations of our thinking.'[11] For another early theorist, Pierre Quesnoy writing in 1928, film can *feel* time and memory in ways similar to the novels of Marcel Proust – superimpositions and shifts to markedly different scenes painting the psychological evolution of characters (subjective experience and triggered memories, for instance).[12] The philosopher Henri Bergson also noticed a link between cinema and memory (namely, mental imagery) and wondered whether it was possible to see cinema as a model of consciousness itself. In an interview with *Le Journal* in 1914 Bergson remarked:

> As a witness to its beginnings, I realised [the cinema] could suggest new things to a philosopher. It might be able to assist in the synthesis of memory, or even of the thinking process. If the circumference [of a circle] is composed of a series of points, memory is, like the cinema, composed of a series of images. Immobile, it is in neutral state; in movement it is life itself.[13]

Commentating on Bergson in 1992, Paul Douglass found him to be realising that, like philosophy, cinema 'has evolved toward a greater awareness of reality-as-mobility', and that early cinema can be seen as 'an example of the spatialising tendency of the mind'.[14] But Bergson was hostile to cinema, and attacked the 'cinematograph-ical illusion' for breaking up movement, and cutting up the fluidity of life into 'still lifes'.

Yet while hardly convincing – cinema and memory are both 'composed of a series of images' – the analogy floats in a relationship between the intentional colouring of (past) experience in human memory (my rosy childhood), and the way cinema can colour its objects and subjects with all the elements of film form. Cinema *believes* in its objects just as we have a *belief* about our past. Film can thus possibly help us understand our own forms of memory and recollection. Metaphors and illustrations of memory are a starting point for realising film's capacities of thinking. That film not only 'resembles' thinking, but that using 'thinking' as a concept for understanding film helps us solve some questions around film's intention and meaning.

Perhaps the next level of theorising links film to our subconscious life (rather than conscious thoughts). As we saw at the beginning of this chapter, Emile Vuillermoz noted film's cerebral connections way back in 1917 – frames as cells, camera as per-ception, editing as imagination – and a year later suggested that film is 'an explora-tion of the subconscious', adding that 'some day one might photograph the music of the soul and fix its changing visage on the screen in rhythmic images'.[15] For the 'cerebralist' Ricciotto Canudo (who inspired Abel Gance's filmmaking), film presents and must exactly develop, 'the extraordinary and striking faculty of *representing im-materiality*'[16] – that is, of representing the subconscious. Film presents (reveals) mo-ments (slow or close or backwards or linked) that we could not ourselves experience normally. For Canudo, writing in 1923, cinema was like arrested thought, transmitted to others, and capable of expressing the *soul* of the artist – and this is significantly *another kind of thought* rather than a representation of our thought.

Usually hanging off these accounts of 'subconscious film' are propositions (less frequently arguments) of film as dream. For Paul Ramain, writing in 1925: 'All the ex-pressive and visual processes of the cinema are found in dream'.[17] And for Jean Gou-dal, writing in the same year as Ramain, film is a 'conscious hallucination',[18] a waking dream. Yet for Deleuze, the dream is 'much too individual' to be a template for film's internal monologue – 'the dream is too easy a solution to the "problem" of thought', he writes.[19] And as Stanley Cavell argued, 'dreams are boring narratives', and that to talk of films as dreams 'is a dream of dreams'.[20] In the end, dreams do not match up to the ways of film – film can be much more expressive than dreams, which actu-ally seem quite ordered, with recognisable symbols and logic. Apart from any other argument, how people dream is usually very far removed from cinema, as we are never merely *watching* our dreams but rather *being* our dreams.[21]

Subjective minds

If a film has a person in it then an immediate possibility offers itself in the guise of that person's indicated thoughts and perceptions. Remembering, dreaming, imagining as well as simply seeing. This is the realm of the fictional character's mind. The writers of this section illustrate film as character eye, as character experience, or as character mind – and perhaps try to suggest that film is mostly character-subjective. For example, Yhcam, inspired by the Futurists, envisioned a type of ciné-theatre which would involve 'projecting the characters and, simultaneously, their states of mind', not in the realm of hallucination or dream, but in everyday walking states – character thoughts '*made material by means of the cinematic image*'.[22] And Christian Metz, writing in 1973, notes 'the purely *mental* image: what a character imagines, dreams, the things he envisages in a state of fear, terror, desire, hope, etc.; in short what he does not *see*'.[23]

The great actor and writer Antonin Artaud also saw the possibilities for showing subjective states in cinema, and referred to *The Seashell and the Clergyman* (directed by Dulac, scenario by Artaud) as a 'film of subjective images'.[24] He also wrote scenarios for numerous unmade films which revolved around the possibilities of filming (character) thought – as with 'Eighteen Seconds', in which the events to be on screen would be almost entirely made up of one character's thoughts, such that his eighteen seconds of thinking take and hour or two to show on screen. Artaud's flights of fancy are still largely unrealised in both today's films and current film theory. What would we see, what could we see in purely subjective cinema? *The Age of Innocence* clumsily gives us an impression of saccades (the way our eyes flit between fixation points) in its thinking of one person's opera-glass sweep of the audience below their box. *The Lady in the Lake* offers facile subjectivity for a whole film, while *Halloween* cheats and teases with its floating killer.[25]

For a 1978 book, Bruce Kawin watched some films and came up with the name of 'mindscreen narration' to describe parts of their action. Kawin divides his attention between the 'mental images of characters', 'third-person narration' and a late stab at the 'mind's eye of the film' – in the end allocating it to the author. (Throughout the book he seems concerned with just spotting 'mindscreens', without extending his comments to what we should do with this new knowledge about film, and furthermore stunts the flow of his theory with mechanistic terms.) For Kawin, confusingly, a *film* can give us the mindscreen of a character by presenting their subjective world, but the *character* also presents his view of himself and his world in a mindscreen moment or sequence. Kawin wants the definition of 'mindscreen' to be the character actively presenting his view and world and feeling, but he cannot quite square this with the film's remaining control over the character. Whichever way though, 'mind-screen' is intended to be the presentation of what a character thinks – 'the field of the mind's eye' of the character[26] – rather than a general term for visual narration, as mindscreens are narrated in the first-person; that is, they give us the mind of a character. For Kawin, characters do have specific minds and do enable first-person images, but he distinguishes these from what a character sees, as that is signalled by a 'subjective' camera.

The main problem with Kawin's attempt at a unified category of first-person narration is that it rests on the idea that once the film starts showing us a 'mindscreen' it has completely let go, and what we see and hear *is* what the character 'thinks'. Kawin notes a sequence in Vsevold Pudovkin's *The Mother* when Pavel's mother remembers an earlier event, and 'a series of dissolves goes on to make her *thinking* manifest'.[27] On the one hand this limits the film 'mind' to a literal enactment of human thought, and on the other constricts the possibilities of the *film's* engagement with the characters. It is exactly not 'a question of making clear that this shot is first-person, this shot third-person' as Kawin would have us believe.[28] This clinging to the first-person does not reflect the powerful free-play of film, and disallows the possibility of 'false' character thoughts or memories. Kawin cannot find the words, cannot make the leap, to escape all that seems 'first-person'. George Wilson wrote that the idea of 'mindscreen' 'is likely to mask and blur distinctions that we need to keep sharp if talk of first-person film narration is to have any use at all'.[29] Yet, for me, Kawin does not go far enough in reinterpreting 'first-person' film, and Wilson should realise that *strict* 'first-person' narration offers little power to film. It is another term borrowed from literature, and merely collapses the moving sound-image into brain-grounded literalness. Film does gain power from the fictional intents of characters, but their implication in the film's sounds and images is much more complicated than an old novelistic term can handle. Of course the film may introduce them, say, as the recalled experience of an accused murder claiming innocence, but to always name these images 'mind pictures' disallows us any sceptical movement concerning the validity of such images. Film talk is full of handy linguistic shortcuts, but these primary assignations of thought and sense cannot be shown to do justice to film's range.

In 1916 Hugo Münsterberg published *The Photoplay*, a study of how film not only works like the mind but almost responds to the mind of the filmgoer. Münsterberg was a Harvard psychologist and philosopher, and part of a neo-Kantian school devoted to value-theoretical criticism which concentrated on attempts to separate a level of (knowable) objectivity in things from their 'value', which is attributed by subjects. In *The Photoplay* he wrote about how film creates its own space, and talked of the unique isolation of the film-world: '*The work of art shows us the things and events perfectly complete in themselves, freed from all connections which lead beyond their own limits, that is, in perfect isolation.*[30] This recognition of the independent, autonomous nature of the film drama led to his double linking of film and mind: how the filmgoer has his anticipations followed through, and, certainly more forcefully, how film resembles the mind itself.

In persuading his readers of the latter thesis Münsterberg makes continual comparison to and distinction from the 'outer world', indicating the use and transfiguration film makes of reality: 'This fountainlike spray of pictures has completely overcome the causal world.'[31] In moving away from reality, Münsterberg understands film to be moving towards the mind, and obedient only to its laws: 'The massive outer world has lost its weight, it has been freed from space, time and causality, and it has been clothed in the forms of our own consciousness. The mind has triumphed over matter and the pictures roll on with the ease of musical tones.'[32] Münsterberg (who believed there to be a fundamental principle underlying all arts) thus relates film's forms to different conscious states, such as memory, attention, imagination and emotion. For example, the flashback is really the film objectifying the function of human memory – and this would be fine, if slightly obvious, but Münsterberg goes on to relate this memory function either to the filmgoer (remembering an earlier scene?) or, in an astoundingly strange way, to the characters' 'own minds'.[33] This either/or somewhat negates any possible indication of the film having its own mind, and we are only left with the simple statement that flashbacks and close-ups are similar (phenomenologically) in manner to our acts of memory and attention.

Andrew Wicclair comes to this conclusion in his 1978 discussion of Münsterberg, and adds his own version of a film-being: an 'agent', where a close-up, for example, is either the agent moving towards the object, or vice versa. He thus argues that the 'point of view' of this film-being, this 'agent', is the main force behind narrative construction. Wicclair is an astute commentator on Münsterberg, and uses his theories to arrive at the conclusion that 'the analogue between filmic devices and mental processes should be construed *functionally* rather than phenomenologically',[34] though it is not clear how Wicclair could hold this and keep his obviously human-like 'agent'. Then in 1988 Noël Carroll set about disproving Münsterberg's central premise, the attempt 'to conceptualise cinema as an analogue to the human mind'.[35] I agree with him that film is not analogous to the mind, but Carroll argues this not in relation to how film works, but as regards our knowledge of the mind itself. He holds that one cannot use the mind to theorise film because we do not know enough about how the mind itself works. Yet Münsterberg was obviously making a comparison with common 'experience', and Carroll's critique seems better suited to those who propose that film can show mental states. With these sorts of lightweight exegeses it seems that Dudley Andrew's pondering thought of 1976 still holds: 'Perhaps Münsterberg's full impact is still to come.'[36]

Future minds

But beyond anthropomorphically subjective concepts of film there lies a few theorist-philosophers who see in film a stretching of our idea of thought. The straight analogy of film and thinking appears to be limiting, and a different concept of a particularly filmic thinking seems to hold a better future. In fact it is this distinction between analogy (film as like our thinking) and poetic concept (film as its own kind of thinking) that will be continuously emphasised in this book. Virginia Woolf understood the power of an artistic reconception of thought: 'The *likeness* of the thought is, for some reason, more beautiful, more comprehensible, more available than the thought itself.'[37] And as Richard Allen and Murray Smith perceptively realise, either cinema is seen as manipulative, 'or it is celebrated as a new art form with the potential not simply to model but to *engineer a state of liberated consciousness* that is historically unprecedented'.[38]

No longer tied to subjective ideas, these writers were testing out more objective and transsubjective concepts. In the 1930s Monny de Boully was arguing (according to Richard Abel) 'that the film image could act magically as a medium for the primordial images of the universal mind, just as did trances, sorcery and the totemic ceremonies'.[39] V. F. Perkins also recognised the metaphysical conundrum of film, which seemed to him to have objectivity (vision) without subjectivity (perception). And he also holds out for a particularly filmic kind of idea-creation – films may not replace language in its ability to clearly state ideas and concepts, but film can contribute in its own way: 'The movie's claim to significance lies in its embodiment of tensions, complexities and ambiguities. It has a built-in tendency to favour the communication of vision and experience as against programme.'[40] It is those natural complexities, previously only the concern of aesthetics, that might hold the key to understanding film as thinking.

In 1933, while reportedly addicted to opiates, Roger Gilbert-Lecomte wrote an essay called 'The Alchemy of the Eye', wherein cinema resembles 'a rag lying amongst the bric-a-brac in the junk-room of the human mind'.[41] A member of the group *Le Grand Jeu* (along with Artaud, Robert Desnos and other ex-dadaists and ex-surrealists), who opposed automatism to consciousness and sought to destroy logocentrism, Gilbert-Lecomte nevertheless argued that cinema needs to locate its own essential nature. He was pointing to a cinema that for him did not yet exist (he only mentions Soviet propaganda films and nature documentaries), a possible, future

cinema in which the photography should impress upon its objects, such that any
real thing may appear

> as it is perceived by human consciousness through the clouded states of mind
> which metamorphose it, though a film of tears, for example, or through the in-
> tensely focused light of inspiration, terror or enchantment ... the Himalayas can
> appear in the stone of a ring; a train can turn around a man's head, a posse in the
> Far West and the swell of the sea occur on a sleeper's pillow; a drama is played out
> on a blackened fingernail.[42]

Taking the magic of Georges Méliès and finding 'thought' is just one of the extraordinary intuitions of Gilbert-Lecomte – for modern-day malleable (digitalised) film
increasingly requires a similar revolution in our conception of the language we use
to describe film. His future cinema thus performs like a mind: 'The fact that film is a
rhythm, that is to say a movement linked with absence, is the first condition which
allows us to envisage the possibility of a dialectical cinema, of a cinema which has
the form of the mind.'[43] His idea of 'mind-like' being identifiable dialectical reasoning, where edit shifts, for instance, offer a classic 'relational' style of thinking: for
example, the *taking away* (his 'absence') of an image, or the *comparison* of images.
He continues:

> This is the only, but immense *raison d'être* of the cinema: it is the mediator between
> the mind and nature, and can express in movement and visible forms the develop-
> ment of the forms of the mind. If man decides that this is the role of film, it could
> become the means of expression whose 'invention' would be almost as important
> as that of language and writing; indeed it would become a plastic language.
>   Thus film, a tool of research and experience, would become a mode of know-
> ledge, a form of the mind.[44]

Here the idea of reflection of nature, of an in-between thought and reality crops up
– the film is the mind in a pure out-of-body state, yet still recognisable. And though
Gilbert-Lecomte looks like he is going to ruin it by bringing it back down to language
(though the sentiment of film being as important as language comes through un-
bruised), he then begins to stretch the analogy, turning it around so that film becomes now a (separate) form of the mind – another mind. This is strengthened when
he calls for the aim of cinema to be 'the highest experience of mind, such as poetry
and metaphysics [where] only a psychology of expanded states of mind will bring
out all the possibilities of a cinema whose function is the visual representation of the

changing forms of the mind'.[45] Now the cinema, Gilbert-Lecomte's future cinema, is asked to go beyond the replication of our mind, and toward the installation of a new way of thinking.

In 1945 Béla Balázs constructed a theory of 'absolute' film that drew on a kind of conscious film-thinking. The Hungarian writer and filmmaker, who died in 1949, based his virtual manifesto for future film on his realisation that film can show us 'invisible emotions' and the 'process of thinking' through such means as the slow fade-out: 'the pictures shown are not those of real objects but images of the mind'.[46] For Balázs the camera has turned inwards in order to show how reality is reflected in the mind. Instinctively Balázs saw that film resembles our selective mix of what we perceive – how our mind, a partial mirror, only 'reflects' a certain amount of the world presented. Absolute film was not only interested in representing human psychology through an actor's bodily expressions, but was attempting 'to project inner conceptions of the mind directly on the screen', with the aim of reproducing 'not the soul in the world, but the world in the soul … to show introspectively the images of the outer world as reflected in the soul. Not the soul in the face but the face of the soul'.[47]

Balázs cites Walter Ruttmann's *Berlin* and Karl Grune's *The Street* as films that are neither pure documentaries nor pure abstraction, but 'mental documentaries', absolute films whose abstract montage and superimpositions project a mind onto the screen. Balázs also argues that the montage of Hans Richter's *Inflation* – images of money, empty shops, ticker-tape and panicking people – moves beyond the psychological to create images that become almost conceptual. But still we are dealing here with the image of 'things' being the link to thoughts and concepts, and not so much the ways and means and formations of the images themselves. Where Balázs steps on an interesting stone, and where he links up with Gilbert-Lecomte in leading us beyond the strict analogy, is through his closing in on the uniqueness of film's soul: 'like visions seen with closed eyes. No reality, neither space nor time nor causality, were valid here any longer. The mental processes represented in the absolute film knew only one law: that of association of ideas'.[48] This points beyond the comparison with mental imagery, and begins to lay the ground for a particularly filmic mode of rationalism.

Interesting in the different approaches of all these authors is the extent to which they actually see the filmic (movements and shifts and colourings) as the site of 'thinking'. Apart from the now unsurprising paucity of examples, and thus their tendency to state and run, most fluff the line between seeing film as somewhat like thought because it sometimes shows symbolic and metaphorical events (leaving just blind rhetoric to prove the link), and seeing film as thinking because it *arranges* what it shows as though it were a mind, or in a similar way to which we control our experience. But more importantly, those that *do* hold that the filmic organises like our minds – or, like our eyes, our 'I', our brain, consciousness, experience, soul – are in the end *limiting* film to our realm of experience and thought. To make such a link is to *prescribe* that film can only mirror our mental emotions. To find objectifications of the mental – to theorise an external consciousness, to see a mirror to the soul – is to drag film down to our cognitive-rational level. Film is more than this.

The type or kind of thinking that film enacts is somewhat gained from realising what kind or type of 'knowledge' a film engenders or produces. In a interview in 1970 Stanley Kubrick said that film 'avoids intellectual verbalisation and reaches the viewer's subconscious in a way that is essentially poetic and philosophic'.[49] Kubrick was saying that images, of a certain non-literary form, can create a rough, perhaps even *vague* kind of 'knowledge'. The movements and sounds of Kubrick's films do not rely on language and verbalisation, but speak to another side of us. Yvette Biró similarly asked us to realise: 'If the camera is an extension of our eyes, the broadening of our vision, then it is also an extension of our intellect.'[50] But Virginia Woolf wrote most precisely on whether film communicates to us in some direct and sub-linguistic way: 'Is there, we ask, some secret language which we feel and see, but never speak, and, if so, could this be made visible to the eye? Is there any characteristic which thought possesses that can be rendered visible without the help of words?'[51] To truly understand this world we must accept that film has a unique way of 'thinking', and the next chapter will therefore continue the conversation of this chapter, and ask: who or what is doing this thinking?

two | **film-beings**

He can do whatever thought can do, he represents without any of reality's fetters, he stages events without care for physical impossibility, he is endowed with all the powers of nature and the mind.

– Otto Ludwig (1871)[1]

Eventually, the investigation into whether film creates a new thinking world begins to turn on the kind of 'being' we put at the head of the table. Filmosophy is partly a philosophy of film-being, of how the film-world is created and reconfigured: how it works and means. This concept is key, because it steers how the filmgoer under-stands the manipulation of the film-world. 'Film-being' is a general term for what we understand to be the origin(ator) of the images and sounds we experience. Who or what provides the images that we see? Why do we see this character, at this moment, from this angle? Beyond or prior to the creation of a narrative (narrative is only one avenue for film to go down) and any possible narrator, where do these sounds and images come from? In this chapter I will survey the different film-beings explored by writers in the twentieth century – film as camera 'I' or virtual creator, as ghostly or absent author, or as some kind of narratological or post-narratological being.

But threading through just about all the approaches is the premise that it is only with the structure and phenomenology of human thinking and perception that any analogies can be made. Whether film is merely compared to *the* mind, or actively seen as an objective human consciousness with its particular laws obeyed to the last, all install some sort of *mirror* between film-thinking and human thinking. For ex-ample, Parker Tyler, in 1972, makes an analogy with the detective: 'when the camera was invented, the idea was intuitively and forcefully grasped that this magic mecha-nism was a figure of speech for the searching eye and the responding mind of the detective himself'.[2] For Tyler the classic way in is through Robert Montgomery's *The Lady in the Lake*, in which the film only shows us the point of view of the detective

– the camera becomes his eyes and body. The camera of Tyler's 'maximal' film 'has photographed a psychology of creativity, so that the exposed film roll is now to be termed *objectified mind*'[3] – and here Tyler links up with all those other commentators who only find 'creativity' in a *moving* camera, or *active* montage.

In 1988 William Rothman struck the camera and author as one stone; for him the camera is author: a knowing 'I'. And it is the anticipation of discovering the camera's *human* touch that possesses Rothman, as when he compares the transfiguring camera Stanley Cavell discovers in, say, Max Ophuls' *Letter from an Unknown Woman*, with the murderous camera of Hitchcock's *Vertigo* or *Psycho*. Rothman wants to find out how film expresses these qualities. Introducing these examples, Rothman asserts: 'these films are thinking; they are thinking about thinking, and they are thinking about film, meditating on the powers and limits of their medium'.[4] Declarations of the 'camera' abound (when Rothman can interpret no further), not only as a technicist way of describing the actions of the film, but also in reference to those moments where the camera wantonly signals its own presence. In being fixated with the camera, and fixed on *subjectivity*, Rothman builds up a picture of a technical self very conscious of its attitude and position. As Daniel Herwitz has noticed, in a 1995 article, Rothman relates the camera to 'speech acts' of 'assertion, self-declaration, questioning, acknowledging and thinking'.[5] In reading it via the author's voice, Rothman's camera has a relationship to the film-world that can be anywhere between indifferent and committed – in this he makes the significant move of seeing film as a *knowing intention*, reflecting on and interpreting the film's drama.

Rothman declares his essays to be 'a way of viewing film as thinking' and not only hopes that 'reading the essays together will help impart familiarity with their way of thinking' but further makes film-thinking '*less* familiar – more provocative, more critical, more demanding'.[6] Thus (although he does not himself write this conclusion) Rothman rightly sees this way of conceiving film as at once helpfully revealing everyday film, but also as planting the possibilities of meaning and poetics of future film. For example, Rothman discusses King Vidor's *Stella Dallas*, arguing that the camera shows, or *declares* its thinking by either possessing or freeing the main character from its gaze – leading to the interpretation that the film acknowledges Stella's otherness rather than the film being a lesson in how to install a woman in the patriarchal order (although the film only frees her at the last moment of the film). For Rothman, in classical cinema the camera is thus analogous to the novel's narrator. Also, Jean Renoir's *La Règle du jeu* problematises the camera's relationship to the world and its human figures: the camera 'denies the power of a character's interiority to motivate a framing or a cut [and] can appear unresponsive, expressing indifference to the events unfolding within and around the frame'.[7]

In his commentary on Rothman, Herwitz follows through the idea of the camera 'I', and argues that the film 'I' not only shows mastery of its images, but can also show itself to be indecisive and contradictory. For Herwitz film can thus also shame and deform its world – the camera is 'a full correlate of a human subject, its identity or "I-ness" involves the kind of capacity for self-reflection and for working through that the human being has'.[8] The camera's eye sees into the narrative world, but also into itself, the 'I'. This puts film at the edge of philosophical self-declaration, and thus possibly self-investigation. Herwitz perceptively brings this out in his discussion of Manet's *Rag Pickers* (aka *The Philosophers*): 'This castigation of our ordinary, post-Renaissance position of perspectival viewing alienates us from the assumption that the space of pictures (like the minds of persons and the furniture of the world) is naturally available to us from our objective, all-knowing and all-possessing position.'[9] It is this powerful possibility of subjectiveness that leads Herwitz to pose Rothman's camera as one-dimensional subjectivity, weirdly free of ambivalence.

Author beings

A short stop on this slope of positions are authorial theories of narrative (distinct from 'auteur theory' which does not necessarily claim the whole film as constantly authored). The writers below seem to argue that each film is ultimately the expression of the thoughts of the filmmaker, and therefore a film's moving sound-images should be conceived of as the *virtual mind* of the production's director. For instance, Rothman obviously intends to use authorship to *reveal* the films, but steering towards authorship is at once a get-out clause (when interpretation finds itself at a dead end), and a rhetoric that removes us from the film, denying the film its own meaning creativeness. When film events end up as assertions of author control whole stretches of film can be consigned to stylistic megalomania without need of creative explanation. For example, Rothman writes: 'Hitchcock's signatures are expressions of his unwillingness or inability ever to forsake his mark, ever to absorb himself unconditionally in the destinies of his characters, ever to leave his own story untold.'[10] And in his consideration of cinema's movement from realism to playdoh-mobility, Tyler indicates that 'a work of film should be precisely, in theory, the *photographic reproduction of what has happened in the creator's brain*, not anything that has happened *outside it*.'[11] Interestingly Susan Sontag finds that film can in fact never match up to the author's vision: 'The ultimate first-person in Godard's movies, his particular version of the filmmaker, is the person responsible for the film who stands outside it as a mind beset by more complex, fluctuating concerns than any single film can represent or incarnate.'[12] Deleuze, for his part, is inoffensively auteurist, and finds a link between the 'experience' of the character and the joint expression of the director and filmgoer. The director and the filmgoer are involved in the expression of the character: author, film and filmgoer together as one.

Kawin's attempt to configure a larger 'mind's eye' helpfully introduces the problems these writers have had in trying to understand the impetus behind every filmworld. He begins tentatively: an image 'is the result, and the indicator, of directed attention',[13] and the hope is there that he might not tie film down to *our* particular type of attention. But Kawin is writing in the tradition of authorship theory and finds it hard to ignore the star and cultural qualities of the solo genius – the director. It is in those films that so *obviously* contort movement and image that Kawin finds the thinking of the filmmaker. Initially Kawin argues that just certain types of film narration can be seen as the visualised 'mentations' of their makers, whereas experimental films completely represent the mindscreens of their makers. Mindscreen's role is meant to be explanatory here, in that the filmgoer can better handle stylistic events with the concept of a authorial persona, yet obviously this just delivers another human consciousness into film. Kawin is on the right track though, as all the images of film should be attended to as 'intended'.

For Kawin 'all films are *mentally presentational*',[14] and Kawin *really* means 'mentally', namely that film presents a mental state. George Wilson's critique of Kawin's mindscreen theory seems right, as the (whole) film is not, and should not be understood as 'the visual experience of a fictional or fictionalised observer'.[15] Thus in Kawin's filmworld (where composition is still likened to a language): a character's mindscreen is unimpinged by a larger film-thinking; film is only really thinking when a character is 'thinking'; and every other image is just 'third-person' provided by some other 'mind's eye'.[16] (He also talks of self-conscious films creating a metaphor for the activity of a self-conscious mind.) But it is the theorising of mindscreen within *reflexive* film that leads Kawin to designate an *authorial* consciousness overseeing the whole caboodle. Nevertheless, he does at one point concede that a self-conscious film can be its own mindscreen, but stops short of elaborating on this type of film style, and merely poses the idea of an origin 'outside the image field ... who is not necessarily the auteur'.[17]

Director-based writing is very easy – it is so handy to talk of 'Kubrick cutting to the face of an actor', of 'Scorsese panning round the room of men', but this is the star-struck language of newspaper film reviews – and if the writer does not happen to know the director, the film is back to just being a chance happening. But more importantly, as a conceptual being through which the filmgoer might understand the film, the 'author' is singularly limiting. Watching a film with the idea that the film's actions are directly the result of an external historical person removes the filmgoer from the film. Each action of form reminds them of the director making decisions and the mechanics of filmmaking. Many films do have (culturally) recognisable marks of their directors – winks, signatures – and these can be revealed and discussed in film culture, but the singular films remain; the first-time naïve experience will always be there. It is certainly important to recognise the work of the filmmaker, but during the experience of the film they are not always helpful to our attention.

Ghostly beings

In-between these anthropomorphic fumblings and the beyond of a neo-thinking film-being lies another stepping stone in this story: theories that call in other, ghostly beings as models for cinematic intention. These writers seem to reach a dead end in theorising via human thinking and push outwards towards any other point of origin they can envisage. Considering the limitations of pasting the (actual) creator's imagination onto the film, some simply call on *invisible* beings to explain film's twists and turns. These writers put forward peripheral minds that nevertheless still remain rooted to a humanistic type of thinking. Kaja Silverman finds that the gaze which directs the filmgoer's attention seems to belong to another fictional character, while in 1957 Rudolf Arnheim tried to get round the problem of the external author; he found that the camera 'can search and hesitate, explore, turn its attention suddenly to see some event or object, leap at its prey. Such complex motions are not neutral. They portray an invisible self, which assumes the active role of a character in the plot.'[18] And in 1970, taking his cue from Arnheim, George W. Linden saw film as presenting us with 'the poetry of an invisible self', but moves on to align this self with the director: 'The camera becomes his virtual head. It sees as his eyes see or as he directs it to see.'[19] Four years later in 1974, Daniel Dayan, following on from Jean-Pierre Oudart who proposed the term 'absent-one' (*l'absent*), proposed that the film view is always the personal view of some unseen human perceiver. Again this posits narrative cinema as always human-subjective. For Dayan a film's narrative, its enunciation system, is a kind of guiding tutor, showing us things and revealing plot points and clues, leading us along its path of vision, of representation and signification. Film is thus either character subjective or 'absent-one' subjective: for the filmgoer 'the visual field *means* the presence of the absent-one as the owner of the glance that constitutes the image'.[20] The absent-one constitutes the image, and Dayan and Oudart's move outside the physical would mark a significant step if it were not for their retention of some sort of human mind as originator.

Those that at first saw an author (actual or invisible) as responsible for the film may attempt to move on past such a spongy relationship towards something more ethereal. We have discussed his narrational subjectivities in the previous chapter, but, as a stab at a concept of film-being, Kawin's 'mind's eye' sometimes provides (a fictional character's) mindscreen and sometimes just third-person narration, thus putting into relief his indecision over where to lay the blame for film's actions. He finds that Alain Resnais' 1977 film *Providence*, for example, may be 'a systemically third-person film populated largely by mindscreens; but its title suggests … a latent, offscreen, systemic self-awareness'.[21] Taken literally, this film-being is still limited to the cognitive parameters of human thinking outside the film, 'images which depict stretches of perceptual thinking on the part of the filmmaker … a visual slice of his cogitating mind' as George Wilson puts it, believing this to be a 'bizarre manner' in which to configure the workings of film.[22] In the end Kawin does attempt to find 'mentation' in the film, rather than via the filmmaker. Here, if only in certain films (of Ingmar Bergman and Jean-Luc Godard), 'minded' narration forms, controls and cognitively responds to its own moving sound-images – and he hits some clear notes when he asserts that the mind 'reaches out to film and finds its own landscape, a version of its own process'.[23]

Apart from their linking of human thinking to film-thinking, what also connects all these writers is their reliance on 'active' moments of film: obvious movements, weird framings, metaphorical montage. Ranging from those that just teleologically bring in select examples of forced congruence, to those that only see film-thinking in completely reflexive film. As we head to more advanced analogies of film and mind the importance of *examples*, of the backing up of theories with illustration, becomes at once crucial and sadly lacking. None seem confident enough to allow 'thinking' into the plainest of films. The reason most writers hold this view is that they are not able to get past the idea of thinking as 'obvious' or 'ostensibly intentional'. For example, in 1987 Ian Jarvie argued that replicated 'mental processes' can only be seen in reflexive film, merely because these films are often referred to as 'self-conscious' movies – 'mimicking the mind, which can think and also think about itself and its own thinking, movies can externalise their own processes'.[24] As we have seen, Kawin also aligns mindscreen narration with reflexivity or filmic self-consciousness. This is a common misjudgement of many film theories, finding 'active' film form only in 'active' film stories and narratives, confusing film externalising its processes with film doing some thinking. It seems at first that Kawin cannot quite stretch himself to allow his mindscreens a place in non-active films, and only later does Kawin try to make amends by indicating that a film can be full of mindscreens even if it is not systemically self-conscious. Reflexive film can be fun (and interesting – film considering its own thinking), but it is not a good route for initial theorising. Kawin continues to tie himself in knots when he argues that in Samuel Beckett's *Film*, the 'subjective camera can function as mindscreen in the context of a self-conscious film'.[25] For Wilson the problem is the idea of self-conscious and subjective narration being collapsed together as subjective. By the end of his book Kawin is hitting the ceiling of his terms, and you can almost hear his desperation as his once pure and simple 'mindscreen' attempts to cope with less friendly films. Finally Kawin admits that it is not necessary, 'to limit the application of "mindscreen" to sequences that present what a character sees, or relates, in his mind's eye'.[26]

Narrator beings

It is interesting to note how close narratology tries to come to a theory of film-being. Over the past three decades or so film theorists have taken it in turn to come up with an adequate theory of narration, and have gone through quite a line-up of entities: sender, author, grand imagier, master image-maker, overriding consciousness, overseeing entity, monstrator, omniscient narrator, implied author, invisible observer, impersonal narrator, narrator, character-narrator. But all these theorists are linked by whether or not they accept the premise that film is a matter of communication. There is certainly a receiver, the filmgoer, and it seems reasonable to say the film is a message of some sort (no matter how indefinite it might be), but do we then say that there must be a 'sender' of this message? A lot of film does seem to be anonymously sent – by a secret film agent? For someone like Emile Benveniste the events of film simply 'narrate themselves'.[27] We follow characters and events but might not feel a 'sender', a guiding hand – and this is the view of many narrative theorists.

In 1985 David Bordwell asked, 'must we go beyond the process of narration to locate an entity which is its source?'[28] And filmosophy would agree with Bordwell's answer: 'To give every film a narrator or implied author is to indulge in an anthropomorphic fiction.'[29] For Bordwell, cinema is not a matter of direct communication: films certainly have perceivers, and can be said to be messages (of art or morality or entertainment), but we do not need a 'sender' to reveal all this. Bordwell argues that notions like implied authors are not useful for studying film, and himself simply refers to the abstract process of 'narration'. Some films may ask the filmgoer to construct a narrator, but having one hang over every film is unnecessary. Sometimes this narrator might show its authority by engaging in overt commentary – but still, for Bordwell, any concept of an 'invisible observer' should not become the basis of film style but should only be understood as one *figure* of style. Bordwell also refers to omniscient narration 'choosing' to show something in certain way: in a scene in Antonioni's *La Notte* the narration 'chooses to dedramatise' a conversation by not allowing us to hear it all.[30] And he also finds moments in Resnais' *La Guerre est finie* where an omniscient narrator – this time he terms it an 'overriding consciousness'[31] – plays with the filmgoer's expectations. The fact that Bordwell returns to this idea to cope with the film's more oblique passages indicates its usefulness.

For Edward Branigan, writing seven years later in *Narrative Comprehension and Film*, not only does the film experience entail a sender and a receiver, but multiple combinations: there is the actual author/filmmaker, an implied author, a narrator, characters, and various focalisers. Focalisers are characters whose point of view we are given – we get to see and/or hear what they are experiencing. In film there are thus objective shots (e.g. a location shot), character-based shots (e.g. over the shoulder shots), actual character point of view shots, and shots that are of character thoughts and imaginings. But who is it that allows us to see or hear this experience? What is it that chooses which experience we get to see? For Branigan it is the narrator – the omniscient controller of the film's images and sounds; a film agent that is not immanent in the film, but only part of the filmgoer's narrative schema. He argues that the concept of 'narration' is enough for the filmgoer, and any stylistic intention in the film can simply be labelled as such. Francesco Casetti prefers to posit an 'enunciator', a mix of implied author and external narrator, a role which can be strangely 'given' to characters in the film,[32] while the philosopher Gregory Currie follows the narratologist Seymour Chatman and uses what he calls 'Implied Author Intentionalism'.[33] For Chatman film is certainly a message, and therefore a sender is inscribed in every moment – the whole of film is intended. His 'implied author', 'instructs us silently, through the design of the whole'.[34] This author-narrator presents the film-world, but significantly does not bring it into being – it does not even have the power to communicate with the filmgoer. The contents of film are 'presented' – that is, we are quietly, simply, presented with image and sound.

Post-narratorial beings

But so far none of these film-beings account for the complete *creation* of the film-world. And those that do allow for an agent that filmgoers can hold responsible for the meaning of the film still create an *anthropomorphised* narration. Branigan's agents (narrators, authors, characters, director), these 'epistemological boundaries',[35] simply leave the filmgoer confused – to most fruitfully and least distractedly enjoy film, the filmgoer needs to have a concept of film-being that grounds all these agents *in the film itself*. For example, writing in 1987 André Gaudreault recognised the problems that arise when characters become narrators, and so forth, and so delineated between narration (to narrate) and monstration (to show). Film shows things, but does it narrate? Is film the narration of past events, or the showing of present things?

Gaudreault argues that films have both a monstrator, or 'grand image-maker', and a narrator. In other words, films contain both mimetic and non-mimetic diegesis: 'The filmic monstrator-narrator brings about syncretically the union, the merging of the two basic modes of narrative communication: narration and monstration.'[36] But monstration is a particularly 'present-tense' form, and only second-level narration can change that and move the film into the past or the future. For Gaudreault, film presents and refigures through shot and edit – editing reveals a narrator, a second-level intermediary look or helper (obviously a limited formal design, as film can of course 'narrate' through many other film forms, movement or focusing for example). But Gaudreault is too concerned with the past event of making the film – the monstrator is apparently constrained by 'reality' – to realise film's stand-alone poetic nature.

Following up Gaudreault's article, in 1990 Robert Burgoyne wrote about the possibility of theorising 'impersonal' narration, which 'both creates or constructs the fictional world while at the same time referring to it as if it had an autonomous existence.'[37] Burgoyne notes the way *Blue Velvet*'s discourse of heightened, ironic imagery is set off against its fictional world: 'This discrepancy can be accounted for only by resorting to the concept of a narrator whose intent is to present the fictional world and to qualify it at the same time … to produce, in short, a guided reading of the fictional universe.'[38] 'Narrators' can be passive and watch the film as much as anyone, or they can direct the images to do things (the voiceover might even say, 'let's go back to see what Jennifer is up to'). Films can be impersonal or personality-full, but both are narrational processes. A film's impersonal narrator encloses and oversees the film's 'personal' narrators (character-narrators who report on or show us things in the pre-existing film-world). The impersonal narrator can comment on the film-world, and can reveal the lies of a personal narrator – and this is its main purpose for Burgoyne, to validate or undercut a film's personal narrations. Most significantly it helps the filmgoer find the authentic in unreliable narration: lying flashbacks, untrue 'recollections' (the murderer only 'finding' the body and calling the police), which are always produced through personal narration. Burgoyne's guiding lights are thus facts, truth, authenticity – a theory of narration should help fill all gaps, should hold up against the waxing and waning of the film.

Yet these 'impersonal' narrators are still attempts at *empirical descriptions* of film. These kinds of super-narrators might plug the latest 'unreliable narrative' gap, but what they do not really advance is our *understanding* of film-worlds. Narrators are also said to give us select portions of the world – but it is nonsensical to say there is a world which we are given *portions* of, because we do not see any other world than the film-world presented. The filmgoer has no choice – there is only one film-world, one sequence of images. And ultimately these 'impersonal' or anonymous narrators still have the flavour of *human-like control*. Burgoyne tries to de-humanise narration, by saying that impersonal narration oversees personal narrations, but it still remains an anthropomorphic fiction, an attempt to find a novelistic voice in film. There is no other human presence (even though particular films may use a narrating voiceover presence as part of the drama). When narratology is moving towards impersonal invisible 'voices' it is time to replace the narrational path laid down for film by literary theory with something more suitable. At this edge of narratology, where narrators are becoming 'unreliable' anyway, we can hear film calling out for a less restrictive conceptual description.

George Wilson's philosophical nature immediately led him to see film as a kind of time machine tour of a secondary world – a new kind of reality, and thus a place that can handle the rehearsal of metaphysical theories. And I get the feeling that Wilson wants to see film as a thinking film-being in his 1986 book *Narration in Light*. When he puzzles over the narrational figures he finds in complex films, he realises that some sort of paradigm is needed 'to ostend those objects, properties and relations, out of all that appear on screen, that are to have a weighted explanatory function in the film'.[39] Wilson simply asks what we take to be objective about the way in which film presents a narrative. Is it a transparent 'window'? He rules out the idea that the shifts and actions of the film image are the work of some other consciousness. And he is right, within his line of argument. For Wilson is here considering the idea that film's actions are the design of an 'ideal observer' who takes up and shifts positions so as to relay the best points of view – the sort of views and shifts of attention that we would engender if we were an actual spectator to the scene at hand. His own analogy is that of the filmgoer sitting in a time-machine looking through a big window which is directed by some sort of prescient intelligence to present a coherent narrative. In considering whether all films have a visual narrator who mediates the action, he finds that the views of the film-world that are changed so often and sometimes so abstractly that the filmgoer feels a guiding mind. In seeking to understand this *other mind*, Wilson begins to consider some sort of omniscient force, or 'meta-narrative observer', a 'narrating intelligence that exists outside the secondary world of the film and designs an "ideal" overview of the narrative occurrences'.[40]

In chapter seven, 'On Narrators and Narration in Film', Wilson sets out to answer this question of whether it can be said that there is some kind of 'being' who shows the narrative to the filmgoer, and immediately questions how such a film-being relates to the narration as it unfolds. Looking to the narration of *Letter from an Unknown Woman*, Wilson acknowledges that it both enforces and complicates our view of the characters. He then proposes 'a visual narrator who is not a character in the narrative but is a kind of invisible but visual Other whose perceptual conscious-ness informs the imagery throughout'.[41] He more or less finds it self-evident that filmgoers are supposed to feel the character's experience directly, unimpeded by direction, and the standpoint from which Wilson dismisses the idea of an obvious metanarrator is that of a realist – 'it is an important aspect of our movie-based per-ceptual transaction with these circumstances that we regard it as a *direct* connec-tion and not as one that has been filtered through the idiosyncratic mechanisms of another perceiver's field of vision'.[42] Here Wilson is again incapable of separating film's actions from either human perception or an implied author, and thus cannot see how a metanarrative could be anything other than 'subjectivity' forced on top of 'objectivity'. Wilson goes on to struggle with the idea that we see through film *and* feel ourselves to be guided by it, and considers yet another kind of 'fictional figure' who is demonstrative in showing fictional events to the filmgoer, but concludes that there is no basis for accepting such a fictional being. Even if he allows 'a *version* – an implicit projection – of the actual filmmaker *implied* by the work', and then admits 'it seems that some severely restricted version of the concept [of a filmic narrator] might have a limited use', Wilson still ends up sitting back on square one: 'this is an abstract possibility of point of view whose nature and interest we ought to be able to discuss accurately'.[43]

Thirteen years later Wilson set out to reconsider his position, looking over and above any possible narrator, and toward a *grand imagier*, or 'master imager'. In an article for the journal *Philosophical Topics* he begins by arguing that film images are 'naturally iconic' for filmgoers, who

> imagine the movie shots before them as offering a perspectival view of those con-tents, and it is the function of the shots to prescribe an imagining of this kind. So, it is in this sense that the shots of a film *present* a view of or perspective on some spatio-temporal slice of the 'story world' and *show* us what that view contains.[44]

Wilson reasons that because it seems impossible for a 'narrator' to show us the imag-es and story, so a *grand imagier* is necessitated. But this does not seem such a good line of reasoning, because if we can pose that question, using the same logic we can just as well ask how a *grand imagier* shows us the story? What Wilson means is that *conceptually* it feels wrong to say that a 'narrator' creates or shows or originates the images, because that is not traditionally within the remit of a filmic narrator. He cites in his favour Jerrold Levinson, who also distinguishes between fictional showings of fictional events in movies, and the *'perceptual enabler'* or 'presenter' of the movie itself.[45] Wilson calls this the 'Fictional Showing Hypothesis', distinguishing between the presenting (which he says belongs to the world of narration) and the presented (belonging to the world of the narrative).

But it is when Wilson analyses the effect on the filmgoer of the narratorial perspective that he begins to formulate the concept of the *grand imagier*. The concept of a narrator, and especially it's humanistic trappings, brings with it a point of perspective. If a filmgoer experiences a film via the concept of a narrator then they will perceive the film events as though directed by an invisible person in a particular location outside the film. But Wilson argues that, philosophically, we *can* imagine scenes without a determinate 'place' of perspective, and uses this argument to forward the idea that film can issue images without needing a *narrational location or body*. This is a very important step – *to bring the conceptualisation of film-being back 'into' the film, and not suggest an external perspective*. For Wilson this enabling-being should be seen as part of the film work; he thus returns the intention of film-being to the 'film' itself – filmgoers do not need to imagine an agent who shows us the film – 'we imagine motion picture shots as motion picture shots'.[46] Conceptualising any 'enabler' as an *outside* force does not really help the filmgoer, they should see the enabling as organically part of the film.

It seems that we therefore need to radically resituate film-being – we need to understand film as issuing from itself. The film becomes the creator of its own world, not from a 'point' of view, but from a realm, a no-place, that still gives us some things and not others. Conceptualising the right kind of film-being gives film a character, a personality, and style becomes a calling card for that film-personality – it tells us what the film is thinking and how the film regards its characters and events. The next chapter will ask whether phenomenology might provide some clues to the right kind of film-being.

three | film phenomenology

> Motion pictures are first and foremost a technical invention in which philosophy counts for nothing.
>
> – Maurice Merleau-Ponty (1945)[1]

As regards film studies, phenomenology has almost exclusively been brought in to help clarify questions of *filmgoer* experience and interpretation, but, with the idea of film-thinking, the intersection with phenomenology becomes much more interesting. Asking of any particular film-being: what does 'it' experience, and how? Should we call the film-being's relationship with the content of film 'experience'? Unlike our inescapable human phenomenology, the film can become other characters, can freeze moments, can rewind images, can alter colours and speeds. There is certainly a phenomenology of our film experience, but is there a distinctly film-phenomenology of film-being? Other questions arise: How might phenomenology help filmosophy conceptualise the new fluid-thinking film – where it might be argued that the *profilmic* has disappeared and the *filmic* takes over, inserting itself into characters (e.g. face-morphing) and settings (e.g. sky-colouring)? From another vantage point, film can help phenomenology clarify its terms and aims: film stands in for the body – how do we regard its perceptions? Are we privileged to see an Other's perceptions? Here in this chapter I will be looking at the work of Maurice Merleau-Ponty and Vivian Sobchack in relation to these questions.

Phenomenology is the philosophy of experience – the study of consciousness and the phenomena (objects/appearance) of direct experience. That is, it attempts to describe our *experience* of things (the appearance of things to us), marking out phenomenal states – also known as sensations, sense data or qualia. For phenomenologists, subject and object are seen as *inseparable*. This endorsement of the philosophical primacy of the lived world means that experience is distinguished from rationality. Merleau-Ponty's *existential* phenomenology is significantly different from the *transcendental* phenomenology of Edmund Husserl, in that it stresses the em-

bodied nature of human consciousness. Existential phenomenology rejects the universal or 'essential' descriptions of transcendental phenomenology, preferring an embodied, historicised description – space and time should be described in terms of how they are in lived experience; it is in this sense that existential phenomenology sets itself against metaphysics (there is no 'triangle', only particular triangles). Here phenomenological analysis provides an interpretation of phenomena that illustrates the *lived* significance they have for the subject.

In being the study of human experience, and of the ways things present themselves to us *in and through* such experience, phenomenology deals with 'appearances', asserting that appearances are real, that they belong to being. Seeing a cube, moving it around in front of me, I see only two or three sides at any moment, and I *intend* (and therefore experience) the sides that are (given as) absent. We intend these absences and presences – consciousness is always 'of' something in the sense that it intends the identity of objects. The *identity* of the cube thus belongs to a different dimension. We *think* the identity of the cube, and when we realise it is we who give the cube its identity, we begin to discover more about our subjectivity in the world – we discover our 'self', as it were. With film we might thus say that, at any one moment, one scene is *present* to the film, with off-frame action being *absent* but intended – we feel it is there (just as we feel the previous image 'over' the present one). Also, film-facts can be told in a manifold of ways. For example, films show people talking in many different ways (close to, from afar, one at a time, both in one image, and so on). A phenomenology of any film-subject would describe these various *manifolds* by which films express themselves (filmosophy describes the various thinkings of films).

Phenomenology reveals how, in 'thinking' the objects before us, we in some sense 'own' them – as Merleau-Ponty writes: 'To see is to *have* at a distance.'[2] When we see an object we take that object and make it our own. This 'strange possession' of the world, as Merleau-Ponty puts it,[3] mirrors film's possession of its characters and settings. For Merleau-Ponty this is why philosophy is suited to film – because philosophy consists in 'describing the mingling of consciousness with the world, its involvement in a body, and its coexistence with others; and because this is movie material *par excellence*'.[4] The film's attention/intention mingles with the objects we recognise, making new 'intended-objects' (thought-things) – film shows us the expression of mind in the world. Perhaps the major difference, as we shall discuss, is that, for human beings, to have an object is to 'change' that object towards oneself; for film-being, to have an object *is to be that object*. Cinema intends and creates at one and the same moment. Film owns the objects it 'sees', because the object is already included in the act of seeing, as it were. Cinematic vision *holds* objects. What

Merleau-Ponty helps us realise then, is the double nature of experience in the cinema: *the filmgoer's experience of the film, and the film's 'experience' of its characters and objects.*

For Vivian Sobchack, following on from Merleau-Ponty, film is understood to be itself a 'subject', an 'object-subject' that sees and is seen. For her film is both presentational and representational, both a viewing subject and a visible object for the filmgoer – film is existentially embodied (mechanical) perception. There seem to be four levels to Sobchack's phenomenology of film's 'experience': that film sees and expresses its seeing; that it is subjective; that it is embodied; and that the filmgoer feels this presence, this other. For Sobchack film is both an *'instrumental mediation* necessary to *cinematic communication'* and *'a direct means* of having and expressing a world', that is given to itself 'as the immediate experience of consciousness'.[5] Film is both a means of expression, and an expression of intention, but from a *particular consciousness* – film brings to visibility its 'certain hold' upon the world. For Sobchack this mingling reveals a 'subjectivity' of the film – a film-subject which 'experiences' a 'world' from a subjective viewpoint.

In both seeing and expressing its seeing, film is not just a view (an image or a scene) for Sobchack, it is a 'viewing view'. The viewing view *presents* (the body-subject of vision), the moving sound-image *represents* (the visible objective body for vision). Film's viewing view is its meaningful choice-making gaze, and thus a new organisation of the whole, a new *mode of attention*. This viewing view thus consists in having and expressing perception: that is, film simultaneously has vision and intention, it sees objects and expresses intention about those objects. The expressive 'camera' brings the viewing view into visibility (i.e. making film's intentionality obvious). This viewing view thus makes the film a spectator as much as a subject. But, how can film have 'vision', and is it not somewhat confusing, rhetorically, to say that film has 'vision'? Furthermore, who or what is creating the objects under film's 'vision'? Is the filmgoer meant to equate the action of film (as a present event on screen) with the historical filming event? If so, if film is forever 'recording' via 'vision', then how can film manipulate these profilmic events?

In any case, this viewing view is termed as 'subjective'. Now, confusingly, Sobchack asserts that this film-subjectivity is both analogous with *and* different to human-subjectivity. The former position, the anthropomorphic position, might perhaps be traced back to the existence of a filmmaker (or filmmakers). Sobchack's film-subject is an embodied life – significantly a *'past'* life: 'the filmmaker's perceptual life mediated and enunciated'.[6] Yet Sobchack goes on to acknowledge that filmgoers do not actually see 'filmmaking', they see film *being*, recognising that for the filmgoer the film is 'an inscribing autobiography of exploration . . . the immediate and direct enunciation of its own *present* engagement with a world'.[7] Yet this about turn does not dissuade Sobchack from seeing human-type subjectivity in film subjectivity: film shows us how human embodied vision works. For Sobchack, film images plainly, simply, represent a Renaissance perspective: representing the visible as originating in and organised by an individual, centred subject. The filmgoer thus experiences film as subjective and intentional.

Yet it seems obvious that film 'experience' looks very different to our experience. A phenomenologically correct flashback should show what the character is seeing and what they are remembering, at the same time – as when you stare at an object while picturing in your mind an old friend. *Film does not make human thinking visible to us*, and if film phenomenology did continue down this path, it would then only find *human-like* styles in film form. Seeing film anthropomorphically thus restricts the possible interpretations of film form. So it seems that if we were to call film-being 'subjective', it would be a different subjectivity to that which we express and hold. Now, it is possible that Sobchack sees film as subjective, but not human-like in its actions (then why call it 'subjective' – why give it 'vision'?). This angle is brought out when Sobchack refers to film as always 'subjectively and existentially Becoming before us',[8] and to film's perceptive and expressive activity as *intra*subjective – it is for itself, by itself (but is made available *inter*subjectively for the filmgoers).

Film-body

In Sobchack's more interesting position a *film-body* emerges, as a 'visible action and gesture' of film-perception, a 'singular intentionality', with its own 'existential presence', its '*own* perceptive and intentional life'.[9] This singular, somewhat less-human, more unique subjectivity, simultaneously 'inhabits, possesses, and signifies' the film-world.[10] Integral to Sobchack's conception of film-being as a subject is thus its *embodied* nature. Film has a body which drives and steers its representations. In phenomenology this is brought out in the move from transcendentalism to existentialism: 'I perceive in a total way with my whole being', wrote Merleau-Ponty.[11] Human bodily existence, material flesh, is the first *premise* of sense and signification – our human body should no longer be seen as a passive machine registering and decoding reality, but as actively engaged in processes of world-making (world-thinking). As George Lakoff and Mark Johnson argue in *Philosophy in the Flesh*: 'What is important is not just that we have bodies and that thought is somehow embodied. What is important is that the very peculiar nature of our bodies shapes our very possibilities for conceptualisation and categorisation.'[12] Flesh is the common ground of all being – and subject/being and object/consciousness are two inseparable aspects.

In seeing film as a body, then, Sobchack makes us realise that film moves towards its scenes, bringing its nature to bear on objects and events that we know but perhaps have never seen (thought) in this way (a love *loved*, a baddie *hated*, a hero *worshiped*). To make clear, Sobchack does not conceptualise film as a lived-body in order to emphasise its physical, mechanical body: camera, projector, screen, celluloid, etc. No, just as our mind transcends our body, so the film transcends its mechanics. Nor is it to be understood metaphorically – for Sobchack, the film's lived-body is an empirical fact, a functioning subject-object (offscreen space, for one, affirms its existence). Sobchack conceptualises film as a lived-body so as to reveal its animated, intentional body – it is a higher-level body than the physical. The film-body creates a modification in the way film articulates its intentions (its thinkings), and thus in the way film is presented to us. The film's body is its 'sensing and sensible being', 'an embodied and intending consciousness'.[13] This film-body (invisible in its own vision) is the subject of the film's image and space and dynamism, inscribing its 'presence to, at, and in the world in the visible motility of its "viewing view"'.[14]

What is important about Sobchack's move to seeing film as a body is the way that it allows for social meaning – allows for a historical, situated film: a body that intends in relation to the world and other films. This other-body is thus ethically invested. The materiality of the (non-metaphorical) film-body *claims* its world – the vagaries of time and space are brought together, are synthesised in its experience. Marking film as a body allows for a coherence of the cinematic. Body is to reality as film is to its world. Cinema is thus a 'becoming', an organic life, that almost necessitates the creation of a sensible body. Yet conceptualising film as a body *separates* it from the film-world – *this is the main problem with translating phenomenology to film*. We are separate yet mingled with our world, but film *'is'* its world. Merleau-Ponty remarks that films 'are particularly suited to make manifest the union of mind and body, mind and world, and the expression of one in the other'.[15] The film-world and the film-intention are one (they are, as I will argue, one mind, a new mind). Sobchack compounds this problem by talking of 'film experience' and 'film vision', which implicates a gap, an anthropomorphic attention, from film to film-world. How can film have experience of 'separate things' when film is its things. The film-body and the film-image should be seen as one and the same. The result of this is the realisation that we need to give film its own terms, not second-hand phenomenological ones.

But, conceptually, where is this body – where does the filmgoer position the origin of this intention? How does Sobchack rhetorically conceptualise film-being? In phenomenology the human mind is a constituting consciousness – it is part of the world – so what kind of constituting consciousness does film have? And does it feel the *real signification* of the cinema world? Sobchack asks in what way the film can be said to exist (perceptually and expressively) for itself – how should we describe this 'invisible presence'. To start to answer this question she begins by realising that filmgoers only see the result or 'terminus' of this embodied film-subject – they see intentional images and sounds and so presume or feel a 'presence' that provides them. Film is an intentional activity and, because the filmmakers and cinematic machinery that created the film are not visible, 'the enabled film emerges and inscribes an existence of its own'.[16] The filmgoer does not see the film's creators (human or technological), so we must accept film's unique existence: we transcend our physiology and film transcends its machinery. Thus Sobchack does seem to allow film a *unique self-intention* – film thinking to itself: 'At the cinema, we see seeing writing itself. We hear speaking listening to and recording itself'.[17] The film-body inscribes this presence, as well as causing the filmgoer to sense its existence.

To name this presence for the filmgoer Sobchack settles on simply conceptualising the film-body as 'an animate, conscious "other" who visually, audibly and kinetically intends toward the world or toward its own conscious activity in a structure of embodied engagement with the world and others that is similar in structure to our own'.[18] Here Sobchack continues her confusing mixture of film as unique being *and* film as 'experientially' recording the world. The film-other intends towards its own conscious creation or the world – even though the 'world' is its own conscious creation. One might say that the film-other is present at the site/sight of the visible – present at both the location and the intention of the visible. Also, this 'other' is the subject of its own vision – so does that mean it is always self-conscious? Is it always reflexive? Is it always 'knowing', perhaps? This other is an autonomous, anonymous, embodied subject which 'experiences' a world. For Sobchack, film allows us to see an existential activity (rather than a uniquely filmic thinking?) that is always becoming and always signifying.

Space and movement

This subjective becoming is made clear through the techniques of cinema. For Sobchack, this other, this film-body, this 'ungraspable *presence*',[19] creates meaning through space and movement (but not through time strangely). As Merleau-Ponty notes, cinema 'offers us yet another chance to confirm that modes of thought correspond to technical methods and that, to use Goethe's phrase, "What is inside is also outside"'.[20] For Sobchack, cinema externalises internal subjectivity, and movement is at the heart of cinematic meaning; even when apparently dormant, film is still a subjective intention. Movement in cinema – whether of the camera, the zoom lens, or the characters – makes the visual visible (seeing becomes seen, perception becomes expression). A film about a character now becomes a dance of two subjectively intending bodies. As Sobchack points out, to show a man running, film can either hold the world or the man static (watch him go by, or keep up with him). The camera is thus the bodily agent, bringing the viewing view into visibility (i.e. making film's intentionality obvious). Sobchack incisively recognises that film needs to unhook itself from merely following character movement, to finding its own movements, its own thoughtful possibilities – think of Murnau's floatings, Tarkovsky's meanderings, Tarr's linking and questioning movements. These gestures of film movement almost force the filmgoer to recognise an intending being surveying its world. It is in these kinds of movements that film 'visibly signifies the activity of becoming'.[21]

A different kind of movement, an 'optical' movement, is apparent in image-displacing zooms. This internal movement of the lens (static camera, displaced space) also makes the filmgoer aware of the consciousness of the film's viewing view: 'It brings that consciousness to visibility as a transformation of the "moving image", as a change of "mind" about the production of vision.'[22] In other words, zooms and the like (active cinema), allows us to see film-intention in action. Sobchack also calls this 'intention' film's 'attention' – a lived-body movement (rather than a physical movement), a creative, questioning act, altering the film's relationship to its world. With the zoom the camera may, technically, stay rooted, but does the filmgoer? But we can see what Sobchack is indicating: the image changes, distance is collapsed and the body is transcended. Yet Sobchack does not see zooms as expressive, only 'impressive', being lured by the object, rather than actively moving towards it, as in a 'camera track in' (a visible gesture for Sobchack). I think directors such as Robert Altman and Paul Thomas Anderson, master and disciple of the internal optical movement, would disagree – the zoom is a very expressive thought, sometimes searching and finding, sometimes receding and denying, sometimes questioning and inquisitive.[23] Apart from being overly concerned with reflexive, active, expressionistic cinema (bodily film movements are apparently 'pre-reflective'; only editing makes a film 'reflective'), Sobchack's technological questions obscure possible poetic ones. An accurate description of the difference between optical and actual movement in cinema (zoom and track) may be clarifying for film theorists, but does it provide a way into the thoughtful and poetic usages of these forms?

Postphenomenology

Sobchack's writings mark a significant moment in the literature on 'film-being', in that they take seriously the question of film 'experience', and the paradox of film both creating and spectating the film-world. Phenomenology has helped Sobchack understand the way that film intends towards its characters and objects – how film thinks its objects. But phenomenology also pushed the view that film is subjective. The problem (repeated in virtually all interdisciplinary studies) lies in the somewhat inflexible adoption of phenomenological terms. Phenomenological terminology provides illumination of film-being as much as it takes its uniqueness away. Phenomenology encourages Sobchack to see film as an intending being, but then limits her analysis to human-like terms (subject, vision, experience). Phenomenology concerns human engagement with reality. Film-being is not human, and the film-world is not real. Film is its own reality, its own world, and the *attention* of any possible, conceptual film-being must be theorised as being part of that world, not separate and observational. We are subjective beings, but film seems more fluid in its place of intent.

The main problem with Sobchack's film-body is thus its anthropomorphism – even though at points she tentatively asserts the unique, non-human-like nature of film. One cause of this anthropomorphism is the attempt to include the creators of cinema within the concept of film-being. Thus film's subjectivity is inscribed with the creator's experience, and so the film becomes human in its expression. Filmmakers *do* create films with their own human intentions and emotions, but the filmgoer's *experience* is of *another* kind of thinking, a mechanical transsubjective being whose 'film-emotions' are ever so slightly askew to our own emotions. To conceptualise this film-being using human-like terms is, I would argue, forced and limiting. These starting points of phenomenology and filmmaker creativity lead Sobchack to make a direct comparison between human perception and film 'perception'. She holds that film vision is similar in form, or corresponds to human vision; that optical movement (zooms) 'makes visible' acts of consciousness; that film and filmgoer both 'inhabit their vision'; that film '*duplicates* the structure and activity' of human vision; that film enacts 'the seeing of another who is like myself, but not myself'; that film is an 'analogue' of human experience.[24] For Sobchack, then, film's viewing view is virtually isomorphic with human vision.

Furthermore, for Sobchack film has a language that is grounded in the parallel language of 'embodied existence' – with structures common to filmmaker, film and filmgoer. Phenomenological theories of film are usually there to undermine semiotics, but Sobchack sees constant, identifiable signification in the actions of the film-body. The body-subject of film is thus inherently semiotic – signifying and significant, intentional and material – film being both the subject and object.[25] The crux of this approach lies in the fact that Sobchack seems more interested in how film 're-veals' *our* consciousness, rather than investigating how we might describe cinema's 'new-consciousness'. For Sobchack film reflects on human subjectivity – film uses particularly human modes of embodied existence (seeing, hearing, movement) to enact its intentions. It also uses the structures of direct experience, situating itself as regards objects and characters. Film's forms are thus able to present memories and moods through a subjective spatial-temporality.

I would certainly agree with Sobchack that film 'thinks' moods and desires through movement and colour and framing etc., but not in the same way as we experience our moods and desires. The way in which the film 'thinks' does not phenomenologically mirror the way our consciousness audio-visually thinks. When I am in love with someone they do not always appear to me in soft-focus. When I am envious of another, or feeling sick, the world does not turn green suddenly. Desire does not cloud my vision in a red haze. We cannot see in black and white, nor actually 'zoom in' on things. As George Wilson notes, we do not see 'tracking or panning shots as corresponding to the continuous reorientation in space of the visual field of people such as ourselves ... we do not see a straight cut, even within a scene, as representing the phenomenology of a shift in a perceiver's visual attention'.[26] It is limiting to talk about film form in terms of our perceptual capabilities – film can do more than us, differently to us. Cinema may *attempt* to function in a phenomenological way (and often tries, sometimes beautifully) but that does not mean that film becomes phenomenological *per se*. Any resemblance is functional rather than exact. If I am frantically nervous and paranoid, my world might look similar to Henry Hill's world in the later parts of *GoodFellas* (fast jerky movement, flitting attention). But even then, the 'similarity' here is a functional one, rather than a phenomenological one: film enacts *its own version* of franticness and paranoia.

But then Sobchack does at times indicate that *she does not* believe film to be phenomenologically the same as human vision/experience: unlike the film frame, our vision 'ends gently rather than geometrically'; unlike film focusing, our eyes do not necessarily 'perceive figures as "blurred" or "out of focus" for them to exist as visible and yet latent in the visual field'; film *amplifies* perceptual experience, 'offers "more" as well as "less" in relation to direct lived-body engagement with phenomena'.[27] At these points Sobchack does seem to indicate that the film-subject is not strictly analogous with the human-subject in its actions and attentions, but her language (of subject, experience, vision) betrays a continuing belief in a straight link. Film cannot show us human thinking, it shows us 'film-thinking'. Film is not a human-like mind, it is, uniquely, a 'filmind'. Sobchack's film-subject 'experiences' a 'world' from a subjective viewpoint; filmosophy's filmind *is* the film-world, though from a transsubjective no-place. This distinction (between 'subjectively having a world' and 'transsubjectively being a world') is the main difference between Sobchack's theory of the film-subject and filmosophy's theory of the filmind. In the next chapter I will therefore consider those writers who have rejected this direct comparison, in favour of a new kind of thinking.

four | **film neominds**

The imaginary gaze makes the real something imaginary.

– Gilles Deleuze (1985)[1]

Germaine Dulac was perhaps the first to use the term 'cinematic thought',[2] in 1925, though without particular explanation, and only in relation to avant-garde or pure cinema. Prompted by this idea of specifically *cinematic* thought, this chapter looks at those writers who have attempted to theorise a particularly *new* kind of thinking for cinema. With the use of a straight analogy between film-being and the human mind now appearing circular and flawed, some authors took tentative steps into independent areas. Here – variously in the work of Jean Epstein, Antonin Artaud, Sergei Eisenstein, Jean Louis Schefer, Gilles Deleuze and others – film is technically non-human, or consciousness perfected, or the unconscious unveiled; or perhaps pure dialectic, and thus an independent, expanded mind. Locating intention within the film is one step towards seeing film-being as it's own particular and new kind of thinking. One can see indications of this direction with Parker Tyler, who writes:

> what injected a new spirit into both photography and painting was an impulse to *move toward* the subject of interest as if to see it more deeply and precisely and variously, and thus to move the spectator's viewpoint inside a scene as if it were another environmental factor, not passively to remain outside it.[3]

Film does not merely present objects, but reveals a way of seeing them – a way of seeing that results from a way of thinking.

In the introduction to Gerard Fort Buckle's 1926 book *The Mind and the Film*, J. D. Williams, then Managing Director of British National Pictures, wrote that film 'cannot be established as an art until we have explored and understood what I may call the Mind of the motion picture camera'.[4] In film studies the rhetoric of the 'camera' has a long history of sheep-like repetitiveness. For those who idolised the technology and wanted a reflexive signal of their love to saunter through their writing, the camera offered a crucial crutch. You may make the claim that this is *just* a question of rhetoric, of using 'camera' over 'author' or some other term for narrative master – but a theory consists of its rhetoric, and is steered uncontrollably by it. To make plain: the filmgoer does not see a camera, they see a film-world; and further, the rhetoric of the 'camera' can't account for other forms, such as sound effects and editing. Yet the 'camera' was a non-mind, a technological mind, and so offered a different mode of thinking.

For Dziga Vertov and the Cine-Eyes group the camera, the cine-eye, captures its own reality, self-consciously. In being linked to the 'camera', the mechanical recording machine, Vertov's version of film-thinking is thus specifically *nonhuman*. Vertov is most interesting when he emphasises this camera-perception, which makes movement-image facts of people.[5] The cine-eye puts perception *into* matter, and so recalls Leibniz's monadology (wherein even a stone has a point of view). In distinction to Eisenstein, Vertov's film-thinking, his sublime materialism, was impressionistic, and aimed to question our experience of reality, rather than provide theses and dialectical positions. Vertov and the Cine-Eyes group *thought* about ordinary events by extracting them, closing in on them, and montaging them with other events and moments. There then exists a personality in the seeing or recording of these moments; and this personality is the thinking, the angle of thought. The selecting (this over that, before that not this, at this moment not later or earlier) is a thinking. For Balázs, these kinds of factual films 'will form the most significant, the richest, the most filmic art form of that lyrical film-poetry which is yet to be born'.[6]

Those that theorise via the 'camera' are close to a unique sense of thinking as they grapple with ideas of 'camera-perception', wherein film reveals a new appearance to things, a restructuring and segregation of real space. In the end, though, all this is hampered by the very rhetoric of the 'camera': biased towards the visual, virtually ignorant of the thoughtful sounds and intentional shifts and cuts, and magnetised to the technique of the author and the artistry of the lens. Also, the mechanical nature of the camera might contrast with rather than mirror the subjectivity of human perception. George Linden adds to this movement when he questions whether film 'is really neither objective nor subjective but a moving synthesis of both'.[7] And when Balázs sees film giving us reality from a unique angle, he asks whether this point of view might not be determined by 'the perspective of the picture', where the image of an object is really 'the subjectivity of the object'.[8] Here he not only understands that we cannot see an object without seeing it in some particular way, but tugs at the idea that film shows us things from perspectives that we could never hold. Paul Sharits, self-proclaimed artisan of 'infrastructural cinema', saw a need for films that amplified just those general infrastructures, in which he saw a conceptual system and therefore deep levels of meaning. Sharits's hope, sketched in a 1978 article for *Afterimage*, was that his various films would 'synchronically reflect off each other and that which is deflected outwards through this undoubtedly flawed paradigmatic system will perhaps amount to a definition of cognition'.[9]

For someone at the very birth of narrational moving pictures Hugo Münsterberg was incredibly perceptive in understanding the possibilities of film. He was not only one of the first writers to link mind with film, but one of the first to write seriously about film at all. In his 1916 book, *The Photoplay* (at that time, in America at least, 'cinema' was the gadgetry, and 'photoplay' the narrative drama) Münsterberg notes that filmmakers might be 'haunted by the fear that the supply of new sensations may be exhausted',[10] that they are running out of jungles and seas and wonders to photograph, and incisively argues that it is not what you show but how you show it that allows for the true advance in film. That film may give us something slow or fast, in sharp detail or blurred, in reversed or broken order, or even, in a description which preempts some current film forms (the 180° whiplash movements of Scorsese's *Cape Fear*, for example), the effect of putting the camera 'on a slightly rocking support and then every point must move in strange curves and every motion takes an uncanny whirling character'.[11] This thought leads Münsterberg to continue:

> there is no doubt that the formal changes of the pictoral representation will be legion as soon as the photoartists give their attention to this neglected aspect. The value of these formal changes for the expression of the emotions may become remarkable. The characteristic features of many an attitude and feeling which cannot be expressed without words today will then be aroused in the mind of the spectator through the subtle art of the camera.[12]

Jean Epstein and Antonin Artaud

Early avant-garde filmmaking resulted in much forward-thinking prose, especially in relation to a cinema of pure visual idea. What is surprising is how much of this work has been forgotten as film theory matured. Perhaps this is because of the theoretically lackadaisical nature of their writings. But the use we should make of them comes exactly from the power of their rhetoric, which cuts through cold analysis with a happy sword. Jean Epstein and Antonin Artaud exemplify this mode.

Born in Warsaw in 1897, Epstein studied medicine in Switzerland before moving to France in 1921, where he began writing on the cinema (via the influence of

French theorist Louis Delluc). He drew a theory of *lyrosophy*, a singing of knowledge, producing reason and emotion in one fell swoop. For Epstein film has that unique quality, 'that of *being an eye independent of the eye*, of *escaping the tyrannical egocentrism* of our personal vision ... *the lens is itself*'.[13] And when he notes that 'there has never been an emotive process so homogeneously, so exclusively optical as the cinema. Truly, the cinema creates *a particular system of consciousness limited to a single sense*',[14] he is not finding a duplication of the work of the eye, but searching for a way to understand cinema's *neo-eye* quality. For Richard Abel, Epstein left behind the conception of cinema as a wavering system of signs, and moved on to the idea that cinema acted out a new kind of 'lyrosophical' thinking, one that could reveal 'the unconscious mysteries of nature, and human nature, through its epistemological exploration of time as well as space'.[15] Epstein also included the concept of *photogénie*, being that sublime, indefinable, ineffable quality given by film to the objects and people within it (and found most readily in close-ups and slow-motion).[16]

But most presciently, Epstein saw a future of film where subjective and objective viewpoints could be shown together, as one.[17] This idea grew in concert with his larger philosophy of film – Epstein posed narrative waxing as being omniscient, rather than subjectivist like the Impressionists' cinema. But this idea of simultaneously showing subjective and objective viewpoints brilliantly sums up the power of film-thinking in many ways – that film offers *another* view. Plus, it breaks any link with real-world experience. For Epstein film breaks free of human perception and moves towards revealing an omniscient eye – perhaps revealing the workings or 'logic' of the subconscious. As Abel notes, Epstein's lyrosophical thought (mediated through the human filmmaker) sought to bring this other consciousnes to light, 'through the hyperextension of a single sense – that of seeing'.[18] Film *sees* transsubjectively: one 'eye' seeing objectively and subjectively.

Antonin Artaud was born just a year before Epstein, in Marseille in 1896, and suffered throughout his life from neuralgia and depression (sparked by a severe attack of meningitis when aged four). He spent much of youth in a sanatorium – only interrupted by a spell in the army in 1916 (he was apparently discharged due to sleepwalking). He moved to Paris in 1920 and became an actor, playing Jean Paul Marat in Abel Gance's *Napoleon*, and the monk Jean Massieu in Carl Theodor Dreyer's *The Passion of Joan of Arc*. Artaud's writings of this period trace an uneven progress from identifying a hidden life or waking dream in film, to finding an expression of the mind, and then the realisation that film is more a 'disruption' of normal thought and an escape from the mind. Artaud conceived of three kinds of cinema, and his version of 'pure cinema' (actively experimental) was the only one that took the form of the

mind (if lacking emotion). The other two were narrative cinema, from basic psychology, executed along literary lines – a sort of 'venial hybrid art';[19] and 'true cinema', a
combination of narrative and pure cinema (way ahead of his cinematic time, the surrealist and actor was asking for a cinema that was a mix of plot and abstraction – as
pure abstraction has little relation to the human).

To achieve 'pure' thoughtful cinema, Artaud demanded 'poetic films in the intense,
philosophical sense of the word … films in which feelings and thoughts undergo a
process of trituration, in order to adopt that cinematographic quality *which still has
to be found*'.[20] Here we find an inkling of the movement Artaud was making, that of
understanding the transformation that film necessarily makes to the rough reality it
seemingly records – grinding it down into something else, a mixture of expression
and reality. Artaud was seeking a unifying concept of this transformative quality, an
idea that would take cinema to a new height of expression. In his essay 'Witchcraft
and the Cinema' Artaud considers that the direct affect of images on the mind may
be the key to understanding how film can think:

> the cinema is made primarily to express matters of the mind, the inner conscious-
> ness, not by a succession of images so much as by something more imponder-
> able which restores them to us with their direct matter, with no interpositions or
> representations … There will not be one cinema which represents life and another
> which represents the function of the mind. Because life, what we call life, becomes
> ever more inseparable from the mind.[21]

Which brings to my mind films such as Ken Loach's *Raining Stones* and Mike Leigh's
High Hopes, 'realistic' films which are often ignored for their *cinematic* qualities, their
cinematic 'extra character' or 'hidden life' as Artaud would call it,[22] leading the filmgoer to see things in a particular way. In his foreword to his scenario for *The Seashell and the Clergyman* Artaud wrote of his desire to engender film that draws on
'the very substance of the eye' to produce a 'visual cinema where psychology itself
is devoured by the action',[23] in other words, where thought is produced by the images. Distancing his ideas from language and dreams, Artaud powerfully identifies
the ur-ness, the ground of images, proclaiming that his scenario 'searches for the
sombre truth of the mind in images', images which draw their meaning 'from a sort
of powerful inner necessity which projects them into the light of a merciless evidence'.[24] Here Artaud really does seem to acknowledge the *unique* thoughtfulness of
film, whose meaning reaches us with direct force and distinctness. (This conception
clearly steers a further reconception of the role of the filmgoer in encountering the
thinking of film, a process I will discuss in chapter eight.)

Sergei Eisenstein

A year after sketching the idea of a filmic 'inner monologue' in his 1929 essay 'Beyond the Shot', Sergei Eisenstein met James Joyce in Paris. Eisenstein was impressed
by the stream of consciousness writing in *Ulysses*, and he and Joyce discussed the
possibility of depicting processes of thought in film.[25] Through his conversations
with Joyce, Eisenstein aimed to cinematically show these inner monologues in an
adaptation of *Ulysses* – but it remained his great unborn project. A few years later,
Eisenstein wrote more on the possibility of depicting inner thought – he was essentially reacting to the advent of sound, and the crass possibilities of talking images. The cinematic inner monologue would capture a character's internal process:
their memories, impressions, streams of linking thoughts. A similar conception to
Boris Eikhenbaum's 'inner speech': internal, private dialogue – a mental version of
normal social speech. But Eisenstein's inner monologue is not about language, but
about concepts, ideas and sensory, emotional qualities. The aim was to fix on film
the particular reality that the character experiences – the camera should go 'inside'
the character, and 'fix aurally and visually the feverish train of thought'.[26] The internal
monologue would reveal thought processes in film without resorting to theatrical
dialogue, and, significantly, might remove 'the boundaries between the subjective
and the objective'.[27] Eisenstein's laws of form came to be determined by their similarity to the laws of human thought – filmic discourse is thus seen to be similar to sensory or prelogical thought. To be effective, a film must find a balance between logical
and prelogical forms of thought – between what the film makes you understand
(plots, places, people) and what it makes you feel (danger, love, empathy).

Eisenstein spoke of film 'reconstructing' the actions and events of the human mind
– 'montage form as structure is a reconstruction of the laws of the thought process'[28]
– and his theories of progressive, associative montage were his attempt to show that
visual dialectics are an *expression* of thought. For Eisenstein, art requires conflict, and
conflict produces vibrations: physiological sensations ('I feel'). ('Stimulants' as Richard Taylor translates it, 'provocations' as Jey Leyda sees it.) Montage is an idea that
derives from the collision between two independent shots. Attractions are elements
within shots that we are drawn to through the narrative. Some are dominant, and
Eisenstein's early (machinic) concept of montage centred on those dominant attractions. One of the best examples is from Eisenstein's 1924 film *Strike*, which montages
a Cossack killing a child with a bull being slaughtered. The filmgoer can almost do
nothing except *feel the meaning* of the montage, can only *receive the shock* and *feel
the thought*. A carefully chosen pair of shots can 'explode into a concept'.[29] Like stereo-
scopy, two images combine to make another, a new idea, but in a way that (at this

stage in Eisenstein's thinking, in 1929) is still analogous to human thinking. For the early Eisenstein, not only does film think like us, but cinema should follow the methodology of language in order to refine its construction of new concepts and ideas. Using theories of ideogrammatic writing (similar to hieroglyphics), Eisenstein thus formulated a rhetorical, mechanical, Pavlovian concept of film, which thus became a highly manipulatable pictorial language.

But the sensual and emotional effect of montage leads to thought by bringing body and mind together. The filmgoer's shock to thought produces an intelligence of the senses. The 'intellectual' version of montage produces vibrations, not of the body this time, but of the mind, creating a new form of knowledge. Intellectual montage is the last stage in the creation of Eisenstein's 'intellectual cinema', which was originally posed against literary and theatrical cinema, as well as warning of the possible takeover of cinema by dialogue – the talkie having a vulgar naturalism for Eisenstein. It is the highest form of cinema, and the true and authentic expression of dialectical materialism (philosophy can now step aside). The montage of various gods and icons in *October* is a basic example – religious icons edited together, moving from the elaborate to the simple (a block of wood) – a montage that enacts a process of logical deduction for Eisenstein. The 'gods sequence' is a basic example because Eisenstein eventually saw a future cinema combining body and brain: 'Intellectual cinema will be the cinema that *resolves* the conflicting combination of physiological overtones and intellectual overtones, creating an unheard-of form of cinema'.[30]

And indeed, it is his later writings that brought out the many other opportunities for film form, and which led to his theorising the 'organic' whole of a film. For the later Eisenstein, montage is a much more fluid concept that now also takes place *within* a shot (within a fragment, a colour, a sound), as well as between film sequences and scenes.[31] The 'image' created by montage is the final idea or theme of the film. Eisenstein thus moved from mechanical rhetoric to *organic process*, creating films that delivered a transhistorical 'image' through an ecstatic process of resonance rather than shock. Film becomes an organic-machine, an organically unfolding creative process, bridging the poles: organic/machinic; art/rhetoric; speech/inner speech. The culmination of Eisenstein's theories, 'organic montage' produces pathos in the work, and thus an ecstatic reaction in the filmgoer.[32]

The method of organic montage is based on 'the vitalising characteristics and innate features common to every human being, just as they are common to every humane and vital art form'.[33] Taking a real-world experience, analysing what makes that experience (that image) special and unique, and translating that into film form – for Eisenstein that translation is *organic*, akin to a birth: the desired image or theme is born in the filmgoer's mind, allowing them to powerfully experience completing the film's 'theme'. Each film is a life-organism that develops and grows through its images and sounds. Each filmgoer sees a different film because the film-life can adapt to different perceptions, but without actually altering itself. Each film procreates by feeding into other films (through reference and homages) and into the filmgoers themselves, altering, affecting, infecting their lives, for a couple of hours in the cinema and sometimes beyond. And each film-life-organism exists 'for itself' (unlike a machine), as a work of independent art.

In a sense Eisenstein's thesis is this: the filmmaker apprehends in nature an idea or 'theme', and then translates this theme into the form of cinema (depictions and parts in conflict, organised through leaps and jumps in their quality), such that the filmgoer will come out with a similar 'image' of thought to the one the filmmaker first apprehended. Theme, depictions, conflicts, leaps, image; from the singular to the singular, via the multiple. The best films, according to Eisenstein, are thus targeted on a uniting *theme* (a soul, a concept, an idea or emotion), a theme that steers its choices and direction, towards its proper form, its almost preordained shape. Each instance of montage, each 'cell', serves this theme in a polyphonic montage to result in a single multiplicity – and the act of making the film is where the filmmakers discover the theme.[34] The filmmaker must realise the true form underlying the real-world event, and then reduce this theme 'into two or three *partial depictions*, which in combination and juxtaposition will evoke in the mind and emotions of their perceiver precisely that initial generalised image'.[35]

The theme of a film permeates every depiction, is the source of each depiction and unifies all depictions. There is thus a dialectical relationship between depiction and theme.[36] The depictions and the theme are two types of the same organic movement. The set (closed) and the Whole (open) inform each other – the set, for example a sequence of shots (cells), relates to other sets, informing and changing the meaning of the Whole, while the very growing of the 'wholes' *when perceived in this way* eases open the set relations for our greater understanding.[37] All parts of the film are thus *interrelated* and self-sustaining, and are abstracted and integrated by the filmgoer into the image of the film. Organic montage serves this theme, to create in the filmgoer's mind an image which arises out of the depictions in the film's story.

For Eisenstein, the basic themes of life are reducible to *conflict*. Opposites in collision give rise to a higher synthesis, and as the film progresses so the parts in opposition grow in size, until they become the work itself (the image, the whole).[38] Again, in two shots, the second gains impact via the first, and so there is a qualitative *jump*, a dialectical *leap*. Eisenstein wanted filmmakers to discover the dialectical form of events in nature, such that they might then translate this form into cinema. The principle or internal law behind the organic, generative growth within film is the Golden

Section, a ratio of parts to the whole, roughly 2:3, making a work that has unequal yet harmonious parts. The five-act tragedy of Eisenstein's *Battleship Potemkin* is structured according to this organic 'golden section' – the end of part three and the beginning of part four (62% of the way though the film, at the point 2:3, or 8:13 to be more precise) marks the dramatic crux, or main 'leap' of the film. This is where the red flag is raised on the mast of the battleship; and this is where the theme of revolutionary fraternity is fused. The leap is the introduction of the most decisive element of the film's image or theme, *'a revolutionary explosion'.*[39] Eisenstein compares these moments of culmination to when ice becomes water, or water becomes steam: an *ecstatic* movement from one state to another, from one quality to another.

The structure of the film is united towards this theme, developed using the formula of 'growth'. The film's first three sections grow marginally, just as in mathematics, from 1, to 2, to 4, such that the fourth act leaps to 8, and the fifth to 16 (as it were). The filmgoer's engagement and knowledge about the theme takes these leaps and jumps, growing organically in a logarithmic kind of spiral toward the Eisensteinian 'image'. The series 1–16 can be seen as such a spiral, doubling and increasing in speed and coverage. Organic montage is thus a great event of genesis, growth and development, born out of conflict – and the drama grows by these leaps or jumps between acts:

> not simply a sudden jump to *another* mood, to *another* rhythm, to *another* event, but each time it is a transition to a *distinct opposite*. Not contrastive, but *opposite*, for each time it gives *the image of that same theme from the opposite point of view and at the same time unavoidably grows out of it.*[40]

These are thus exponential leaps, from one quality to another, creating an expanding whole through *sensuous shift-thinkings*. Natural leaps as it were, because *nature is dialectical* (it is not 'indifferent'). Organic montage therefore pathetically produces expressive qualities – ideas drenched in emotion (pathos).[41] The collision of film cells (moments, acts, scenes) generates this 'pathos' through these revolutionary explosions. The pathos of the theme of *Battleship Potemkin* is embodied in the pathos of the form of the film: the rushing-movement filming of the people rushing down the steps helps the filmgoer to see the theme of pathos in the thinking of the film's style, thus allowing the filmgoer to *feel* the pathos. A film structured with pathos compels the filmgoer *'to experience the moments of culmination and becoming* of the norms of dialectic processes'.[42]

Furthermore, in order for the filmgoer to receive the image of the theme of the film they must leave their normal state of comprehension and reach another, ex-static state.[43] The film produces that ecstasy through pathos – an exalted feeling, a sense of being taken away by the film, an empathy; we participate in the film's thinking. Pathos, especially the colour sequences of *Ivan the Terrible*,

> is what forces the viewer to jump out of his seat. It is what forces him to flee from his place. It is what forces him to clap, to cry out. It is what forces his eyes to gleam with ecstasy before tears of ecstasy appear in them … it is everything that forces the viewer to 'be beside himself'.[44]

The powerfully organic-dialectical unity of the film creates a direct link to the filmgoer's mind.[45] The filmgoer is brought to this state by the *metaphoricity* of the depictions and the *organic organisation* of the depictions. For Eisenstein the filmgoer is tuned to this kind of film-thinking because the law of the film's structuring 'is also the law governing those who perceive the work, for they too are part of organic nature'; the filmgoer feels 'organically tied, merged and united with a work of this type, just as he feels himself one with and merged with the organic environment and nature surrounding him'.[46]

The filmmaker's theme thus lays out a path for the filmgoer to follow/interpret, such that they might derive an *image* of the film's theme; the filmgoer synthesises the depictions into an image of this theme. In fact each depiction, if it has that metaphorical open quality, has also a possible image – a felt meaning not reducible to the facts of the depiction itself. For instance, there is the graphic design of a frame (what is in it and how it looks: e.g. a barricade in a street), and then its image (a metaphor of its contents: e.g. the idea of revolution). A sequence then gains an image: a generalisation expressing the central idea of the scene, the truth of its content. Organic montage produces '*separate depictions … fused into an image*' by the filmgoer – an emotional image, a feeling; 'from a mass of particular details and depictions we shall observe the perceptible build-up of an image'.[47] But the filmgoer does not just 're-produce' the theme – Eisenstein is here allowing the filmgoer some intelligence and control over their meaningful experience of the film.[48] The filmgoer's mind energises the attractions before him, ultimately gaining, receiving, their particular image of the theme. Each filmgoer has a unique experience of this theme, and thus a unique and active way of creating their image of the theme. The desired/filmgoer's image 'is not something *ready-made* but *has to arise or be born from something else*'[49] – a virtual image.

These depictions and collisions and leaps are organised through melodious forms of polyphonic and vertical montage, weaving together dominant and overtonal elements, to achieve a resonant *synthetic, unified whole*. Contrast and counterpoint should still run through the course towards synthesis and unity – opposites (conflicts) have both unity and struggle inherent in their purpose. The filmgoer's image of the film represents this synthesis or unity of organic montage – a unity of nature and consciousness. The image that the filmgoer receives is a unitary image, an 'intellectual-emotional image'.[50] In a good film the thinking of the forms thus work together to create a *unified impression* – in a truly happy film (to choose a nice example) the shifts are happy, the colours are happy, the movement is happy, etc. Or as Eisenstein's example puts it: 'The hero grieves and nature, lighting, sometimes the composition of the frame, less often the rhythm of montage, and most of all the music pasted onto it, grieve with him in unison.'[51]

Film-thinking becomes a *personality*; the colours and framing have a personality, a way of thinking about the objects and subjects they surround and merge with. Representation and composition are united in thought – the film has an emotional relationship to its objects. Film-thinking should gain it's intentional style from an Other's viewpoint about the object, should tell us something about the object that cannot be gained from the object itself. Speaking of two characters, a German officer and a prostitute, from Maupassant's story 'Mademoiselle Fifi', Eisenstein clarifies this (reversal) dialectic:

The structure of the image of the 'noble officer' is assigned to the prostitute.
The structure of the image of the prostitute in its most unattractive resolution is the skeleton of the treatment of the German officer.
...
The structure of the image of the Frenchwoman is woven out of all the characteristics of nobility connected with the bourgeois presentation of an officer.
And it is quite revealing that by the very same method the German officer is revealed in his *essence – in his prostitute-like nature*.[52]

The film *thinks* the officer a prostitute – sees the officer through a prostitute form (perhaps the film image might be red and blurry with lechery). The organic unity of a film thus comes about 'when the law of the construction of this work corresponds to the laws of *the structure of organic phenomena of nature*'.[53] The filmgoer, as part of nature themselves, simply has to emotionally connect with the film in order to feel its theme.

The generalisation of depiction to image by the filmgoer requires a kind of *sensuous* thinking, and, in parallel, the depictions of film achieve their resonance through being a sensuous (emotional, organic) mode of film-thinking. In attempting to overcome the perceived idealism of the inner monologue, Eisenstein attempted to develop a model of mental imaging derived from naïve, intuitive, savage art, wherein pure line and form might amount to a more sensuous kind of thought. He drew on the work of anthropologist Lucien Lévy-Brühl to form a concept of cinema as 'sensuous thought'. Feelings, thoughts, concepts and action are on the same level of imagistic thinking. Film-thinking (image-structuring) can thus be seen as both logical (narrative and dialogue) and prelogical (colours and movements).

In the real world our imagination helps us unify the various perspectives and images given by our senses. Eisenstein argued that at the heart of cinema is the reflection of this primary, eidetic process of thought. The audio-visual counterpoint of montage thus mirrors the becoming of consciousness: our mind analyses the world, breaking it up into fragments, before creating a whole picture from those parts. Man creates cinema via this process, and cinema becomes a playing out of this process. It is in this sense that filmgoers create concepts by generalising a depiction – film-thinking is a reflection of the eidetic process of thought, a (perhaps 'purer') imagistic, transsubjective version of this process. Organic film-thinking conveys brutal (imagistic, direct) reasoning through the action-thoughts of the film form.[54] This film-thinking combines or fuses an idea with form; for Eisenstein, a film has two forms, internal (idea) and external (colour, shape). In *The General Line*, the metaphorical images of the fountains of milk from the cream separator, followed by shots of fireworks and streams of water, expresses the joy of the peasants that their machinery is working – a plastic rather than dramatic representation for Eisenstein.[55] An expressive organic film will thus induce the filmgoer to grasp a metaphorical significance deeper than the external form.[56] Eisenstein questions his own use of 'metaphor', and proposes to use 'fresh' metaphors only: emergent, nascent metaphors. As Geoffrey Nowell-Smith notes, for Eisenstein image, metaphor and montage are much the same thing: montage produces metaphors that produce images of thought in the mind of the filmgoer – thus montage's aim is the 'association, through the image, of object and idea'.[57] Montage is a figure of thought, in the sense of being a direct *reflection* of human thought, and the filmgoer's ecstasy results from the natural affiliation between human thought and the efficient thinking of montage.

Classic Eisensteinian montage, with its readable shift-thinkings, thus enacts a classic movement from image to thought.[58] Classic montage forces a concept or idea into the mind of the filmgoer. With later Eisenstein, sensuous film-thinking produces sensuous filmgoer thinking – previously only found in primitive myths and prelogical thought (inner speech). Organic montage, and its syntax of figures (metaphor, metonymy, synecdoche), simultaneously produces a figure-image, which causes another shock within the mind of the filmgoer. This double-shock returns the filmgoer to the images of the film. Thus organic montage also creates a second movement, from thought to the image: the filmgoer is made to think, and this thinking is of the image of the theme of the film.

Gilles Deleuze

Gilles Deleuze offers a variation and extension of Eisenstein's theories, and sees a third link between image and thought: the identity of one in the other. Deleuze used the theories of Eisenstein to grow his conception of a 'thinking image',[59] and his two-volume *Cinema*, completed in 1985, stands at the culmination of our history of film minds: it is a developmental, natural history of images; a taxonomy of cinema's signs; a pure semiotics. For Deleuze, the *image* is almost legible, in the sense of being a table of information; and he goes on to define image types according their content (rather than their 'meaning', as in semiotics). In the cinema the image is different from what it represents; cinema is beyond the bounds of representation; it is the image that is the real 'thing' present to the filmgoer.

In the first volume of *Cinema* Deleuze reclassifies classical narrative filmmaking as a cinema of movement-images – naturally structured stories in which we do not usually feel the attitude of the camera (for example, the film will normally simply follow and react to characters' movements), and where edit shifts are there to deliver an indirect (realistic) image of time, time in its empirical form.[60] But at the end of this first volume Deleuze notes a crisis in the reigning form of the movement-image (the action-image, where situations are changed by events into new situations, in a logically flowing narrative). He finds this crisis, or change, coming about in Italy towards the end of the 1940s, in France at the end of the 1950s, and then in West Germany around the late 1960s. The change concerns the structure of time in film, with a proliferation of fractured voyages and seemingly random spaces and images. Where the movement-image released an indirect representation of time, flowing from chronological montage, the time-image subverts this smooth passage and so gives a 'direct' image of time, shattering the sensory-motor schema. The time-image is the crisis of 'representability' – its opening-up, or deconstruction. In a sense the movement-image and time-image represent two kinds or structures of thinking (linear and non-linear, to oversimplify).

The relationship between cinema and thought is theorised differently for the movement-image and the time-image. Deleuze outlines three relationships between cinema and thought to be found in the movement-image: cinema and a higher Whole (how we think about the gathering, increasing meaning of the whole film); cinema and thought, through the unfolding of images (that is the thinking we do image by image); and cinema and the relationship between world/nature and man/

thought (the infusing of the filmgoer's thought by image). On the other hand, the modern cinema of the time-image develops three *new relations* with thought:

> the obliteration of a whole or of a totalisation of images, in favour of an *outside* which is inserted between them; the erasure of the internal monologue as whole of the film, in favour of a free indirect discourse and vision; the erasure of the unity of man and the world, in favour of a break which now leaves us with only belief in this world.[61]

In other words the break-up of flow, the instantiation of gaps and fissures in movement, and the splitting of subjectivity and objectivity, thus undermining traditional meaning structures and causing the jump to transcendent belief. Deleuze's 'mental image' takes on three different movements or forms in the cinema of the time-image: *image to concept*; *concept to image*; and *image as concept*.

Deleuze's first movement, of image to thought or concept, is deeply indebted to Eisenstein and Artaud (as is his whole 'thought-cinema'), and develops out of their conceptions of the 'shock' or 'vibration' to thought. Eisensteinian montage, as we have seen, produces a shock to the brain, awakening thought. Artaud also saw this unique aspect of cinema (neuro-physiological vibrations) that caused a shock to consciousness, and thus a birth of thought – he drew this from the way film *transforms*: 'The cinema implies a total reversal of values, a complete disruption of optics, perspective and logic.'[62] Film always produces an effect in the filmgoer, but, in Deleuzian terms, the time-image has a direct relation to (real) thought, and produces *thinking* in the filmgoer.

Deleuze's 'relation-image' is part of this first movement, creating a mental image, 'which takes as objects of thought, objects which have their existence outside thought, just as the objects of perception have their own existence outside perception. *It is an image which takes as its object, relations*, symbolic acts, intellectual feelings.'[63] The 'symbolic acts' and 'intellectual feelings' are similar to those we find in the story 'thinking' of intelligent drama (characters discussing ideas; stories with symbolic meanings). 'Relations' comes closer to the neominds of this stage: simply put, Deleuze argued that certain types of cinema contain images that make 'relation' their object – that is, images that, however formed, work as conjunctions.[64] Deleuze points to when the film gets bored of moving only with the characters, and takes off on it own movement, thus subordinating 'description of space to the functions of thought'.[65] These movements and reframings take on the *functions* of thinking. It is exactly the blurring of subjective and objective, the real and the imaginary

which will endow the camera with a rich array of functions, and entail a new conception of the frame and reframings ... a camera-consciousness which would no
longer be defined by the movements it is able to follow or make, but by the mental
connections it is able to enter into. And it becomes questioning, responding, ob-
jecting, provoking, theorematising, hypothesising, experimenting, in accordance
with the open list of logical conjunctions ('or', 'therefore', 'if', 'because', 'actually', 'although...').[66]

Film is capable of presenting the 'and' of our relational philosophies; and this con-
junction, that we struggle to solidify, to place, through the language of metaphorical
philosophy, becomes the flow of images in film.[67]

For Deleuze (in a 1983 conversation following the French publication of the first
volume of *Cinema*) this interpreting, hypothesising camera is 'a sort of third eye, the
mind's eye', as with Hitchcock, who 'frames the action in a whole network of relations
... symbolic acts that have a purely mental existence', where 'framing and camera
movement display mental relations'.[68] It is Hitchcock who introduces (what Deleuze
terms) the mental image into cinema – a consummation or saturation of the previous
types of images in Deleuze's history of images. But, significantly, Deleuze differenti-
ates the image from the 'camera' – the film image 'is able to catch the mechanisms of
thought, while the camera takes on various functions strictly comparable to propositional functions'.[69] This allows Deleuze to theorise a particularly movement-based
'camera-consciousness' as only one part of his larger 'thought-cinema'. In Hitchcock
the relation-image is also found in short shots, each illustrating a differing relation
to, or interpretation of, the action – 'relation' becomes the very object of the image.
In these images actions only come with sets of relations which alter their meaning:
for example, as mentioned in the Introduction to this volume, it is not dialogue, but
the camera which shows us why Jeffries has a broken leg in *Rear Window*. Deleuze
also cites the continual interpretation of Hitchcock's 1950 film *Stage Fright*, where
the film actively steers our knowledge all the way through, as well as the process of
reasoning in *Rope*'s 'single' shot.

But Deleuze, like Artaud and Eisenstein, saw a further possible thoughtfulness
of cinema: a second movement, from thought to (back to the) image. As Deleuze
replays, for Artaud the image has as its object 'the functioning of thought, and that
the functioning of thought is also the real subject which brings us back to the images'.[70] There are thus *two* shocks, from the image to concept (through *our* conscious
thought), and from concept to image: 'the thinking in figures which takes us back to
the images and gives us an affective shock again', as Deleuze puts it.[71] A basic metaphorical sequence will cause the filmgoer to think, cause them to receive a fairly

distinct idea. A somewhat more irrational sequence will cause the filmgoer to think and receive (a less exact) idea, and the shock of this 'new' idea will cause the filmgoer to go back to the images, re-experience them, and see *within* them a belief or inter-pretation that caused the idea. In other words, the shock effect of false movement and irrational cuts (forms of the time-image) provokes the filmgoer's 'new' thought, which brings them back to the image, and the interpretation or belief *within* the im-age itself. Deleuze did make the important step of actually trying to work out how the image might work to think, and my interest here is in finding out how Deleuze sets out this thought *within* the image – this interpretation or belief within cinema.

So for Deleuze, beyond the mutation of the movement-images, the mental image was also to 'do' thinking, rather than merely reflect or provoke it – to become a cin-ema of the seer rather than the agent. This is one of the most important moves in our history of film minds and film-beings. Thus the mental image, this new image, this new mutation of cinema, 'had not to be content with weaving a set of relations, but had to form a new substance. It had to become truly thought and thinking, even if it had to become "difficult" in order to do this.'[72] To make the mental the *object* of the image cinema must create and enact its own figures of thought, transforming narra-tive cinema by penetrating inside it – becoming a re-examination of its nature; this is why Deleuze sees the mental image as the summation or completion of cinema – all its images perfected. The mental image is here 'a primitive language or thought, or rather an internal monologue, a drunken monologue, working through figures, me-tonymies, synecdoches, metaphors, inversions, attractions….'[73] Drunk because it is blurry in its meaning, loose in its movement, becoming pre-verbal content. Deleuze means his mental image to embody the two 'faces' of the image, one which attends to the characters and events, and one which steers the whole film. A kind of thinking that informs our knowledge of what is happening, while also being in full control of the film's overall concerns. As Deleuze writes: 'The soul of the cinema demands increasing thought, even if it begins by undoing the system of actions, perceptions and affections on which the cinema had fed up to that point.'[74]

But the real importance of Deleuze's new situations (images or sequences) is their power, the power of pure image and sound, to 'replace, obliterate and re-create the object itself', to 'give rise to a seeing function'.[75] This is important because it recog-nises the ability of cinematic form to completely reinterpret the objects it is osten-sibly representing. Deleuze continues (including a quote from Jean Louis Schefer's *L'Homme ordinaire du cinéma*):

> the object of cinema is not to reconstitute a presence of bodies, in perception and
> action, but to carry out a primordial genesis of bodies in terms of a white, or a black

or a grey (or even in terms of colours), in terms of a 'beginning of visible which is not yet a figure, which is not yet an action'.[76]

Here the sense is of cinema being able to think anew, to create a new way of seeing bodies, producing a uniquely cinematic 'presence'.

For Deleuze both the film and the filmgoer can be referred to as 'automatons', either psychological or spiritual: these represent modes of thought (comparable to Heidegger's calculative and meditative thinkings). A *psychological automaton* is either a film or a filmgoer who enacts normal law-bound (unthinking) thought. The movement-image is just this, an automaton who 'no longer depends on the outside because he is autonomous but because he is dispossessed of his own thought, and obeys an internal impression which develops solely in visions or rudimentary actions'[77] – somnambulists and hypnotisers like Dr Caligari or Dr Mabuse. Deleuze's *spiritual automaton* refers to a mode of thought that is alien and outside to this normal thinking. Artaud noted that the cinema resembled automatic writing, *simultaneously* conscious and unconscious, a spiritual automaton. The time-image is like a spiritual automaton for Deleuze, 'the highest exercise of thought, the way in which thought thinks and itself thinks itself in the fantastic effort of an autonomy'.[78] This is automatism become spiritual art, and heralds a cinema of true self-specificness (eventually creating a thought specific to cinema). For Deleuze this cinema resembles no language, but consists of 'pre-linguistic images' and 'pre-signifying signs':

> It constitutes a whole 'psychomechanics', the spiritual automaton, the utterable of a language system which has its own logic. The language system takes utterances of language, with signifying units and operations from it, but the utterable itself, its images and signs, are of another nature.[79]

This contrast with language is a necessary starting point, as images will always be, in one way or another, linked to language. Deleuze is saying that *images have their own logic of non-linguistic communication*. The time-image film-being is itself a spiritual automaton, a psychomechanics with its own logic, enacting a free indirect (trans-subjective) film-thinking. The image is thus 'the utterable itself' – pure automatic or psychomechanical utterance (emitting from itself, a no-place). Significantly it is an autonomous thinking machine: as Deleuze relays, for Jean Louis Schefer the cinema is a 'giant in the back of our heads, Cartesian diver, dummy or machine, mechanical man without birth who brings the world into suspense'.[80]

Deleuze sees film-being as the 'brain' of this spiritual automaton: the film-world is a brain-world. Love, death, memory, future, reality: Deleuze's cinema of the brain (the stories of Kubrick and Resnais) and cinema of the body (the interacting bodies in Godard and Cassavetes) become the thinking of the film. (Antonioni passes through both – the tirednesses of the world, and its possibilities of creativity.) In Kubrick's films the brain is there in the mise-en-scène for Deleuze, and the scale and sets of his films make us see the world itself as a brain. But even though Deleuze states his interest in how film might work as a brain, his is not about an image of *someone's* thought, nor a pure thought by a pure thinker; he is using the term 'brain' in a much more metaphorical way (edit shifts can be like cinematic synapses, linking and un-linking different circuits). And when Deleuze introduces the 180° continuity shots of Ozu, and the multiple orientations of *The Central Region*,[81] he is showing that the im-age requires a more fluid conception than that so far provided. The image becomes a panel of information, a mesh of messages, and film no longer contains images like those formed for the eye, but 'an overloaded brain endlessly absorbing information: it is the brain-information, brain-city couple which replaces that of eye-Nature'.[82]

Film paraminds

The final step in our history of film minds and film-beings is that of the para-thought-ful film. Here it is mainly Deleuze who finds film starting to be able to think *more* than us, finds a cinematic thought that can do so much more than our own. At this point film truly becomes something very different to, something more (and less) than, our own thinking – becoming sensory thought, emotional intelligence: the exploration of a thought *outside* itself.

But, as we have already seen, Deleuze would never have got this far without Ar-taud. In his scenario for *The Seashell and the Clergyman* Artaud saw a film that 'de-velops a sequence of states of mind deduced the one from the other, as thought is deduced from thought *without this thought reproducing the reasonable sequence of facts*'.[83] That is, a film that achieves thought without reasoning. In this film Artaud intended to isolate an element of cinema: 'This element, which differs from every sort of representation attached to images, has the characteristics of the very vibra-tion, the profound, unconscious source of thought'.[84] In an essay from 1933, Artaud attempts to explain why the cinema *looks* as it does, and realises that the lens of the camera, 'which pierces to the centre of objects *creates its own world*'.[85] And although he understands this as corresponding to the ways of the mind, he follows through this line of enquiry, and asks if the cinema could

> carry the experiment further and offer us not only certain rhythms of habitual life as the eye or ear recognises them, but those darker, slow-motion encounters with

all that is concealed beneath things, the images – crushed, trampled, slackened, or dense – of all that swarms in the lower depths of the mind.[86]

These are images that *we cannot think; images beyond our experience*. Artaud calls cinema 'a succession of mechanical apparitions which *escaped* from the very laws and structures of thought'[87] – for him cinematic images have moved *beyond* human thought, have *liberated* the forces of the mind.

After working through the 'shock to thought' of the first 'image to concept' movement, and the appropriation by cinema of rhetorical forms in the second 'concept to image' movement, Deleuze proposes the *identity of image and concept* to be the third movement: 'The concept is in itself in the image, and the image is for itself in the concept ... no longer organic and pathetic but dramatic, pragmatic, praxis, or action-thought'.[88] Violence, for example, can be communicated by the vibrations coming off the image, rather than that of the represented, while a concept such as 'grandeur' should be brought out by composition, and also not by any attempted representation. Here cinema seeks to be its own thought – for Deleuze the essence of cinema takes on the *functions* of thought. Recurring through this final conception is the realm of the *unthought*, the way that film thinks what we cannot think, or are not yet able to think. For the moment it is enough to sketch its idea: formally, that of gaps and dissonances in the form of images, and, in its reception, an indication of the impower of *our* thought in the face of this new thinking. Deleuze's 'problematic images' and 'irrational cuts' go to make up a paramind of the unthought. Necessary for this movement into the unthought is the recognition of film's autonomy: film controls its own images, and thinks anew. And the thinking is self-perpetuating, not a thinking that can be translated.[89] Here film moves into real creative 'choice' – for Deleuze it is filmmakers such as Pasolini and Dreyer and Bresson who, beyond the interpretive relation-image, show film to be 'capable of revealing to us this higher determination of thought, choice, this point deeper than any link with the world'.[90]

As Deleuze pursues the thinking of the image he extends the mechanics of that thinking, making for some difficult reading. Deleuze finds depth-of-field, say in Renoir and Welles, not to be merely metaphorically figurative, but more demanding, almost 'theorematic', the chain of images working more like a theorem, making thought immanent to each image. Film-thinking here is no longer relational (e.g. figurative metaphors and linkages) but immanent to the film – automatic almost. The filmgoer feels the *intention* of the film, whether posing a problem or staging a theorem. Again, thought is presented as 'belief' – *outside* interiority or knowledge.[91] Deleuze unites the thinking of cinema with an inescapable *believing* – a thinking towards the world. He finds this in Godard's novelistic free indirect cinema, which erases the unity of man and world to leave us only with belief in this world. When Deleuze introduces the idea that cinema 'must film, not the world, but belief in this world',[92] he is advocating a cinematic thinking *towards* the world, interpreting it, changing it (creating a film-world). Film bypasses our deadened interaction with the world by feeling it, relating to it intuitively. In philosophy Deleuze compares this to the replacing of the model of knowledge with belief. But importantly for Deleuze, it must be a belief in *this* world, not another, transformed one.

Inextricably linked with the mental image is the time-image which brings in irrational cuts and interstices – inextricably linked because cinema needs to be thinking before it can attempt to give a direct representation of time. The time-image is at once a re-examination of the nature and status of the movement-image, and the very crisis of the movement-image. It heralds the autotemporalisation of the image, most obviously leading to open plots and multiple flashbacks and flashforwards. The chronosigns of the time-image give, in D. N. Rodowick's words, 'the appearance of time as a nonlinear and nonchronological *force*'.[93] Film, here, is helping us understand time, openness and the whole. Deleuze found in Schefer (along with Artaud and Eisenstein, a major influence on Deleuze) a similar attention to time. Though Schefer feels that cinema can only produce the effects of memory, can only imitate thinking (an eye without a memory), he understands that this gives rise to a new kind of thinking – film offers us a new direct experience of time; the film is a mind that has a direct feeling for time.

Where the movement-image is empirical time (the indirect representation of time), the time-image is transcendental – presenting time in its pure state. Purely optical and sound situations (opsigns and sonsigns) are the foundations of the time-image. These extend into recollection-images and dream-images rather than action. The time-image 'shows time through its tiredness and waitings' (citing Antonioni); time 'appears for itself'.[94] False movement and false continuity – *irrational cuts* – make visible 'relationships of time which cannot be seen in the represented object', creating 'a coexistence of distinct durations ... which can only appear in a creation of the image'.[95] It is also the breaking down of the action-image (situation, followed by action, creating a new situation).[96] Films such as Tarantino's *Pulp Fiction* and Resnais' *Last Year in Marienbad* make obvious examples, shifting, as they do, layers of time over each other. But also films such as Angelopoulos's *Ulysses' Gaze* or Straub and Huillet's *Too Early, Too Late*, inhabiting time, almost leaving time behind, via their pure optical states. Here it is less a case of film cutting images from reality (the whole which is the outside), than images 'plucked from the void',[97] and differentiated by interstices through shifts to images of productive potential (frequent in Godard). *Not a chain or association of images, but a 'method of BETWEEN'.*[98] The montage of the direct presentation of time (irrational shifts) produces an unthought, a kind of irrationality that is proper to thought.

The time-image is part of this movement into the 'unthought'. Deleuze recognises that it is Artaud who makes cinema the thinking of the unthought – gaps, fissures, nothings: 'on the one hand there is no longer a whole thinkable through montage, on the other hand there is no longer an internal monologue utterable through image'.[99] Godard's recent video work is instructive here. Iconographic montage-thinkings such as *Histoire(s) du cinéma* and *The Old Place* are exercises of thought, using a souped-up version of Eisenstein's intellectual montage in sequences infused with melancholia. And there are differing intensities of the interstice: superimposition gives the filmgoer time to think, while sharp shifts and sounds cut short awake us with shocks to thought. But images also emerge from the centre of other images (iris-like), perhaps thinking a sense of one thought growing from within another. Here irrational cuts create an original re-linkage of images:

> This is why thought, as power which has not always existed, is born from an outside more distant than any external world, and, as power which does not yet exist, confronts an inside, an unthinkable or unthought, deeper than any internal world. … There is no longer any movement of internalisation or externalisation, integration or differentiation, but a confrontation of an outside and an inside independent of distance, this thought outside itself and this un-thought within thought.[100]

For Deleuze our thought is born from experience of much more that just reality (an 'outside' of proud and straight knowledge). In cinema this thought is confronted by the profound emotional thought of moving sound-images. The unthought is a thought 'outside' thought. Deleuze's new *cerebral* images define themselves through this relation of the inside and the outside – an unsummonable, inexplicable, undecidable, incommensurable outside.

Deleuze adds to this conception Schefer's views from his 1981 book *L'Homme ordinaire du cinéma*. Deleuze remarks that for Schefer,

> the cinematographic image, as soon as it takes on its aberration of movement, carries out a *suspension of the world* or affects the visible with a *disturbance* … directed to what does not let itself be thought in thought, and equally to what does not let itself be seen in the vision.[101]

The time-image, in its 'aberration of movement', is not of our perception or thought, being a furtherance or parallel thinking. This suspension of the world gives the visible to thought in that it replaces our regular vision (thought) of the world with a different view. Deleuze reads Schefer's cinema to be 'a thought whose essential character is not yet to be ... not that it is here a matter of thought become visible, the visible is affected and irremediably infected by the initial incoherence of thought, this inchoate quality'.[102] The 'ordinary man of cinema' is this incoherence – spiritual automaton, experimental dummy. The cinematic image takes on what we cannot think; it reflects our initial 'incoherent' thoughts (unformulated linguistically) – those thoughts that are powerful but unnameable, uncontrollable.

Now that this film-thinking has successfully ruptured our confidence in our knowledge of the world, Deleuze argues that film can also re-establish the link between man and world by bringing in the unthought of that relationship. Film shows us the impower of our thinking in relation with the world. Deleuze's realisation of cinema's para-thoughtful state comes through his reading of Artaud: that cinema shows us the impower of our own thought. For Artaud cinema is uniquely suited to reveal this powerlessness. By bringing 'the *unconscious mechanisms of thought* to consciousness'[103] film alights on this impower. Filmgoer and film: thought brought face to face with its own impossibility: the impossibility of our thinking its thoughts; the *powerlessness of our thought* in contrast with film-thought. In sum, film shows the unthinkable, forcing us (the filmgoers) to face up to our limited thinking. All this points to the (Heideggerian) fact that we are not yet *thinking*: a 'being of thought which is always to come'.[104] If theatre gives us presence, cinema offers a different objective for Deleuze (after Schefer):

> it spreads an 'experimental night' or a white space over us; it works with 'dancing seeds' and a 'luminous dust'; it affects the visible with a fundamental disturbance, and the world with a suspension, which contradicts all natural perception. What it produces in this way is the genesis of an 'unknown body' which we have in the back of our heads, like the unthought in thought, the birth of the visible which is still hidden from view.[105]

A birth in the image and shock to *rebirth* in the filmgoer – this unthought lying dormant at the back of thought. Film's dancing grains, its primary forms, are recognised here as the site of the birth of this 'other' thought. The first chapter of Part Two will attempt to conceptualise the origin of these dancing grains: a filmind. A concept that will hopefully help us design a practical, applicable theory of this other thought, this new film-thinking.

part **two**

five | **filmind**

I have been interested in how we can move this point of consciousness over and
through our bodies and out over the things of the world … I want to make my camera become the air itself. To become the substance of time and the mind.

– Bill Viola (1995)[1]

Filmosophy is partly a philosophy of film-being, and the 'filmind' is its particular conceptualisation of film-being. The concept of the filmind offers a radical yet practical
framework with which to understand the creation and intention of moving sound-
images – it is essentially behind the 'primordial genesis of bodies' (Deleuze).[2] It is
not an empirical description of film, but is rather a *conceptual* understanding of the
origin of film's actions and events. Being a conceptual construct and not an empirical
explanation it resembles an urconcept, or urtheory of film – the kind of theory that
comes before aesthetics and evaluation. For instance, as the ultimate controlling
force (behind and before any possible 'narrative'), the filmind can construct an autonomous invented world (such as *Final Fantasy*), significantly embellish a fictional one
(such as *Amelie*), or apparently show realistic events (such as *Rosetta*). The concept
of the filmind is there to help us equally understand *Rosetta and Amelie*, subtlety
and extravagance. But significantly for a 'film-being', filmosophy wishes to place the
origin of film-thinking 'in' the film itself. There is no 'external' force, no mystical being
or invisible other. It is the film that is steering its own (dis)course.[3]

It is called the 'filmind' because, simply, it is not a human mind. It is another kind
of mind, its own mind, a new mind. It is the next step on from the use of 'mind' as
a metaphor for film's actions – those actions have their *own* mindfulness. When I
say film is a mind of its own, the meaning of 'mind' has been changed towards its
expression through film. The extension of this process is the coining of 'filmind', so
as to make clear the meaning, but also to allow the idea's rhetorical progression in
talk about film. The term also designates that the dramatic meaning of film comes
from 'within' the film rather than from some outside force. For instance, it certainly

does not represent the sort of 'sentient being' that George Wilson looked for in his *Narration in Light*, but is rather a shorthand for the abstract bucket from which film's sounds and images spring. Essentially the filmind is just the film, so the terms will later become interchangeable, and eventually the term 'filmind' will not be necessary ('the film does this', instead of, 'the filmind thinks this'). The term itself need only reappear infrequently, and only when absolutely necessary in any film interpretations – but will be central to philosophical discussion later in this work. The filmind becomes just 'the film' – speaking of 'the film' believing this, questioning that, will be enough to designate the working of the filmind.

Deleuze has described film-being as the brain of a spiritual automaton. While the term 'brain' may still be anthropomorphic and limiting (making film a mirror of activity), Deleuze is led to this idea not only because cinema is more than an eye, a perception of a world, but also because the concept of the brain identifies that film has a content and a structure and a working nature. But it has no 'self'. Reflexive cinema (postmodern referencing, Brechtian wake-up calls, playful nods, and so forth) simply calls attention to the event of film-being and film-thinking, possibly forcing the filmgoer to look outside the film for further information. The filmind is thus a rhetorical extension of Deleuze's spiritual automaton, a 'psychomechanics' with its own logic, enacting a transsubjectively free-indirect film-thinking, a union of the material and the spiritual. The filmind can be anonymous and neutral, and quietly show the drama, allowing the film-world to respond to characters' movements and actions – this kind of film-thinking defers to the characters, letting the filmgoer see their progress without too much presence. But it can also be expressively controlling, moving about independently of the characters or fluidly re-creating the film-world. Either way it expresses itself dramatically through its film-thinking: being calculating like *π*, or meditative like *Badlands*, or ethical like *The Son*.

Here the charge of solipsism arises. Is the filmind therefore a Cartesian, Hobbesian, or Lockean mind, one that is conscious only of itself, its own thinkings? The filmind as a brain in a vat? If the filmind is enclosed in its own thinking, how can it appropriate other films, make in-jokes about the actual creators or actors, or comment on real-world events? Almost exactly halfway through his 1938 novel *Murphy*, Samuel Beckett decides he must speak of his central character's mind:

> Murphy's mind pictured itself as a large hollow sphere, hermetically closed to the universe without. This was not an impoverishment, for it excluded nothing that it did not contain. Nothing ever had been, was or would be in the universe outside it but was already present as virtual, or actual, or virtual rising into the actual, or actual falling into the virtual, in the universe inside it.[4]

Beckett's words could also describe the solo-intention of film – an intention that conceptually seems to have no other origin than itself. In human phenomenology we are minds plus reality – as Merleau-Ponty points out: 'I do not think the world in the act of perception: it organises itself in front of me.'[5] Filmosophy argues that the filmind and the film-world are one and the same: the film-world does not organise itself independently of the filmind. Yet a solipsistic philosophy of mind is very different to the pre-designed, yet enclosed thought of the filmind. Film-thinking may be enclosed, but the filmind is conscious of external events because it is designed by real people, with real desires and motives. Artists and cameras and technicians and writers and microphones and actors and nature and best boys all play a part.

Film-thinking is always 'created', by filmmakers – David Lynch orchestrates his films along planes of narrative that are made to either intersect or run parallel; Martin Scorsese designs images with bold colouring and descriptive movements that reveal a judgement about the characters in the drama; Béla Tarr creates film-worlds with lengthy thought-images that reveal the gapless nature of experience and the fluid linkages between characters. These filmmakers translate ideas into the form of cinema by harnessing and mobilising different strategies of film-thinking, but they cannot transcend the concept of 'film-thinking'; using this concept, the film-goer experiences the film in ways that the mechanics of artistic filmmaking and the creative intentions of filmmakers cannot completely control or limit. Filmmakers are film-creators, but they are also simple conduits for film-thinking, and conceptually it seems better to initially divorce the creators in order to begin to purely understand this film-thinking. By conceptualising film this way filmosophy does not aim to sideline the creators of cinema, but simply attempts to re-invigorate the experience of film.

Filmosophy is therefore interested in the philosophical question of how film creates the meanings filmgoers feel, beyond mechanics and creative intention. And to do this the argument must start with the film as pure sound-image experience. This approach also has the advantage of revealing the pure poetry of cinema, before films are mangled by contextual knowledge. While information can certainly be added to larger interpretive strategies or filtered through a particular person's knowledge about a film, filmosophy does want to find out what the films *alone* are thinking, and just how poetic a private experience of film can be. We all initially experience films as new film-worlds – especially with 'new' films by new directors – and the 'naïve' experience of those films has the potential to reveal new concepts of film-thinking, and that is what filmosophy is interested in.

It is contemporary film that cries out for this new conceptualisation of film as thinking. Current image forms are malleable and free to show virtually anything, and both the unreliable narrator and non-subjective 'point of view' shot are becoming more apparent. This affects film theory and criticism, indicating a need for a more poetic (rather then technicist) descriptive language, and thus comprehension, of film form. The fluidity and scope of the moving sound-image deserves (requires) such a conceptualisation: all film is thinking. The contemporary film can go anywhere and show anything – it is *asking* for a new conceptualisation. When the film arrives at us, when the film begins, the filmind is there, thinking has started. This means that the whole film is intended, all formal moves are thus possibly important or meaningful; the film becomes alive with intention. The concept of the filmind is there to help the filmgoer *relate* to the formal twists and turns of film; it is there to assist in their *experience* of film. Thus beyond any 'essence' to the conceptual existence of the filmind, what is more important for our knowledge of cinema (philosophy is another matter) is *what it does*. My aim in this chapter is thus to set out the conceptual and working descriptions of this intending filmind.

Film-world creation

There are two aspects to the filmind: the film-being that creates the basic film-world of recognisable people and objects, and the film-being that designs and refigures this film-world. We shall call these two aspects film-world creation and film-thinking. The filmind *exists* in its activities of film-world creation and film-thinking. André Gaudreault, Robert Burgoyne and George Wilson all recognised the need to conceptualise this simultaneous presenting and refiguring. In conceptualising a filmind behind film-world creation filmosophy is attempting to see film for the first time: film is flat and it can show anything; it gives us moving sound-images (we do not see a director or a camera); it is a careful construction, and physically appears as just light and sound in the experience of the filmgoer.

Let us look at the not obviously conceptual question of film-world creation. Not obvious because a car or a chair in a film does not seem to require a conceptual reason for appearing as they do. The indexical nature of celluloid or digital tape is the reason a car looks like a car and a chair looks like a chair. Filmosophy *does* theoretically account for the basic film-world, but this account does not impact on the meaning of this film-world. Conceptually accounting for a car looking like a car does not give that car a more meaningful quality for the filmgoer. That the filmind creates the film-world (of cars and people and buildings) is therefore relatively useless for the filmgoer's experience of most films. But a coherent and comprehensive concept of film-being must be able to account for both film objects and film style. It is in this sense that filmosophy *wants* to theoretically account for film-world creation, that is,

in order to work through its philosophy of film-being. But it also *needs* to theoretically account for its creation in order to help the filmgoer eventually understand fluid
film-thinking. The idea sits at the back of the filmgoer's head, resting there until a
particular film engages in film-thinking that re-creates this basic film-world (through
special effects or computer-generated imagery).

So, in this theoretical account, the filmind creates everything we see and hear in
a film, conjuring it all up: people, buildings, settings. It creates, composes, inhabits,
and controls the film-world, for instance it is the creator of the dinosaurs and the
people in *Jurassic Park*. Film-world creation is the unstudied 'intention' of the filmind (while re-creative film-thinking is something like the studied 'will'; but there is a
significant poetic grey area of thinking in-between). This 'pre-reflective' side of the
filmind creates the basic coherent world of the film. The filmind thus has a basic
belief in the film-world; an *Ur-doxa* or *world belief*. In this unstudied natural intention, the film-world obeys normal and natural laws (light, shadow, dimension). In this
natural attitude we simply see objects as neutrally as possible. This base creation is a
simple likeness of the real world we know, with gravity and shadow and people and
buildings. For Merleau-Ponty, phenomenology 'must rediscover ... a presence to the
world which is older than intelligence',[6] and the filmind has the feeling of this presence – this natural intuitive immediacy – to its world.

This relation between the filmind and reality is important here. The basic film-
world is not a copy of reality. The event of filmmaking does usually begin with the
unique recording of the real world (we might call this the debt of images), but even
technically, the film camera is never merely an autotelic device, an end in itself, reproducing a sliver of reality: the film's image of the world is no longer 'formed automatically, without the creative intervention of man' (Bazin),[7] nor has it ever really
been since the beginning of cinema. The filmind thus creates its own film-objects
(via the mechanics of filmmaking) within a unique film-world. This does not mean
that we do not eventually relate a film such as *Rosetta* to our real world and its poli-
tics and humanity, rather it just means that we are *ready* (conceptually) to accept
whatever 'kind' of image-reality the film decides to give us. Filmosophy is interested
in 'conceptualising' *all* film, where 'reality' can often be heavily disguised by slow-
motion and space-shifts and digital morphing. Film has moved on and our concepts
need to adapt. We must resist the desire to always 'reference' film to real-world physical laws and properties, exactly because contemporary film is leaving those laws and
properties behind.

Strictly then, within this theoretical account, the filmind thus creates or visually
produces the 'objects' (characters, sounds, buildings) we see. The filmind in a sense
becomes the 'objects' in its own particular, unique film-world. And unlike our con-

sciousness, these objects are totally 'within' the filmind. As indicated above, a solipsistic theory of the filmind would therefore say that there are no objects, there
is only appearances (the two-dimensional film event). This possible idealism of the
filmind provokes many questions – some of which were posed in chapter three. If
the filmind 'is' its objects, how do we term the 'relationship' it has with the objects the
filmgoer plainly sees? Is the film's 'experience' of things similar to our experience of
things? Indeed, should we even call the film-being's relationship with the content of
film 'experience'? If there are no objects how can there be an 'experience' of those objects? For Vivian Sobchack, the film-subject 'experiences' a 'world' from a subjective
viewpoint.[8] These phenomenological theories of the film's 'experience' argue that
the film has a vision of objects – but are these theories confusing the mechanical
perception of 'filming' with the pure moving sound-image event of 'film'? Talking of
'film experience' and 'film vision' surely implicates a gap, an anthropomorphic attention, from film to film-world. How can film have experience of 'separate things' when
film *is its things*.

The answer to this paradox lies in the filmgoer's experience of the film. The filmgoer does see objects, recognisable objects, within a film-world. We say that 'the
film moves towards a chair', when it is strangely more correct to say that the film
thinks the movement and the chair as one, as one changing image (the chair gets
bigger). But the chair in the room is not seen by the filmgoer as being part of 'film-
world creation', it is seen as a chair in a room, and the filmgoer feels themselves being
brought nearer to the chair. The filmind and the film-world may be strictly one and
the same thing, but *film-thinking* is (most often) realised, correctly, as an *intention
towards recognisable objects* (characters, sunsets, guns). Most films do present their
film-thinking as if it were an 'experience' of objects – the better reason not to use the
term 'experience' may derive from the argument that film is not human, nor simply
subjective.

So why theorise this strict level of the filmind? Why say that the filmind creates
the film-world? Because this normally dormant fact (of filmind's creation of the film-
world) becomes more interesting when film begins to reveal this ability to re-think
the film-world it has created. Let us consider two very different films. *Rosetta*'s film-
world (of people and caravans and rain and roads and mopeds) is only re-thought,
only intended upon, by classical film stylings: movement, shifts, framing, sound
level, image grain, colour tone, and so on. *Amelie*'s film-world (of people and cafés
and sunshine and canals and mopeds) is re-thought by these classic film-thinkings
and fluid, film-world re-thinkings. The fluid film-thinking filmind of *Amelie* decides to
turn our heroine into water, or animate photobooth images. A film such as *Amelie*
stretches our understanding of 'form and content', mixing and uniting them until

the film has no 'objects' except itself. In theoretically accounting for the 'person' of Amelie in the film, the filmgoer can organically understand the way that the filmind can show us her heart, beating, colourfully, beneath her clothing and skin.

Simply put, film-thinking is normally colourings and movements and image shifts and sound design – but with the acceptance of the filmind and its film-world creation we can then add another 'formal' mode of film-thinking: fluid film-thinking. (Note: 'fluid' being a starting term that can and should be replaced and updated as film replaces and updates its malleabilities.) Filmosophy's filmind is a response, in part, to this future of film. The filmind can alter the time and space of objects as we normally experience them. It does not 'represent' actual things, it thinks its own film-things: seeing film objects as 'created' does not take away their commonsensical recognisability, *but simply allows for the malleability of that object within the film*. The filmind, as Deleuze would say, 'composes bodies out of granules'.[9]

Conceptualising such film-world creation allows for a flexibility of film-thinking, and allows for the film to re-think its creation via fluid film-thinking. We know from the beginning of *Rosetta* that we will not need this concept; we know soon enough in *Amelie* that we may. In filmosophy, the film is an *integrated being*. The filmind is capable of creating un-real worlds and re-creating real-looking worlds – and so a philosophy of film-being, to be inclusive of all films, must be able to handle every type of cinema, from the realistic to the fluid-future. We humans intend both our version of the world and our selves in it; the filmind intends both its world and its self – its *belief* in the objects it itself creates. The filmind *is* its objects and characters, it just does not normally let us know: most characters are just not 'changed' by the filmind in the manner we see in *Amelie*. But we must start with *Amelie*, at the possibility of total manipulation; we must be ready for anything.

This conception of film-thinking *anticipates* that fiction films can be as abstract as experimental and avant-garde filmmaking. Whether it is a matter of *Three Colours: Blue*'s defocusings, or the distortions of *Natural Born Killers*, a good theory of film must be able to cope with the margins of film form, and not relegate it to an 'excess'. A filmgoer who takes on this conceptualisation of film is thus ready, almost anticipating, the possibilities of cinema. The fluidly changing faces of the characters in *Natural Born Killers* no longer provoke confusion about who or what is 'doing that', the filmgoer sees the thinking of the filmind, and moves on with their experience and interpretation. The concept of the filmind makes the filmgoer aware that the film-world can be re-thought – that film-thinking may dig into the film-world to undo or subvert this basic creation. If a filmgoer has the concept of the film-world-creating filmind in their mind as they watch a film, then they will be ready for whatever manipulation the contemporary film throws at them. The filmind is designed around this new future of film, a future of being able to *be* anything anywhere. With this new physics of filmmaking we need this new concept of film-being.

Film-world re-creation

But in order to consider the more important (more commonly apparent) working of the filmind, that is film-thinking, we should make this concept of film-world creation quiet for now. For in most cinema this side of the filmind is relatively unimportant, or rather not helpful, in comparison to its main true (conceptual) role: that of elucidating and illuminating the images and sounds of film. The fact that the filmind conjures up people and places is redundant in most cinema experiences: the filmgoer is not meant to sit there and think how incredible it is that these characters are so real and yet are two-dimensional inscriptions of a filmind. The concept of film-world creation is simply there as a background idea, available for when fluid film-thinking films arrive at our senses. The filmind is thus an all-creating film-being that also *designs* its film-world of people and objects, either through basic image tone and sound level, or by more obvious turns of form such as film movement or digital morphing. These areas we shall call basic, formal and fluid film-thinking – each refigures the recognisable people and places that have been created. Therefore, importantly, interestingly, practically, the filmind thinks *how* we see and hear what we do. The 're-mainder' it still does create, but that it 'thinks' characters and mountains and streets is not (poetically, interpretively) that important for now. *The important film-thinking is that which 'surrounds' recognisable people and objects in film.*

The coherent film-world is thus given a layer of intention in the work of film-thinking. The pre-reflective creation of the film-world (filmind thinking) is reflected upon (filmind Thinking). Let us compare this to our thinking for a moment. Human reflective subjectivity (or attention) questions the objects of consciousness – clarifies their significance. Attention 'as a general and formal activity',[10] as Merleau-Ponty noted, does not exist without objects; attentions transform objects into figures, new objects. This phenomenological attitude is our studied 'will': reflective, philosophical, analytical. *Differently*, the filmind's reflective will contemplates its natural intention, questioning the neutral creation. A change of focus, a colouring of a scene, a shift to an object, a movement towards another character, all are examples of the filmind's attention. Thus the filmind simultaneously creates and *refigures* the film-world. It 'decides' when to shift from one character to another, when to move along a street, when to focus on the background, when to show what a character sees, when to switch into black and white, when to frame a person's face, when to slow the film down. The filmind chooses not to show the face of Gino at the beginning of *Osses-*

sione, that is until he is seen by Giovanna – the filmind knows that it is through their relationship that they reveal each other. Film-thinking is the mobile and intentional action of the filmind. The filmind is always implicated in its thinking – the filmind exists in its act of thinking. Basic film-thinking begins with basic values: a black and white image or a colour one, grainy or sharp, wide or square. Basic film-thinking is not pre-reflective, the design of the basic film-world is as much a 'decision' by the filmind – that people look like people is the pre-reflective part of the filmind, whether a person is shown in grey or colourful tones, for instance, is because of the reflective part of the filmind.

The filmind enables film-thinking to be at the service of many masters. The filmind serves itself, the drama, its characters, its narrator, or even an outside creative force other than just itself (as in reflexive cinema, for example). This ability to engage in the drama at hand and think for itself or for other characters is significant. Later I shall look more closely at how the filmind might be said to think for (or sometimes as if) characters. To begin with, though, the filmind simply thinks for us, from itself – for example, by giving us an idea of what it thinks the characters should do: shot of knife during struggle might mean 'pick up the knife and stab him you idiot' (or it might indicate that one of the characters is thinking about picking up the knife). This aspect of the filmind becomes one that is most important if we consider the confusion that has accompanied disembodied viewpoints and ostensibly detached displays. Realising the film as thinking allows an intention at the very base of film's actions, and moreover helps us understand these moments via the classification of 'thoughtfulness'. A shot of a vista can be allowed its beauty and intrinsic nature, but the idea of a filmind gives a possible further aspect: that of 'comparison' or 'equation' to a previous scene, or silence or peace, or ontology (of nature), or whatever. Though this further aspect is *not* necessary: the concept of a fully intended film does not deny or remove the aesthetic uncertainties that are part of any art object. It is the *way* that the filmind re-thinks the film-world that is interesting here – how this 'intentionality' becomes 'form', how this 'thinking' reveals itself. The filmind presents (film-thinking) a representation (images and sounds). What we come to is an acknowledgement that the filmind (any film) can think the slow fast, the loose tight, the small large, the loud quiet, the tame violent, and the mythic real.

Vivian Sobchack has theorised a particularly *subjective* intention for her film-body, but her conclusions are significant. Her film-body consciousness is 'intentionality incarnate'[11] – human thought is made flesh, made physical in images. Thinking presented in its most extreme form. Her film-body's 'vision', its contingent intentions towards its world, is an inflection or reflection of its existence – it is its existence. As mentioned earlier, her use of the term 'vision' also leads to a strange separation of film and object-images. As Sobchack puts it, film's images are 'visible to the film's vision'.[12] The term 'experience' also contains a sense of this separation: the film-body is said to enact a *subjective experience of things*, is said to 'look at' the objects it has also produced. This would indicate that, during the film's running, Sobchack's film-body simultaneously 'experiences' (previously recorded) real-world objects, *and* creates these objects as unique film-world image-things. Sobchack obviously means that film has a particular experience of its objects; it loves one character, while shows its distaste for another, and so on. This 'experience' is revealed through such things as frame angles, movement, colour. The film frames a person in a certain way, so Sobchack would call this the film-body's subjective experience of the person.

But, again, the filmind does not (somehow) reveal human intention, just its own kind of thinking. The filmind's intentionality 'is' form (colour, movement, framing), and it is perhaps only misleading to say that the filmind 'experiences' its objects using its 'vision' – both create a separation and a sense of passive spectatorship. Filmosophy does say that the filmind creates a world which it then re-thinks (or sometimes fluidly re-creates), that the film-world contains ostensible objects for the filmgoer, and that film-thinking is enacted through the filmind's intention towards those objects. But 'experience' and 'vision' are perhaps not the best terms to apply.

Basic film-thinking

It is now possible to sketch what this film-thinking consists of; the working of film-thinking; how this film-thinking is apparent in film. As previously noted, there are perhaps three main intermingling types of film-thinking: basic film-thinking, formal film-thinking and fluid film-thinking. The basic design of the film-world (black and white or colour, frame ratio), the addition of traditional formal elements (framing, movement, shifts), and the re-creation of the film-world itself (special effects, image morphing, and so forth). Basic film-thinking is the unique base design to the structure and appearance of the film-world. It is reflective attention *on top of* the film-world – the default *attitude* the filmind has about its world and characters. Basic film-thinking is the coherent design of the base film-world. The colour tone of the image is thought; the fact that the film takes place in a wide image is a decision, an intention of the filmind. The filmgoer can then add this dramatic reason to their experience and interpretation of the film. This general intention of the filmind is for itself (for us) and evolves out of the basic film-world (of simply showing a character or a scene).

This kind of film-thinking (the 'animation' of Cavell's 'world pictures') is always explicit description – even when it does not look like it is being explicit. Intentionally, this film-thinking is simultaneously a showing and an analysis or interpretation of what is shown – no image is unthought (in a double sense). It is always an 'attitude' towards recognisable things (people, events) in the film. But it is an intention that comes from within the film: it is not an extradiegetic or ghostly intention. Virginia Woolf, in her 1926 essay 'On Cinema', recognised the organising being of film:

> Something abstract, something which moves with controlled and conscious art, something which calls for the very slightest help from words or music to make itself intelligible, yet justly uses them subserviently – of such movements and abstractions the films may, in time to come, be composed.[13]

The filmind is a model of this *controlled and conscious artistry*, giving each film its own style. The concept and framework of the filmind gives each film a basic character and identity, and we most obviously see this basic film-thinking as composing, ordering, 'choosing' images and sounds. This type of film-thinking is relatively unobtrusive, creating the structure of the film through almost neutral decision-making. The filmind thus works as the decision-making fire of film; the guiding 'attitude' and the only 'agency' or intention to be found. Sometimes it may not seem to be doing anything to a scene, but the very fact that it is showing this scene, now, from this vantage point, with these sounds, and before that next scene, is ample evidence of its thoughtfulness. In this sense it isolates in giving only what it decides to give – becoming *selector, chooser, arranger*. Basic film-thinking is the basic choice structure-thinking (this image over that, that image after this one), marking out the time and space relations of the film. A regular film-world may look familiar, but the filmind is breaking and rupturing and reordering and selecting sound-images (film-thoughts), creating a united space-time film-world that is really very dissimilar to the real world.

Each film is unique then, with its own filmind steering the film-world. These unique filminds are also *autonomous* and free to create or think anything they wish. As William Rothman rightly observed, films are masters of their own languages, images and intentions. Sobchack grasps the autonomy of film-thinking: 'the film may choose whether to attend visually to the world it physically inhabits or to a world it dreams, whether to move falteringly or smoothly, whether to hear or to close itself from the world's sound or the sound of its own feeling'.[14] If a filmgoer decides to use this particular concept of film-being then they will be anticipating this freedom, these possibilities of intention.

A film philosopher such as Stanley Cavell recognises that film is able to show us many things, but seems unable to conceptualise this 'showing'. The concept of a filmind can help Cavell when he ponders the sudden appearance of a still of Jeanne Moreau's character in Truffaut's *Jules et Jim*: 'the image private to the two men appears as if materialised by their desire'.[15] Once we find the film to be 'thinking', there is no conundrum, this becomes exactly what the film is capable of (and perhaps meant to be) doing. Realise just how much thinking film is doing and you will be half-way to an interesting interpretation. The filmind never stops thinking (possibly meaningful) sound-images, and never stops being. Film has a constantly active relationship with its internal object-images. *Being* the film, it is thus always there, and therefore constantly thinking – sometimes quiet, sometimes obvious – it is there even when the film image appears transparent and unintentional. It is an uninterrupted conception of what is shown. It never stops thinking, it is always flickering (just as our minds are always ticking over). Importantly it is an intention that is there even when the film seems inactive (film cannot exist without a form). A filmind can be quiet or loud, realist or expressionist, but there is always thinking, always intention. The filmind's act of intention/attention, choosing this image, this framing, over another, confers importance on that image. Why is this important or useful? *Because it means that every moment of every film is an intended moment – every simple framing and shift is meant.* Every frame is intended, every shift in images is thought by the filmind.

Integral to the power of the filmind is its *knowledge of the whole* – its transcendence. It has in its knowledge the whole film, from opening to finale, which therefore gives it the ability to think expansively, towards (within) its future. Filmosophical film-thinking is by definition organic. The film thinks with its beginning and end 'in mind' – it might show us a clue to the outcome, or frame a person according to their eventual fate. Every image also contains a thinking of the whole, as Deleuze would say. Therefore, apart from its ability to think any scene in any way, or 'privilege' any one of the characters in the film, the filmind can *anticipate* things in the film (it can show us the door that someone is about to come through). As our friend Münsterberg realised: 'The photoplay alone gives us our chance for omnipresence.'[16]

Transsubjectivity

But where does the filmind think from? If we look at the story told in the previous chapters it is clear that anybody can find imagery in film that resembles thinking or perception, but the most useful conception of film-thinking does not necessarily rely on the existence of characters or persons doing the thinking. Making film a thinking medium only when it is character-subjective is reductive and limiting. Making film itself a subjective being is also limiting. Why have others seen film as a subjective gaze? Cognitivists would say that the notion of the 'gaze' is a mythical transcendental entity for which there is no empirical evidence (do filmgoers feel this gaze they ask). Yet its 'empirical' nature is less important then the way it construes the event of film. We really need a less subjective conception, or else film becomes flatly personal – in that slightly weird images are forced to fit as (to become) 'subjective'. Yet a theorist such as Slavoj Zizek would argue that the gaze should not be seen as the action of a subjective being – rather it refers to the way that film's objects regard the filmgoer: the film gazes at us, and subject and object are reversed.[17] Film may not be 'subjective', but it can reveal 'subjectivity' to us, can show us subjective-life in a filmic mirror. For Zizek, 'one can render the Real of subjective experience only in the guise of a fiction'.[18] A handy way to comprehend how the concept of a filmind can help in our understanding of film's actions is thus through characters and 'point of view' images. The first thing to understand is that the filmind always thinks its *own* thoughts, whether they look like the thoughts of a character or not. This simple starting point allows film its playfulness (even if it really is playing it straight) in showing character point of view. It also allows for a greater subtlety of effect. The concept of the filmind should thus help us to understand the authentic within ironic or unreliable point of view.

Many authors cannot make the leap to autonomous film. Even George Wilson, who gets close, cannot see that film may just be thinking *from itself*, and, only if it feels like it, through or 'as' other characters. In a sense auteur theory *lessened* the art of film, exactly by personalising and subjectivising its actions of form. Thus a character never *completely* originates a narrative, the filmind is always giving us its version of what the character tells. This double authoring, where personal narratives are enclosed by the larger filmind, allows us some possible scepticism over what the character is relating, allows us the possibility of not believing the character (and removes any need to call-up an implied author).[19] The filmind can think (imagine, create) the 'contents' of its character's minds. The concept of the filmind gives the filmgoer a grounding for when, say, two characters see the same scene, but with differing emotional states. The filmind can visually and aurally think these differently, and the filmgoer would understand how and why she is seeing two differing visions without trying to work out who is giving these versions. *It is just the film thinking.*

Yet when the film appears as the eyes of a character do we really need to say that the filmind is giving its version of what the character might be seeing? Can we not just say that this is what the character sees? On the one hand, we need to realise that it is a significant and active decision by the film to show us this point of view in the first place. But, more importantly, this way of understanding point of view allows for when we are tricked by this seeming authority (for example, the classic case of the murderer recounting how he only *found* the victim). Furthermore, this allows for more complex interpretations of point of view, and may help us verbalise why a certain point of view shot, for example, does not simply confer 'empowerment'. Looking closer at the relationship between filmind and character, we find many levels: that of the film thinking about or towards the character, the film thinking for the character, and the film thinking as the character (point of view). As the filmind understands everything within the whole it can work its thinking towards any characters. This simply means the formal understanding the film has of its characters (for example distorted image for baddies, soft image for love interest). The filmind has the capability to understand a character and thus 'think the film' in relation to them; it can steer our attitude to characters, looming them tall, colouring them yellow, or by locking on to their eyes. The film may even try second-guessing the filmgoer, giving them the information it presumes they might need to understand the story. All the while the filmind is thinking from itself.

In thinking 'for' a character the film can give an impression of their mental state, perhaps, without aligning itself point of view-style. We may in fact be looking at the character while seeing what they are feeling. Thinking more closely 'as' a character – what they see, what they think, how they describe or recount, what they dream or hallucinate, what they feel – is all held and revealed by the filmind, as I have indicated. Fantasies, dreams, memory, lies, shared reality – the filmind helps us grasp that we sometimes cannot tell the difference (a character may be leading us up the garden path). In only ever thinking its own thoughts, when it decides to provide a sense of a character's thinking it is only ever producing an *inflection* of that character's way of understanding. It can say this character is thinking like this, is seeing this scene like this. (It does not 'show' human thought. It does not make human thought visible.) Thus a film image (a film-thought) from the head height of a character just shown is an *interpretation* of how the filmind feels he or she is thinking. This even applies to films that presume to show direct experience: Robert Montgomery's *Lady in the Lake* and Delmer Daves' *Dark Passage*, both made in 1947, are good examples.[20]

Integral to its neo-thinkingness is the filmind's transsubjective nature. The filmind has *un*certain thoughts (non-definitional images) which are not subjective, even though the idea of a subject is usually presumed in the fact of *our* thinking. Filmosophy finds two main reasons to conceptualise the filmind as transsubjective. Firstly, the filmind intends from a non-place or realm of perspective rather than a singular point of view. The filmind is not outside the film, it is the film. The film's perspective is the whole film. This is somewhat revealed in acentred and deframed images, impossible angles and omniscient positions. Fluid film-thinking brings this home: think of the trip through the garbage bin in *Fight Club*, or through the car engine in *The Fast and the Furious*. As Béla Balázs realised, film has its own 'perspective', and can endow objects with their own subjectivity. Secondly, with film-thinking the same scene can appear as though subjective, and then later as though objective – but both times they must be understood as thought by the filmind. Deleuze theorised this as the movement from the concept of the internal monologue to the notion of free indirect vision. Simply by moving us in and out of the subjective and the objective – comparing, contrasting – the filmind becomes a pure intentionality (there really being *no intentional object*). Filmosophy conceptualises film-being as transsubjective, because all 'subjective' and 'objective' shots within the film are produced through the filmind's 'thinking': the filmind is neither subjective or objective, it is both, it is a transsubjective being. Though it can appear to be subjective or objective like our thinking, it will always remain transsubjective. And this is not an attempt to objectify the subjective, but an offering of metasubjectivity (the real and the imaginary, the one and the many, the me and the you, in one image). The 'I' becomes an 'other' – subject and object can thus become fused, *participating* in each other.

Paul Messaris, in his book *Visual 'Literacy'*, finds a good example of a confusingly subjective/objective shot: thinking for us, then the character, then us again, all in one single movement.[21] Messaris calls this a breaking of convention, but film study cannot rely on toing and froing around whatever happens to be the conventions of the day. For the filmgoer just to understand film as regards other films is impoverishing to film's very possibilities of expression: as Messaris notes later in his book, a person may not come to grips with a new kind of composition simply because they understand an older conventional version of that compositional form.

The filmind shows itself here as a flexible, playful, transsubjective mind, which allows us to move away from reference to what may have previously been 'subjective' and 'objective' styles of film. Again, the filmind operates from a uniquely transsubjective *non-place*, thinking for itself or a 'narrator' or a character, or whatever. The filmind handles all: views of the character *and* that character's point of view – how else could we get a rounded, relational sense of the character's thinking. But importantly, the filmind can also show us a character *via that character's point of view*, can be both itself and the character, objective and subjective – such as when we see a drunk character *through* a drunken swaying defocused haze that would be their point of view. But not only here, each time we see a 'point of view' shot it is the filmind that has decided to give us this point of view, and it is also the filmind that filters this point of view through its own intention. Robert Burgoyne quotes Shlomith Rimmon-Kenan's theory of comprehensive literary narration, and it is applicable to this aspect of the filmind:

Even when a narrative text presents passages of pure dialogue, manuscript found in a bottle, or forgotten letters and diaries, there is in addition to the speakers or writers of this discourse a 'higher' narrational authority responsible for 'quoting' the dialogue or 'transcribing' the written words.[22]

Apart from anything else the concept of the filmind solves the riddle of the film that seems to be enunciating a viewpoint of a character from an impossible position – the filmind enhances film's subjective-objective games without resorting to the muddle of 'who is narrating?' Film always thinks an interpretation of a film character's 'thoughts' (even when it is obviously a fairly truthful interpretation). Writers that attempt to force subjectivity onto film are giving themselves problems of 'enunciation' that need not exist (language *bewitches* their thought, leads them to search for what the language makes them believe should be there).

Where we arrive at is the argument that the term 'subjective' limits the many uses of scenes emanating from a character's position. Filmosophy poetically thickens point of view imagery by collapsing subjectivity and objectivity (the character and the film). If the film gives us something comparable to a character's view filmosophy recognises that it can be interpreting, conditioning, inflecting that view if the film so decides. In filmosophy no point of view is pure, it is always the filmind's thinking. This is the interpretive coherence that will become so important to a filmgoer's experience: the nonconformism and downright trickery of some film narration (such as *The Usual Suspects*) can stump the filmgoer about the origin of the film images – the concept of the filmind helps the filmgoer out of this confusing quagmire. In important contrast to the theories of a phenomenological film philosopher such as Sobchack, the filmind is conceptualised as transsubjective so as to allow the filmgoer to follow its intentional actions without seeing them as emanating from a subjective, singular source. The filmind thinks – there is not a *particular* wizard behind the curtain pulling the strings to move the scenery, the scenery is simply moved by the film.

Formal and fluid film-thinking

Beyond its job of constructing and ordering the film-world, the filmind also re-designs the film-world through formal and fluid film-thinking. In other words, beyond the simple 'intention' of basic film-thinking is an active 'involvement' in the scene at hand. Firstly, fluid film-thinking is that which alters the basic film-world from the inside out; it is re-creative film-thinking. Fluid film-thinking gouges the film-world – it tears and rips into it, morphing it from within. We are thus confronted with a film-being that can imagine anything, can re-create the recognisable world at will. Special effects have been re-creating the film-world since Méliès: as we noted earlier, for Roger Gilbert-Lecomte, 'the Himalayas can appear in the stone of a ring'.[23]

Contemporary (digital) fluid film-thinking forces Sobchack to re-think the embodied nature of her film-body: *'electronic space dis-embodies'* as she puts it.[24] A good example of fluid film-thinking can be found in *Natural Born Killers* – at one point the face of Mickey is twisted and accentuated by the filmind, thinking his demonic nature as physical image. (Again, we might say that the scene of the action is the 'thinking', and the disfigurement the 'Thinking'.) This new fluid film-thinking could have many poetic and transcendent functions, even though so far it has been mainly used at the service of fantasy and horror. To consider the plain world through this kind of film-thinking offers many possible interesting results. But generally, by conceptualising a filmind which creates and re-creates its own film-world, these kinds of self-rupturing can be brought into the general classification of styles.

With fluid film-thinking the paradox (mentioned earlier), of how film can have an attitude to its things when it is its things, arises again. There is one key to remember here: *the filmind is conceptualised in order to assist the filmgoer in getting the most out of cinema.* Therefore, as the filmgoer sees recognisable objects, that are then changed by the filmind, we should say that the filmind intends towards its film-world things. All film-thinking makes objects and characters appear to the filmgoer in various ways. All film-thinking is an attitude or intention towards the film-world and its characters. *The concept of the filmind simply helps to explain how and why film can fluidly re-think the objects we recognise.* It is just that in fluid film-thinking we are made to realise that the filmind inhabits the objects as much as it formally attends to them. Fluid film-thinking is possible because the filmind is an invested *inhabitant* of the film-world. This style of intention, in which objects are truly 'transfigured', reveals the integrated nature of film-being, reveals the fact that film objects are 'created'. In this sense Sobchack is not wrong to say that the film has an *experience* of filmic objects it 'sees', only half-way to a complete understanding of film intention. (Apart from anything else, the concept of 'thinking' allows for a much more refined rhetoric as regards the moving *sound*-image than a rhetoric of vision and perception.) In fluid film-thinking cinema has a greater power: it *inhabits* its objects; it has created them in the way we see them. In fluid film-thinking the film does not have 'experience' of some thing (a character, a setting) – *it is the things already.* In filmosophy the film does not have experience *of* things, it just has film-experience, or not even that, just film-thoughts. We might say that the filmind has a 'film-experience' of the objects and characters – it can never be separated from the images and sounds it shows. The filmind thinks an image which includes its attention and 'objects' as *one*.

Our thinking responds to the world, and moves towards it as it changes before us (a mix of thinking and the unthought/nature – making a phenomenological being-world). In inhabiting film, in being the film, the filmind works from the *inside-out* as it were. Once there were objects and cameras, now there is just film-thinking. Thus the filmind has a dual nature: it both intends towards and 'is' the film-world. It is in control of all it creates and yet it has various attitudes towards itself. The filmind is (part of) the film-world, and yet in intentional possession of it. It creates, organises and manipulates. It *possesses and controls* time and experience. Strictly speaking, the filmind's attitude and its effect on objects is thus *simultaneous* – film both creates the object and necessarily thinks it in a certain way.

But most film-thinking is not as radically film-world-morphing as fluid film-thinking. Most film-thinking is formally layered over recognisably normal-looking characters and settings. (The filmgoer does not see layers though, with the concept of film-thinking they would see a person 'loved', a setting 'believed', a gun 'desired'.) While usually plain and realistic (what others may want to call passive thinking), this formal film-thinking is exactly that which 'surrounds' recognisable people and objects. It is the filmind's engagement with the drama at hand, considering possibilities of intervention and design. Film-thinking is the *way* the filmind rethinks the film-world – the *way* the film shows what it shows. For Parker Tyler film, 'embodies *ways of seeing*'[25] – every object is shown by the film in a particular way. Formal film-thinking thus concerns: zooms, close-ups, fast editing, defocusing, rough image grains, crane shots, reverse motion, colour filters, and so on. Filmosophy basically translates these technical aspects into poetically-thoughtful dramatic workings of the filmind.

Formal film-thinking is not meant as a *replacement* for the tradition of 'mise-en-scène criticism', only an extension of its coverage. Mise-en-scène criticism has been traditionally concerned with a range of film-world elements – such as lighting, costume, acting, set arrangement, props, décor, space – and how the meanings of these elements are further changed by camera angle, movement, colour, framing, and so on. Filmosophy is an attempt to extend and organicise this latter area of mise-en-scène concern: that film is always thinking about its characters and objects, and that this thinking is a dramatic and thoughtful intention of the film itself.

An example from *Casablanca*: a beautiful indication of the filmind's intention comes when we are first shown Rick himself. The filmind teases us by initially resting on his hand which has just signed a slip, and then moves to reveal his face and at that very moment almost recoils a little, stepping back to reveal the man we have been expecting to meet, or perhaps like a customer who with initial intrigue first meets him and suddenly realises they should not be staring so closely at such a figure as Rick. The filmind thinks this revelation or reaction. (The filmind does not think meanings, it thinks formal events through which we possibly feel meaning.) In *Vertigo*, when we see Judy come out of the bathroom of her hotel room, transformation complete, and her image is bathed in a green glow, we should understand that the filmind is directly thinking this whole moment (framing, soundtrack, movement and colour). The filmind reveals its thoughts and beliefs through *discours*, that is though framing and colouring and floating and focusing and closing-in, and so on. Thus film-thinking is the stylistic thinking of the filmind – how the filmind thinks (provides the thoughts of) the film, as in 'the film circles around Jack, feeling his confusion'. There will be an extended discussion of formal film-thinking in chapter seven, so let us return to the question of the nature of the filmind and film-thinking.

Postphenomenological

Phenomenology has been helpful in clarifying the presence of the filmind in its world (its intentions and being-ness), but film itself is not by definition phenomenological, and it is somewhat limiting to conceptualise cinema using a transplanted phenomenology. For Sobchack film is metaphenomenological, in that it tells us things about our own phenomenology: for example, we humans intend the absences of objects we partially see (the other sides to the cube) – the filmind intends only presences; it intends them by thinking them in a particular way (angle, colour, distance). This philosophical aspect to cinema is fine, but somewhat useless for the filmgoer. It follows on from this that attempting to make film enact a phenomenologically correct human experience is also limiting. The filmind can be anything, go anywhere; a fluid existence that is pointedly denied in a film such as *Lady in the Lake*, which, as Sobchack puts it, moves away from realising 'the *transcendent* aspects of its own embodied existence'.[26] The filmind has its own particular film-phenomenology, its own way of attending to its world (it thinks a loved woman with soft-focus, we do not). Film offers another phenomenology. The filmind is something else, and has its own way of thinking what it 'perceives' and 'hears'.

But must we, as Noël Carroll argues, know much more about the human mind before we can in any way 'link' it to film? Well, on the one hand when Carroll takes on the analogy he is narrowly focusing on a formal replacement of vision by thought. Thus his critique of a theory of film finding 'cinematic processes as if they were modelled upon mental processes'[27] is not hard to disagree with. Unlike Münsterberg, unlike the sort of mind-film theory that Carroll critiques, filmosophy does not argue that, for example, the close-up is 'equivalent to the psychological process of attention'.[28] Carroll also argues that one cannot use the mind to theorise film because we do not know enough about how the mind itself works. Exactly, the filmind can make us feel things, and we find it difficult to account for the process. By rhetorically investigating mind-like terms to describe film we are not only giving flesh to films forms, we are perhaps also helping to give an account of our own mind. (Why can film not *help us* in our search for a more *suitable* theory of the mind?) We do not initially need to 'know' about the mind to use it in relation to film. We talk about it normally without that specific knowledge. What is interesting is the language we use to get near to explaining the mind, which, in a way, mirrors the language we use to get near to *describing* film images.

The filmind thinks better than us, as well as thinking beyond us: it can not only show us actual things that before would have been virtually closed off (cells, insect eyes, and so forth), but truly non-actual events and forms. Slow-motion is a good example, bringing us images we could never find for ourselves (even though, paradoxically, slow-motion is most often given a phenomenological interpretation). For Epstein film is *'an eye independent of the eye'*:[29] film sees without eyes, observes without perception, creates images without vision, and thinks without a consciousness. The filmind has less and more capabilities than us; has different capabilities to us. Film-thinking is simply different to our thinking. Filmosophy believes film to be significantly different to human experience – similar structures, yes, but a parallel universe, where everything is slightly askew and different (think of the depth and ratio and colours and lack of saccades of a basic film image). Central to the concept of the filmind is the newness of film-thinking – its parathoughtfulness (and metathoughtfulness, for that matter). Film-thinking is beyond our thinking (and helps us understand our thinking). It is not physical, nor metaphysical, but postmetaphysical in its thoughtfulness. But I shall leave a fuller examination of these ideas for the final chapter.

What is film-thinking?

If the filmind is not strictly analogous with our mind and film-thinking is different from our thinking, then what kind of thinking is going on in the cinema? What film-thinking 'is' can only be shown through examples – and the whole of chapter seven will be taken up with just this project; but it is another matter to explain what 'kind' of thinking film-thinking is. Considering the ideas of the previous chapters we might begin by separating this film-thinking from being tied to specific forms and types of cinema. Film-thinking is not reliant on characters or implied authors; is not aligned merely with the 'camera'; is not simply a reference to philosophical stories and gestures; is not dependent on a creative director; is not analogous with dreaming or the subconscious; is not only applicable to abstract or reflexive cinema; and it is *not* analogous with human thinking and perception. Let us take that final and most important comparison: film-thinking is not analogous with human thinking. This means that the filmind does not 'show' human thought; it is not mirror of our minds; it does not make thought visible; it is not simply the fictional thoughts of a character shown by film; it is not about the conveying of 'internal states'; it does not exhibit metaphors for mental states; and it is not an objectified consciousness (as that too exists in relation to human consciousness).

Well, what is human thinking? It is planning, meditating, problem-solving, reverie, reasoning, daydreaming, figuring, judging, imagining. Human thinking is having ideas or images in the mind. Now, film can show fictional daydreaming and imaginings, but can it show reasoning and judgement? I would say it can and it cannot. It cannot in the sense that our minds can do reasoning without any physical 'showing' of reasoning: there is an outcome, of decision or opinion, but no appearance of 'reasoning'. It 'can' in the sense that a film can show a judgement of a person by showing them in a certain way – we cannot show our judgingness, we can only tell someone our final judgement. Thus film can think less and more than us. This is why the question of 'analogy' is redundant. We must begin from the point that film-thinking and human thinking are different, and then move forward to ask what kind of thinking film shows us, rather than berate it for not being able to exactly show 'multiplication' or 'argument'.

Film-thinking is also not (by definition) metaphorical. The Eisensteinian filmgoer is brought to a state of ecstasy by the metaphoricity of film. Particular depictions (especially containing symbols) refer to a larger meaning; these depictions must be open in order to become or refer to the theme of the film. Montage produces metaphors that become images of thought in the mind of the filmgoer. Film does make us think, makes us relate the film to other ideas, but that is not the reason to call film a thinking thing. A movement in the film is not by definition metaphorical, it is immediately affective, bringing the filmgoer to a knowledge about its subjects without having us think or refer to ideas outside the film. Film-thinking is there in film – the filmgoer can see it if they take on the concepts of filmosophy. Even though it is a conceptual rather than an empirical description of film, the filmind is not transcendental, it is actual and active – we can actually 'see the film thinking' if we accept the conceptualisation that filmosophy offers.

You might obviously ask, then, why call it thinking if it is not like our thinking. The similarity between the human mind and the filmind is functional (or parallel) rather than phenomenological. Andrew Wicclair recognised this in his 1978 discussion of Münsterberg,[30] and for Bruce Kawin the filmgoer's mind sees in film 'a version of its own process'.[31] Film enacts its own version of human thinking. This is not to say that a close-up functions like human attention, because it represents a distinctly different film-attention. Filmosophy recognises that film has always been thinking (questioning, judging), and simply conceptualises it as such. The sense in which the filmind is 'thinking' is that of intention, creation and knowledge. It is its own mind and its own way, or realm of thinking – it designs for itself new thoughts. It is free to think whatever it wants (and, unlike the relative mess of our minds, films are able to think clear, precise images). Inspired by the thought of the (unachievable) possibilities of consciousness, this is a specifically 'film' thinking. That is why new terminology is required: film shows us 'film-thinking', which emanates from a 'filmind'. For Artaud, if you remember, in order for human thoughts to make any kind of appearance in film they must 'undergo a process of trituration'[32] – they must be ground down to their fundamental origins before they can be brought alive again through cinema.

In a general sense there are two classic ways in which film has been said to think. That film causes the filmgoer to think, and that film itself enacts thinking. What we might call the shock thesis and the action/immanence thesis. Filmosophy finds that one usually involves the other: film cannot create new thinking in the filmgoer without itself being said to 'think'.

In the classic shock thesis, it is usually edit-shifts that create concepts in the mind of the filmgoer – two shots combine to create a third image, an idea in the mind of the filmgoer. The two shots shock the idea into the filmgoer. A vibration of the brain immediately provides the filmgoer with the idea the filmind intended. Filmgoers can do little but receive the shock and feel the thought. In the 'shock to thought' version of film-thinking the filmgoer is usually an unthinking and law-bound psychological automaton who can do nothing but react to the shock by beginning to think. Both Eisenstein and Deleuze then theorise a second movement, back to the images. The filmgoer's new thinking takes them back to the film, and the continuous experience of cinema thus becomes a cycle of shocks and thinkings: shock, thought, back to the images, second shock, thought, back to the images, third shock. This shock leads to a new way of thinking, an image-thinking of emotional concepts (a new kind of filmgoer thinking that I shall look at more below).

Deleuze's relation-image is an extension of this shock to thought thesis, and ascribes 'thinking' to the film by the way certain images force the filmgoer to relate that image to other images or thoughts. Deleuze's relation-image transforms the images of perception, action and affection; that is, it gives them a mental aspect (movement becomes relational, the close-up becomes relational, and so forth). These relations are more abstract than natural: the filmind is here attempting to tell us things we would not have presumed ourselves. This is also the case for someone like Gilbert-Lecomte, for whom edit shifts offer a classic 'relational' style of thinking (of this to that). Deleuze argues that Hitchcock's films offer the best example of the relation-image. Hitchcock's filmind leaves the characters behind to make its own 'investigation' into the film-world drama, creating film-thinkings (movements, shifts to objects) that force the filmgoer to *interpret* the relations the film-thinking suggests.[33] When *Rear*

Window tells us how Jeffries broke his leg, the image and the thinking being shown are brought into intelligible relation. The filmind reveals relations between people and objects (between broken leg and racing photograph and broken camera). The filmind's image has an object: relation (of racing photograph and broken camera to Jeffries' broken leg).

This is how film-thinking always ultimately *works*: we feel a notion because of an image, and so tie that notion to that image (leading to, or because we have, the concept of film-thinking in our minds as we watch the film). The notion (the sign, the vague idea) mediates between the image and the filmgoer. The image, and what the filmgoer senses to be the image's thinking, are here brought into relation, and this relation, this 'thirdness' is 'the mental' for Deleuze – via his understanding of C. S. Peirce. Film-thinking thus creates a kind of Peircean thirdness: an image and its 'event', its thoughtful meaning, are brought into relation. The relation-image is thus a mental image for the filmgoer, a figure of thought. We then say that the film was thinking that idea – the shift in images created that idea in the mind of the filmgoer. The filmgoer's figure or image of thought becomes the thought of the film. The image interprets – because the image forces the filmgoer to interpret. So, in the shock thesis the film thinks because the image forces the filmgoer to think.

In the end any concept of film-thinking has to revolve around the thesis that the filmgoer is made to think, to create new thoughts, because of the film. But the concept of film-thinking cannot be *based* on the thesis that the filmgoer is made to think, that is why the shock/relation thesis is only one aspect of film-thinking. Deleuze himself moved on from this rough-hewn shock/relational approach to making the filmgoer think, and towards a concept of film as new-thought, growing rather than shocking ideas in the filmgoer's mind. For Deleuze, the identity of image and concept means a cinema whose essence is 'thought and its functioning'.[34] Film has its own figures of thought, which re-create the objects of film, and re-examine narrative cinema. In film-thinking, images, framings, movements are transsubjective and freely interpretive. Film-thinking also has its own temporalisation – film moves freely through and around time, and can be nonlinear and nonchronological. The filmind can decide to move the drama laterally, moving beyond 'narrative' storytelling into pure image and sound. Classically normal film-thinking is sequential and uses the figures of sensual thinking, but film-thinking can also be manifest itself in the interstice of edit-shifts – the between, the 'and' – to create what Deleuze calls a difference of potential. Film *does* thinking, rather than just *provoking* thinking. Film-thinking is immanent to the film. The filmind reflects on the characters and objects within the film-world. This reflection has poles of intention – it can be calculative or meditative, assertive or questioning, or the many gradations in-between.

Film can recall for us the visibility of the psychological *in* behaviour. Film-thinking is thus a cinematic form of behaviour – film is made up of formal actions, events of movement or time-shifts. These physical film events reveal the *action* of the filmind. In Deleuze's third movement the unity of thought and image is an 'action-thought' (the shocks of the first movement produce 'critical' thoughts, the second movement of thought to image is termed 'hypnotic' thought). For example, the filmind might use a flowing movement over a group of people to think a relationship between those people (see the example of *Werkmeister Harmonies* at the end of chapter seven). As Gerard Fort Buckle noted, the activities of technique (film form) produce a particular conception of the characters and objects in film. Movement thus becomes a key part of film-thinking, though filmosophy may not completely agree with Henri Bergson when he says: 'Immobile, it is in neutral state; in movement it is life itself.'[35] The statically framed image is still a moment of film-thinking, but movement actions film-thinking in multiple ways; making it relational or questioning or historicising, and so forth

Yet, considering that film cannot exactly re-enact 'argument' or 'reasoning', staples of human thinking, should this filmic action not be termed *film-feeling*? Human feelings are instinctive or intuitive, but can develop into emotions (strong feelings). They can also represent a vague or nascent belief or opinion (we feel some way about some thing). Most art expresses feelings or emotions – for Béla Balázs film can show us 'invisible emotions'[36] – and it is true that much film form enacts an emotional side of 'thinking': colours are mood-giving, movements are inexact in their impact, framings can be sensuous – forms that resemble human feelings more than rigid thinkings. So why not term it all film-feeling? First of all, film-thinking is 'film' thinking, and film forms and styles are non-strict in their effect; therefore film-thinking already refers to 'emotional' thinking. But more importantly, film-thinking is an umbrella term, encompassing film-feeling. We think and feel; the filmind thinks and feels; but both can be termed as thinkings. Most film-thinking may be emotional or sensuous, but the term allows for all kinds of intention to be going on in film: the film can intend emotionally or more structurally and strictly towards its characters and objects (think of Eisenstein, or Godard's essay films, or the more precise expressionism of Hitchcock or Scorsese). The concept of film-thinking allows for both of these events.

A creative part of this conception is that of 'choice', 'belief' and 'judgement' – these are important ingredients of film-thinking, and a reason why the concept of thinking as regards film arose. Film cannot think without choice, belief and judgement. For example, it can be a judgement about a vista, or a belief about a character, or a choice of angle – the filmind thinks or taints the scene or character in a certain way, with colour or framing, and so on. The filmgoer sees a world similar to her own, but thought another way. The rhetorical move of seeing film-thinking as intended in these ways also gives its thoughts (framings, movements) added force for the film-goer. The filmind is thus the mechanism, while film-thinking takes on propositional functions: using the objects of the film to enact a reasoning about the drama. This particularly filmic reasoning is primarily made available by the possibilities of choice: the filmind decides to show this or that, decides to bring us these images and not some others, decides to show a character from below and not above. The image becomes an action of new-thinking – a close-up can be inserted by the filmind to make the filmgoer question what they thought they knew. Ostensibly pragmatic, the filmind can in fact be deductive and judgemental, steering the filmgoer's experi-ence while appearing merely responsive and neutral.

Belief is choosing a choice (from the infinite choice the filmind has). Deleuze was the most explicit about this – arguing that cinema does not film the world, but belief in the world.[37] It is a belief, immediate, that lives in the moving sound-images that the filmind 'creates' – we 'see' the filmind's belief about a character; *we see the character and the belief as one*. In the end the filmind almost becomes a synonym of belief – as one involves the other. Filmosophy aims to relight the connection between filmgoer and film (and therefore between humans and reality) by revealing this 'belief'. The filmind can therefore almost neutrally give us an object, or it can give us the object via (with, in, through) an expressive judgement about that object. The filmgoer then sees the object with that judgement, that belief.

Eisenstein helps us realise that films can have a type of film-thinking that runs through the whole film, and that inflects every image, thus giving the whole film a theme. The best films serve this theme by making each image part of this type of film-thinking (the questioning nature of *Magnolia*, the meditative nature of *The Thin Red Line*, the empathetic nature of *Rosetta*). All parts of the film are thus interrelated, giving the filmgoer an accumulated sense of the film's thinking. The filmind thus has doxic modalities: different kinds of intention towards the objects and characters it presents – love, suspicion, rejection, and so on. Film-thinking can thus indeed be in-quisitive like Parker Tyler's 'maximal' film detective, searching out objects that relate to characters. These different types of film-thinking will become apparent over the course of the examples in chapter seven, but there are no hard and fast categories of thinking. The filmind may be seen to think 'causally' (usually through editing), but there is no one particular sequence of images that denotes 'cause'.

Not all film is idea or concept (being kinds of thinking) – and a boring film is still thinking, just not very interestingly – but film can also structure its thinkings to produce a kind of ideational or conceptual thinking. Cavell feels that films such as Resnais' *Hiroshima mon amour* and Antonioni's *L'Avventura* are 'works of cinematic art decisive in modifying concepts … of what constitutes a medium of thought'.[38] And Balázs's absolute film knows 'only one law: that of association of ideas'.[39] But it is also important not to take the filmind too 'intellectually' – it can think jokily, playfully, kinetically, as well as 'philosophically'.

Film-thinking becomes somewhat more intellectual or 'categorical' when it begins to rationally articulate its field of objects and characters. A film may simply give us a close-up of a part of an object, to highlight it, and then give us the whole object, such that the filmgoer now concretely understands the part of the object in relation to its whole. The judgements of film-thinking are usually emotional rather than intellectual – but they are film-judgements that can develop into or produce the conceptual or intellectual. As with organic montage, film-thinking conveys brutal, imagistic, direct reasoning. The filmind gives us the feeling of ideas, *philosophical inklings* that are whispered to us. Film-thinking suggests, hints, gives us a vague notion of (perhaps 'particular') ideas. The filmind thus produces emotional ideas, feelings of thoughts, fragments of concepts – fruitfully vague in structure, intentionally blurry in meaning. These are not bad versions of logical, clear ideas, but distinctly 'film-ideas', existing in a state of image, a state of flow and flux. The filmind is para-thoughtful, and film-thinking is 'outside' our thought – a beyond of pure transsubjective intention.

The filmgoer

In the end this grandly named postmetaphysical, postphenomenological, transsubjective filmind arrives at the thinking of the filmgoer. Therefore, the final question of this chapter revolves around the relationship between the filmind and the filmgoer – because in order to completely answer the question of how film thinks we must look at the filmgoer, and how they see thinking in film. How do the concepts of filmosophy help the filmgoer? What kind of thinking does film-thinking produce in the filmgoer? Here I will give a taste of the questions that will be continued in chapter eight.

First of all, film-thinking is not 'read' but felt. As Eisenstein realised, there is an organic fusion between the principles of human thought and the structure of film-thinking. The thought-images of film are very suited to creating thought-images in the mind of the filmgoer. Filmosophy simply aims to enhance this 'suitability' with its concept of the filmind (which includes or entails the concept of film-thinking). And like any new concept its true habitat is in the *back of our thinking*. In this sense it is filmosophy's toy, the alphabet of filmosophy, to be learnt then forgotten, even though it never goes away. The filmind is the conceptual ladder, to be climbed and then kicked away. Film does not technically need a filmind – filmosophy is not an empirical investigation – it is a decision by filmgoers whether to use this concept when experiencing a film. The film is just light and sound. I am simply arguing that filmgoers *should* use the concept of the filmind, in order to experience film as a *fully expressive* medium. This is not to say that the concept creates the film-thinking: the filmgoer feels the presence of the organising and thoughtful agent, the concepts of filmosophy simply enhance and bring out this feeling, helping them understand the activity of film forms even more. Any filmgoer who experiences a film with the concept of the filmind will see the filmind at work. The filmind then becomes immanent within the film, and film-thinking is immanent within the images and edit-shifts and sounds. With the concept of the filmind and film-thinking the filmgoer will thus 'see' film forms (colours, movement, edit shifts, framing, focusing) as thoughtful intentions. The form of a film can then be understood as 'the film' thinking about its characters and events.

In other words, once understood, the concept of the filmind becomes simply 'the film' – the film is the utterable itself (though it does not represent a language, or language system). This means that, for the filmgoer, it is simply the film that is creating itself and intending towards the characters and objects. This also means that, as we shall see in the next chapter, all narratorial agents are grounded in the film itself, in a singular intention that gives us scene-settings and character thoughts, objective viewpoints and character experience. Filmosophy aims to bring creative intention back into the film, not take the filmgoer out of the film to some external invisible puppeteer. Filmgoers should see film-thinking as just *part of what the film does*.

In order not to 'remove' the filmgoer from the film, filmosophy attempts to enable a poetic rhetoric. The concepts of the filmind and film-thinking create an emotive and fluid language for the filmgoer to experience the film with. As Eisenstein noted, the filmgoer has to think 'sensuously' towards the film in order to get the most out of it, in order to receive the 'sensuous' film-thinking. It is in this sense that filmosophy reacts against the technicist rhetoric of so much film study. Cinema may start with technology, but the filmgoer does not see this mechanism; cranes, tracking shots, camera, and so forth, are in themselves not significant to the filmgoer's experience. As Sobchack perceptively notes, we do not see a track or a dolly, so why should film writing relate to film as if it were 'some objective mechanism like a water heater'?[40] Yes they are a film's means of being in the world, but the filmgoer does not need to 'know' this *during their experience of the film*. Film-thinking *inhabits* and *is* its world, rather than simply 'looking' at it as the 'camera' rhetoric persuades. This is all the more applicable nowadays because of film's new digital (even camera-less) freedom. The only 'technical method' we should see in film is its visual conduct and behaviour.

An example of how technicist rhetoric can infect the poetics of cinema can be found in a textbook such as *Film Art*, written by David Bordwell and Kristin Thompson. *Film Art* finds no *organic reasoning* in film, but only *categories*, formal dissections, of shape and speed and length. Furthermore, the authors will call attention to, say, a multitude of framings, but without giving the reader a way to understand 'framing' *per se*. In their book the two authors catalogue an incredible amount of framing styles, carefully differentiating, for example, between the angle and the height of filming. This technicist rhetoric weighs-down the meaning possibilities of Bordwell and Thompson's film discussions, but also creates a distant 'linking' of form and meaning. Technical terminology is far removed from the expression or reception of emotions, and by starting with this kind of terminology the authors limit their 'interpretations'. A particular type of framing may not have a single meaning in their commonsense pragmatist view, and this is fine, but what opinions of meaning or 'director intention' they do allow themselves are (like much film theory and mise-en-scène criticism) found through a *clunky attachment* of form to meaning, or experience (somewhat better). This is theory of the type: watch out for a low camera angle, as this may be trying to make you feel so-and-so, and may then mean so-and-so. It is not so much that classic film analysis does not have incisive things to say about cinema, just that it has never had a way to intuitively *bind* form to meaning. *Filmosophy aims to organicise the relationship of form and meaning.*

Thus the most important thing to remember here, and one of the most important points of filmosophy, is that the concept of film-thinking *transfigures* actions of film. This is one of the most difficult ideas to get across – how this recognition of film as thinking illuminates our filmgoing experience, and our understanding of film aesthetics. A quick example from *GoodFellas*; the Ray Liotta and Robert De Niro characters are sitting in a diner late on in the film, and the film does a (now classic) track-out while zooming-in action (a track-in zoom-out can be seen in *Jaws* when Roy Schneider is sitting on the beach and a shark attacks). Now, a technicist or formalist description would talk exactly of this camera movement and take some delight in explaining (away) how it was done. *We do not need to be told what the film is technically doing, we can see what it is doing.* A regular film studies description (and here we are exactly not talking about interpretation, or any particular film theory, but about the descriptive language that most film studies uses, and which in turn steers its interpretations) would perhaps talk of the 'director' giving us a 'formal metaphor' for the changing 'world' of the characters. This generalised form of description has been happily used by film studies for a long while. The writer then uses this basic description to build their interpretation of the film. A filmosophical *description* of this scene might go something like this: the filmind understands the change in the relationship of two characters, and thinks (feels) the twist in their world. The film shows us the enclosed world of these two men (by only framing them), and shows how this world is a subverted one by *thinking* (through image form) the relationship between the men, and their relationship to the outside world. Of course the regular description and the filmosophical one may be revolving around similar meanings, but the filmosophical one, with its unifying of form and intention, leads to further possible interpretations. *The uniting of form and content using the concept of film-thinking creates an integral whole for the filmgoer.*

Cinema should never be dissected into low and medium and high camera angles – there will always be in-betweens – so constructing a concept of film-being that adapts itself to whatever a particular film does seems to be a more fruitful way to go. The concept of the filmind offers thoughtful cause and thus thoughtful, possibly poetic effect. The concept of film-thinking not only offers an adaptive framework, but also unites meaning to form. This organic uniting of film and filmgoer allows meaning to be *experienced*. The filmind does not determine meanings, it determines actions of film-thinking by which we receive and create meanings. As Merleau-Ponty argued: 'The meaning of a film is incorporated into its rhythm just as the meaning of a gesture may immediately be read in that gesture: the film does not mean anything but itself.'[41] Meaning becomes immediate and immanent to the rhythm and motion and mood of the film's thoughtful forms.

Narratologists, for example, are primarily concerned with the truthfulness of their narrational entities – which one works with the least errors of narrational validity, which one solves the problem of unreliable narrators. But the whole impetus behind finding the right master imager should be the resulting experience of the filmgoer – how might they best encounter the film. Directly and organically I would argue, without jumping between narrators and characters and authenticity and inauthenticity. The concept of the filmind provides filmgoers with a unitary source of intention, that helps them see how a character point of view is always given by the film, or that a movement is not a question of camera or 'crane' mechanics but of emotion and feeling. So, just as a phenomenologist sees the world as full and thick with affect, so the filmosopher sees film similarly, as fully intended, giving every formal move a possible meaning.

To conceptualise all-film (film-being) in a way that leads to the fullest and most poetic experience for the filmgoer, is to reconfigure film as a unique filmind. What the concept of the filmind does is offer intentional and dramatic cause, and thus possible poetic effect, to all the forms of images a single film may have. The concept of a filmind gives a poetic reason that the film shows us anything at all – poetic because 'normal' shots of people and place become transfigured by understanding them as fully 'intended'. This film-thinking produces virtual images, mental images in the mind of the filmgoer that become their filmosophical inklings of the film's meanings. While the filmind is enacting images of film-thought, filmgoers create their own images of thought: collisions of ideas that fuse or coalesce into images. As Eisenstein realises, the image that the filmgoer receives is an 'intellectual-emotional image'.[42] Our automatic, literal thinking is unsettled in favour of image-thinkings. Film-thinking makes the filmgoer's logical thinking recognise its limits, its impower, its impotence. Film-thinking forces thought to think the unclear, blurry, dispersive, outside. For Deleuze, film causes a major change in the quality of the filmgoer's thinking, and this new thinking is itself a form of spiritual automaton, alien to the filmgoer's normal ways of thinking, revealing the unthought within thought. Just as with Sobchack's metaphenomenology, film reveals the filmgoer's thinking 'to' the filmgoer.

There are four more areas needed to complete our understanding of filmosophy's concepts of the filmind and film-thinking: we need to give examples of film-thinking (chapter seven), flesh out how the concepts of the filmind and film-thinking transform the filmgoer's experience (chapter eight) and their routes of written interpretation (chapter nine), and consider the philosophical implications of understanding film this way (chapter ten). But before that, we should compare and contrast the activity of the filmind with classic theories of narration.

six | film narration

Cinema always narrates what the image's movements and times make it narrate.
– Gilles Deleuze (1985)[1]

Before we flesh-out film-thinking with examples, we should take a moment to consider how traditional theories of narration relate to filmosophy. Let us first of all look
at David Bordwell's theories of film narrative style and comprehension. For Bordwell,
narration is a process in which films provide cues to the filmgoers, who use interpretive schemata to construct the story of the drama. Narration is thus the main influence on filmgoers, who must actively construct meaning (rather than receiving it), in
order to render it coherent. The *plot* (or syuzhet) is the actual form in which events
are recounted, the selection and organisation or story events – the information on
causality and temporal relations for the filmgoer to work out. The *story* (or fabula) is
the ideal story, which the film has within it, but which the filmgoer has to imaginatively reconstruct (for example, with *Pulp Fiction* we realise, gradually, what events
precede and follow others).

  This is Bordwell's rational, cognitivist theory of narrative structure and comprehension: the filmgoer is guided by norms and conventions, called schemata, usually
of a basic canonical story structure, and these cinematic conventions 'are often built
out of ordinary-life behaviours'.[2] According to this theory of narrative comprehension, filmgoers cannot simply absorb the film because the data is not in itself complete – it needs the filmgoer to sort it. Films thus 'cue' filmgoers to generate inferences about what is happening in the film. For example, a cue may be an elliptical
shift, and the filmgoer fills in the blank: man on train, edit shift to same man in city,
therefore the man who was on the train has arrived in a city. Space, time, causation,
all are the sort of things that are inferred by the filmgoer according to Bordwell.

  But there is already an initial sense here that film is simply made to be a plan or
map from which to find the meaning. Bordwell continually refers to 'mise-en-scène
cues', which not only indicates that he believes that cinema is always attempting

specific communication, but that it is cueing us to understand something else, something almost beyond the image. *A cue (an image) to be left behind and forgotten in favour of the meaning it points to.* For Bordwell (and his structuralism) images are only there to tell us something; what else can they be there for?

Bordwell's third element is style – simply put, narration is plot plus style. The film-goer uses the plot and style of the film to mentally construct the film story. Bordwell does have a genuine desire to understand films from their style: art-cinema narration and parametric narration are two kinds of style-laden narration that he discusses. He sees three interlocking schemata in art-cinema narration: objective realism, subjective realism and narrational commentary. This kind of cinema does not just show a plot using objective realism, but delves into characters' subjectivity via point of view shots and overt narrational devices. Art-cinema narration is modernist, as exemplified by the questioning of a character's 'reality', and the use of new forms: long takes, strange angles, ellipses, and so on. Chance and randomness can take over, or even a higher causality. Art-cinema narration is thus more open-ended, with shifting attentions, and very much centred on character rather than plot. Bordwell acknowledges that this kind of cinema does attempt to reveal the thoughts of characters through image and sound.

But for Bordwell, the ultimate self-conscious narration (sometimes serving up hardly any story) is 'parametric' narration: style-centred, permutational, poetic. Parametric cinema is a genre, perhaps a sub-genre of art-cinema, and like all genres it is non-definitional – there will always be films that simultaneously fit in it and do not fit in it. He names this genre parametric because the images of these films are, in a sense, drawn from hundreds of possible variants of chosen parameters, and thus the only parameters for these films' styles are the next film techniques. To work parametric narration must develop simply, not every style at once but certain forms repeated for effect, around an intrinsic stylistic norm. Bordwell uses the example of *Last Year at Marienbad*: its time relations are abstract and non-causal; style becomes dominant at certain moments; the image is often divorced from the soundtrack; eyeline matches are not used; camera movement becomes independent of the action; and offscreen space is rendered incoherent. These kinds of films are open rich texts, with multiple layers of signifiers which almost resist interpretation – and for Bordwell the concept of parametric narration allows us to acknowledge the rich nature of these films. That is, by *understanding* the genre of parametric narration Bordwell believes we can better appreciate these kinds of film – but in analysing typical art-cinema or parametric narratives Bordwell only seems to want to *rationalise* them. Radical cinema is reduced to *principles, systems*, all towards trying to bring artistic cinema into the *rational* fold of classic cinema. Again Bordwell classifies according to a diversion from the norm. Parametric also means 'not just metric', not classically simple, just *more than simple*! How low-impact can you get, how … boring (in the face of such amazing films: is *Europa* simply parametric narration?). Bordwell's theory is truly an analytical film theory – and I will come back to this question of the 'usefulness' of Bordwell's theory.

Having said this, Bordwell is one of the few film theorists to attempt a complete understanding of film style. He interestingly theorises a possible 'scanning' strategy by filmgoers, one that 'compares one stylistic event with preceding ones, giving the earlier one the status of "statement".[3] The filmgoer adapts during the film, learning from the film's emerging styles. One kind of form or style is grasped by the filmgoer in the light of its previous appearance in the film, and its (historical) appearances in other films. Bordwell asks how patterns of stylistic continuity and change can be explained. To achieve a 'a self-conscious historical poetics of the cinema',[4] the film theorist must become a historian of film style in order to analyse how schemas grow and change over time. Bordwell's model thus builds 'from patterns of task-governed decision-making to schemas and thence to norms and their open-ended dynamic across time'.[5] For Bordwell, style is historical, to the extent that a new style can only be seen as deviating from classical norms. Beyond classical cinema, a new way of doing things is an *excess*, meaning that all innovative cinema techniques are rooted in some classical style or other. Style can therefore only be meaningful through its historical growth: every new style is simply a variant on a previous style.

But how does a new style gain meaning? With new digital forms computers can achieve styles completely unlike anything in the history of cinema. Furthermore, the forms of experimental-narrative films such as *Julien Donkey-Boy* do not seem to have any historical precedent, and to tie them to history is limiting to our interpretation of film. The fact that a filmgoer can follow and be affectively moved by innovative films without a great knowledge of the history of film style surely indicates that meaning does not come via history. For some structuralist theorists, such as Noël Burch, film style can become a system in its own right, accomplished by a process of dialectical structure. For Burch, filmmakers should examine the structural possibilities of film style, and develop open, musical narrative forms. In art-cinema and parametric narration Bordwell is concerned with how film style might become a shaping force, beyond aesthetic playfulness, artistic flourishes and 'unjustified' movements.

Bordwell acknowledges that style is as equally important as story, and that it is normally there to help show the story, to expose plot patterns. A good film for Bordwell is one in which the style is in symbiosis with the plot. Sometimes plot is even subordinate to style: style can achieve formal saliency, can become the main source of meaning and interpretation for the filmgoer: 'In parametric narration, style is organised *across the film* according to distinct principles.'⁶ Bordwell even worries that the filmgoer may not notice the stylistic meanings – the filmmakers style their film with ideas and concepts and motives, and can only hope that the filmgoer feels them in some way. He notes that a director such as Godard utilises a wide range of styles, responding and adapting to events with appropriate styles. Compare this with documentary filmmaking, which is usually reactive in style to events. On the other hand he discusses the ascetic style of Bresson, in films with few different stylistic forms, each with a limited range: a style that filters events through a set formal range. Sparse styling can indeed offer more subtle and affecting results: *Secrets and Lies* has only a few 'stylistic moments', but they are all the more powerful for their subtlety and rarity. With subtle filmmaking, the style almost has an 'unseen' structure. Bordwell remarks about minute, almost unrecognisable stylistic changes or events (as in Ozu) but finally says that most cases of parametric narration are fairly obvious to the filmgoer.

Bordwell's analysis of film style is, much like his hypothetical filmgoer, somewhat cold and calculating. For him, filmgoers do not feel the style's meaning but recognise and add and subtract differing devices. Style is consciously perceived and the filmgoer then makes hypotheses about how these moments relate to the plot. Bordwell, for all his attentions, is still ultimately *separating* style and plot, and even asks whether a filmgoer can see film style on its own, separate to the story. Filmosophy argues that films have a direct affectiveness, and that filmgoers cannot *just* perceive style, but perceive a character as thought by the film, or the landscape as the film thinks it. (Filmosophy is about *developing* this mode of attention, rather than empirically *finding out* what the common mode of attention is.) Of course we might 'notice' the 'camera moving', but that depends on our concept of cinema. Filmosophy wants the filmgoer to see that a character is thought a certain way by the film, but it does not want the filmgoer to simply see the thinking, the style. With the concept of film-thinking, filmgoers should be better able to feel the meanings of films, rather than calculating hypotheses – the filmgoer feels an object via the film-thought without actively having to 'realise' it. To help the filmgoer grasp stylistic ideas we must not just give filmgoers an index of formal significations, they need an adaptive and suitable conceptualisation of film.

Bordwell certainly does help us understand the formats of various modernist narratives, but using a very *technicist* language (boundary situations, schemata, and so forth) that break-up our understanding of narrative without necessarily helping us to bring it back together in the filmgoing experience. After reading Bordwell, films become jigsaw puzzles of narrative styles, which we are now tempted to 'work out' – filmosophy attempts to organicise rather than technicise the filmgoer's experience of cinema. His analyses may be coherent, and completely understandable, but they are painfully lacking in resonance: 'the goal-bereft protagonist, the episodic format, the central boundary situation, and the spatiotemporal "expressive" affects'.[7] There is also much 'description', description that does not illuminate our experience of the films. We are left with technical structures haunting our thoughts as we sit down to watch *Vivre sa vie*; a film that does indeed have structure, but that is not the heart of the film's style.

These concerns lead us to the question of science's involvement with aesthetics. One set of emotions that is lacking in cognitivists' talk are aesthetic emotions (beauty, the sublime) – what are the cognitive effects of wonder and awe? Bordwell needs a rationale before he can accept an aesthetic theory, and his analyses do not seem to capture the emotional effects of films, marking out the filmgoer as a controlled machine. Charges of pleonastic scientism at the expense of art can be leveled at a lot of film cognitivists, who seem more interested in facts over opinions or theoretical positions. The psychophysical problems of motion picture viewing do seem more suited to a scientific arena than philosophy or the humanities. Should science grade our art? Should we take empirical tests into the cinema? Will science enrich our experience of film? Richard Allen notes that scientific approaches to art, 'can only have a circumscribed place in relationship to the main intellectual concerns of the humanistic scholar'[8] – knowing that water is H_2O does not change our experience of water. This *rationalism* in the face of irreducible, ineffable beauty needs to be critiqued. Filmosophy certainly does not believe that the natural scientific way of viewing things provides the most significant access to ourselves and the film-world. Filmgoing seems pre-scientific, an activity scored by our emotional and aesthetic persona. What filmosophy learns from cognitivism is that you cannot scientifically theorise the filmgoer, just as you cannot scientifically theorise human beings.

Interpretation

Cognitivist theories of narrative comprehension also assert that rational explanations of films should come before any possible symptomatic interpretation. Cognitivists criticise the 'double-talk' of continental film theory, and not only want to reassert a rational, 'commonsense' understanding of film, but pour scorn on continental readings, which they see as 'hermetic, inflated and tautological', according to Robert Stam.[9] For Gregory Currie recent film theory has been too concerned with 'hidden' or 'deep structural' features of film, 'the supposed codes by which films are "read"'.[10] Psychoanalytical readings are especially targeted for being ambiguous, equivocal and limited to emotive, irrational aspects of films (sexuality, fantasy, surrealism). For the cognitivists, if a scene can be *explained* cognitively, then there is no need for a psychoanalytical *reading*. Currie even argues that interpretation should be a question of hypothesising about the intention behind the work.

Bordwell's analytic theorising can also lead to charges of over-rational reductivism, on two counts: that filmgoing is simply cognitive processing, and that filmgoers should always initially go for the most rational interpretation of a film. He thus subscribes to the rational problem-solving filmgoer theory, arguing that the filmgoer seeks cogency, and uses conventions and principles to gain the most rational interpretation of the material. For Bordwell we have a natural desire for meaning: we are presented with stimuli, and we try to make sense of it, and moreover, all filmgoers will respond to specific visual strategies in more or less the same way. Cognitivist theorists such as Bordwell thus attempt to construct a model of the norms, principles and conventions that will help explain how filmgoers comprehend films. In addition to the question of whether a certain film is cogent or not, Thomas Elsaesser and Warren Buckland note that this approach: 'can focus on the moments where the film goes beyond the spectator's routine and rational ("common sense") way of comprehending a film, and begin to determine how non-rational energy has influenced the film's structure and meaning'.[11] Elsaesser and Buckland are pointing up how cognitivists always see style in relation to a base normality (while for filmosophy it is exactly this 'beyond' that is of interest). Styles are so often seen as *excess derivations*, rather than thinkings in their own right. Seeing new styles as only 'derivations' ignores what a filmgoer might *feel* from the experience of this new form. How does simply knowing that it has a parametric style help the filmgoer better understand *Julien Donkey-Boy*? The filmgoer already notices that the film is not 'normal' (not 'classical' in style). Does Bordwell's 'classification' enhance the filmgoer's experience? Following Bordwell we might just get analyses of stylistically innovative films as simply *deformed* or *abnormal*. Filmosophy wishes to reveal the complexity of film, not attempt to reduce it to norms and non-norms.

Cognitivists would say that a filmgoer's principal pleasure is derived from problem-solving, from the nerdy 'interest' they have in working out the film. The filmgoer's main emotional engagement with narrative film is that of 'interest'; we are simply in a state of 'action readiness' towards the stimuli of film. Yet reading Bordwell making *sense* of *La Guerre est finie* is quite strange, in that he seems set on *reducing* Resnais' film to literality; working it out in order to gain relief from its willful strangeness (and perhaps win a prize for solving the film). And seen through the idea of 'parametric narration', *An Autumn Afternoon* becomes some sort of mechanical tease, adding and subtracting expected shots and 'normal' editing in 'constantly self-correcting shot combinations'.[12] His resistance to interpretation in *Narration in the Fiction Film* is not just a holding back in order to theorise more clearly, but indicates a lack to the system he sets out. Working out a genre of parametric narratives does little for our experience and interpretation of film. We may 'understand' these kinds of films better – understand their structures and modes – but this is a limited and limiting kind of 'understanding'. Bordwell's clarifying ambitions dull these films. They become puzzles to be set straight, mazes to be spoiled by leading you through them: *problems to be solved*.

This begs the question: are films redundant once we have 'understood' them? Why would we want to go back? Are films really puzzles to be solved? As Stam observes: 'Why do we go to films? Is it to make inferences and test hypotheses?'[13] Making sense out of film is not always the purpose of our visit. It seems obvious that we do not always go to the cinema simply to 'work out' what is going on in the film. Filmgoing perception seems to be equally aesthetic and non-practical. We can just as well soak up images and playfully deconstruct the experience (by perhaps always watching a certain peripheral character, or by concentrating on the soundtrack rather than the imagetrack). The filmgoer may have a desire for spectacle, pleasure or even aberration, thus connecting with the abnormal in film.[14] A filmgoer's response to *Mulholland Drive* may be to swim with its images, feed off its sounds and ruptures and come away with a new sense of reality – not to 'make sense' of it. Some filmgoers may not like the film because they 'can't make sense of it', and it is exactly those filmgoers who might benefit from a filmosophical approach.

Filmosophical filmgoers do not want films to be solved, they want films to be illuminated for them. *They do not want sight of the architecture and the scaffolding, they want a rhetoric that allows them to float through a living artwork.* All film theorising and writing should be about helping the filmgoer *feel* the film's forms and actions and styles and meanings *directly*. I say 'all' because ultimately I do not see a point to structuralist writing that exposes the skeleton of films, because we do not see or experience the skeleton on its own. Filmosophy is not asking filmgoers to see the 'thinking' on its own, it is asking them to see form and content *together*: the event *via* the film-thinking, the person *through* the colouring. The interesting route is to attempt to respond to the film in kind: that is, to illuminate the film for others by riffing on its thinkings; by giving weight to its actions of form; by poetically translating its thinkings. Seeing *La Guerre est finie* through filmosophy we might understand a shift from a character to a (distant or random) object as more than the possibles Bordwell provides (e.g. subjective flashforward, or new objective scene). The film may feel a relationship between the character and the object, may think associations beyond 'rational narrative schemata'.

Bordwell is also still in the position of saying that the parametric art-cinema film *reflexively* calls attention to its own processes – rather we should be looking for ways to allow (encourage) the filmgoer to simply see the film thinking, rather than see the film thinking about filmmaking (its own thinking). As noted in chapter two, when writers cannot make dramatic sense of a stylistic moment, they often chuck it in the excess bin of 'reflexivity'. In being somewhat anti-reflexive, filmosophy intends to shine a light on small formal moves, 'trivial aspects' given their due, and perhaps shown to be 'essential'. For Bordwell, the opening of *Vivre sa vie* simply announces 'the "theme" of varying camera/figure orientations'.[15] This opening gambit displays Bordwell's problem: there might be many 'camera/figure orientations' in a difficult Godard film, but it is a little simplistic to see these technical aspects as reflexive 'themes'; it is what these thinkings lead us to understand about the characters and locations that are the real 'themes'. It seems lazy to say a difficult film is simply reflexive. 'Nana's spatial relations with her surroundings will function as material for the stylistic variants', Bordwell continues; a 'true' description, in one sense, but unhelpful in so many more senses. Bordwell does eventually admit that the problem 'is what to do with them', suggesting that they perhaps symbolise 'the distance between people'.[16]

Two further problems with Bordwell's narrational analyses arise. Where is the 'experience' of these films? And how does narration relate to the characters? Firstly there seems to be little or no mention of the *experience* of these films, and the possible ways a filmgoer might *see* a film using, for example, the knowledge they have about the genre of 'parametric narration'. Bordwell seems happy to repeat in words what we see in film: the ellipsis and repetitions of Bresson and Ozu, for example, stating (the obvious): 'the constraints of stylistic patterning are imposing their will on the syuzhet, or at least that the narration limits itself to presenting events that display the style to best advantage'.[17] So we are told how films are structured and how we make sense of the film, but does that tell us anything about film art, about our emotional engagement with the aesthetics of film? Bordwell's analyses do help us understand *how* we comprehend film, but not how we might *better* comprehend film. Cognitive explanations would make a filmgoer realise what they are doing when they watch a film, and may help them analyse films more acutely, but the filmgoing *experience* is little (or even negatively) altered, and excess to the cognitivists' norms will still arise. Bordwell describes possible structures (modernistic, parametric) for stylistic forms, but does not give us a handle on *how we might understand the forms themselves*. It is thus the 'usefulness' of Bordwell's concepts that appears to be the true lack of his enterprise.

Film can think in a modernist way, but the next important question is how does this style of narration relate to the characters? Ellipses may be modernist, but what does that tell us about their appearance in a film such as Steven Soderbergh's *The Limey*. Telling us it is modernist is nice, but filmosophy is interested in how this style thinks a relationship to the characters: 'the film' (as a thinking filmind) 'feels' the world of the central character, and thinks the film via this feeling. The father in *The Limey* searches for knowledge of the whole, but only finds glimpses and gaps, and the film knows this, and 'tells' us this through its formal-thinking. Anatomising the style of Dreyer's *Ordet* still tells us nothing about why that stylist range was used. What do 'slow lateral camera and figure movements'[18] tell us about the figures represented? Asking (and trying, attempting to answer) that question seems infinitely more interesting. And Bordwell still sees these as foregrounded actions of form; the point should rather be to assimilate them into the drama for the filmgoer. *Do not let the filmgoer think of them as 'stylistic moments'*. This is the aim of filmosophy.

Just as style must be tied to history for Bordwell, so stylistic moments must be 'justified' in order to be coherent. He writes of 'gratuitous' movements and 'unjustified' colour shifts, calling these moments 'unmotivated elements',[19] indicating that they are merely stylistic extravagances. So elements must be justified, assigned, or else dropped in another bin of unmotivated excess (next to the reflexivity bin). And reasons, rationalisations, must be found for the rest: subjectivity and Bergson's 'psychological time' might 'justify' slow-motion, for example.[20] The question of whether character or film originates a meaningful style to a sequence (is it subjective or commentative) is for Bordwell the essential ambiguity of art-cinema. Overall though, he places too much emphasis on narrational ambiguity and self-consciousness – art-cinema is not just about forcing multiple interpretations or reflexive stylistics.

The objective/subjective ambiguity is something the concept of film-thinking does not wish to remove, but only freshen and illuminate. Filmosophy would not tie down sources, or ascribe 'meaning' to all these moments, but it would allow the possibility of their being 'thinkings' about a character or situation, and not just the flourish of a craftsman. (In filmosophy, no moment in film is unmotivated.) A Bordwellian filmgoer's schema cannot help them know what images relate to which character – a 'schema' cannot predict which shots represent 'mental imagery', or point of view or objective viewpoints – but a concept of film-thinking might help the filmgoer there. For example, Bordwell cannot resolve whether the flashbacks in Bertolucci's *The Spider's Stratagem*, or the colourings of Antonioni's *Red Desert*, should be 'assigned' to the characters or the narrational commentary: 'That these schemata are mutually exclusive creates the ambiguity.'[21] But are they mutually exclusive? In a sense they are both: as I have argued, the filmind (transsubjective) provides each character's point of view (subjective). Filmosophy's question is: why, for example, cannot a character's 'subjective narration' contain 'narrational' commentary? The thinking of a film should be seen as free and fluid – sometimes a subjective shot is a simple subjective shot, but our concept of cinema *should include the possibility* that it might not be simply subjective (nor objective, nor 'narrational').

Filmind and narration

In chapter two we considered the traditional concept of the narrator, and also saw how some writers have used omniscient narrators as sub-film-beings, but what about the subject of 'narration'? How does the filmind relate to the concept of narration? What is the connection between film-thinking and theories of narration? All fiction films have a narrative, but filmosophy would argue that the concept of narration does not *exhaust* the event of film. As a framework for understanding all fiction filmmaking it is ultimately archaic and limiting. Narrative is a fact of fiction films, it is a process that structures most feature films. So why not just use the idea of 'narration' to describe the 'event' of all film? Most obviously because narrative films are only one particular kind of film. A concept of film-being must be able to handle all kinds of non-narrative film, which may include documentaries, pop promos, art video, experimental film, and so on. Narration only concerns plot events and structure, and not all film is dedicated to storytelling, or *storyshowing*. Narration is a *process*, and to stretch this concept of process into 'being' in order to cover every element of the film (images, characters, edit shifts) is to virtually cut all ties with its original literary meaning, and thus delete any original usefulness.

It also carries a limiting resonance of this literary usage: it denotes 'story construction' and a story-bound entity, rather than the fluid mixture of story and pure, autonomous sound-image-art that we find in the most interesting cinema. Narration is direction of the drama, not the creation of film-worlds, and consequently theories of film narration are overly 'dramatic' and 'literary' in their concerns. The concept of a filmind is not a narratological theory, even though part of its role is to oversee a film's narrative – the filmind is not simply concerned with articulating stories. Considering a film via the concept of narration, filmgoers may well just see a sequence of actions and events, rather than a whole of image and sound and drama. This literary heritage also disallows it from truly being able to handle poetic and emotional imagery. The concept of narration is not 'suited' to the more imagistic, poetic, sublime moments of cinema. It struggles to handle these moments. Narrative theories are simply not suited to the elucidation of film *images*, no matter how much Bordwell and Burgoyne try and stretch the concept over into film form.

Furthermore, as I have argued in regard to Bordwell, the concept of narration does not tell the filmgoer anything about *why* what is narrated is narrated, it does not give them an angle on the sound and vision, or a 'way in' to the drama via the cinematics, only a layering of plot and style. Narration tells us that a film is organised, but it does not give the filmgoer an angle on this organisation, or an organic way to *conceptualise* how this organising relates to the characters and events in the film. By seeing film as thinking the filmgoer understands every element of style as an intended effect, and so every moment as the film thinking through its image-content. The concept of narration tells us that a certain moment of style is assisting the plot, the concept of the filmind tells us that this moment of style is a dramatic imaging of the story.

The filmind is not a replacement for the concept of the 'narrator', as a filmind can decide to give a film a narrator, such as a visible character-narrator, or an invisible voiceover narrator. But film does not essentially, by definition, require the concept of a narrator. Some films have narrators, some do not. Ironically, the concept of narration can run into problems with narrators: it can leave the filmgoer confused when a character becomes a narrator, or a narrator becomes a character, and they find they still need to posit another 'narrator' beyond that character-narrator. (For George Wilson the problem is the idea of both self-conscious and subjective narration being collapsed together as subjective.) The concept of the filmind allows the filmgoer to attribute certain shots to a variety of sources: the film informing us about a character, or a narrator informing us about a character, or a character informing us about another character. Seeing the whole film as thought by a filmind gives the filmgoer choice, and recognises the artistry of filmmaking.

The filmind is a theory of film-being not film narration, and is therefore a controlling construct *beyond* the traditional powers of 'narration' or the cinematic narrator. The filmind's basic film-thinking is structure, which can be either non-narrative (for example, experimental), or narrative (plot-based), or moving from one to the other. Narrative is thus one result of film-thinking, a certain type of thinking, one which lines-up plots and characters to tell a story. In fiction feature films the filmind creates a film-world, basic film-thinking structures a narrative (creates a plot with connected events), and formal film-thinking creates a style for this narrative. The narrative is simply the form that film-thinking takes in most fiction films – whether it be a tragedy, comedy, fable or thriller. The filmind creates a film-world and brings its choices of images together to create scenes and sequences and thus an overall structure with certain limits and coherence. The filmind is active and ethical, and makes its own limits – every film has its own world, a world in which a man being shot by a gun can be funny (*Raiders of the Lost Ark*) or not (*Schindler's List*). The concept of the filmind is therefore not intended as a replacement for the concept of narrative, it only points up the lack in theories of 'narration', and the limits of the idea of 'the narrator'.

We have already seen that narration is limited in that it traditionally only handles that which cannot be attributed to character-narrators – unmotivated colours or movements or edit shifts become an excess, or that which does not conform to norms. Again, filmosophy wishes to reveal the complexity of film, not attempt to reduce it to norms and non-norms. The filmind can change the very nature of the film-world, while 'narration' seems more separate, and only adds structure and style to the film-world. Theories of narration ultimately separate form and content, asserting that filmgoers respond to the fiction and then also to the film. Filmosophy argues that we (should) respond to the whole caboodle: *we cannot see what is 'in' the film without seeing it the way the film thinks it.*

Also, not only are narrative films just one kind of film, but films are not simply reducible to their narrative, and this is where theories of narration really do reveal their limitations. For example, the narrative of *Mulholland Drive* is only one aspect of its event, of its life as a film. Bordwell's theory of narration would analytically describe the bare bones of the film, and would attempt to bring in some of its stylistics as assisting or contrasting with the narrative, but the film would resist such rationalisations. There will always be an excess that theories of narration leave behind.

Filmosophy is concerned to merge form and content via the concept of film-thinking – everything in a film is thought, is intended, and so is possibly poetic, meaningful, affecting. The filmind actualises intention in the realm of film form. Film is not form *and* content, and the filmind arranges everything we see, sometimes subtly integrating and mixing 'form and content'. To hit a workable conceptual film-being one must start from the fact that film can show anything, that film is primarily image and sound, and then work backwards. Narratologists see films as stories, which sometimes stray from the path of storytelling, while filmosophers see films as pure image and sound that can tell stories if they so wish. Thus the concept of the trans-subjective filmind *positively anticipates* the nonconformism and down-right trickery of some film narration (such as *The Usual Suspects*). The filmind controls the time and space of the film-world, and understanding the concept of a 'filmind' allows the filmgoer some organisational comprehension over the film as a whole. It controls the narrative and any narrators, but also importantly designs the images and sounds of the film-world. It is a concept that brings the *imaging* of story back into the filmgoer's comprehension.

Some writers, once they have hit upon the idea that film is a kind of mind, move swiftly on to theorise about the limits of thinking and the possibilities of 'pure' or 'imagistic' thought. But the mistake these theorists make is in not following through with the original idea into the heart of films themselves. The only way we might fully understand the possibilities of film-thought is, firstly, to arrive at a workable conception, and then explore its practice, especially in contemporary cinema. One may also loosely divide its 'types' of thinking between the various forms of cinema – revealing examples of colour thinking, focus thinking, movement thinking, and so on. The next chapter will therefore explore film-thinking through these examples and formal categories.

seven | film-thinking

These past few days, I have seen a film where an actor and a horse, placed side by side, were both partially cut off at the knees; then when the man mounted the horse, he found himself suddenly decapitated. To pass instantaneously from being legless to being headless is really pushing things a bit far.

– Yhcam (1912)[1]

In the following sections I shall be concerned with the loosely defined basic fields of film composition (image, colour, sound, frame, movement and edit-shifts), elucidating filmosophy's attention to these fields with examples from various films. The sections are less about the extent of what film form can do than how general film form is thinking. What will be shown is the life of film, making up its own mind about how it gives us what we experience. Within these sections I will show the *possibilities* of thinking within each filmic field, that is, before dialogue and theatrics; as Eisenstein writes: 'Cinema can – and consequently must – convey on the screen in tangible sensual form the pure, dialectical essence of our ideological debates. Without recourse to intermediaries like plot, story or living man.'[2] The following sections will concentrate on examples that are helpfully bright in their thinking – namely, actions of film form that stand out for whatever reason, though not necessarily because they are wild or extravagant turns of style. The aim of this chapter is not to exhaustively document *all* the thinkings of film form, but to give paradigmatic indications of how film-thinking occurs, and how seeing film as thinking expands meaning possibilities. Obviously, the main problem of this design is that all film forms arrive as one, and are not delineated as individual fields when shown. But my task here is to further our understanding of film-thinking, rather than come to considered and fulsome interpretations of the films mentioned, and these films are certainly strong enough to survive my lopsided analyses. There is certainly a continual interaction and oneness of film-thinking; not an 'addition' of framing and movement, but the thought of the whole moving-shifting-sound-image to be understood.[3]

Image

The basic image (thought) of the film (filmind) is not so basic. Each granule is composed to form the image that the film intends.[4] Think, perhaps, of the director and cinematographer getting together to make some initial decisions about the film they are about to make: academy or widescreen ratio; black and white or colour; type of film stock (grainy or sharp); plus other ideas about filters, special effects, or digital manipulation. They are making decisions that will intrinsically affect our reception of the film; *decisions that we can understand as the thinking of the film.*

We normally understand a regular Hollywood film as giving us a nice window on the world it represents, but even subtle changes of image steer our reception of the characters and events. Of course any filmgoer may be *aware* of these image types, but the move of filmosophy is in crafting an integral understanding of how these image forms work *inseparably* with (as) the drama of the film. A whole film can be given a thoughtful mood of one kind or another with this simple basic film-thinking: grainy realism, soft historicalness, harsh modern living. These possible qualities to the image go against the view that meaning arrives purely via the drama. As already indicated, the change from previous film theory is that these formal qualities are shown to have integral dramatic intention within the whole film.

Whole films can be re-designed to look a certain way: think of the active grain of Korine's *Julien Donkey-Boy*, the fog-bound greys of Tarr's *Damnation*, the bristling and harsh tone of the Dardennes' *Rosetta*, the blurred daze of Sokurov's *Mother and Son*. Modern computer-generated imagery demands of us a great re-thinking of the cinematic image, but it is only as thoughtful as how you use it.[5] With fluid film-thinking the filmind can decide on anything from a minute to a flagrant altering of the filmworld. The filmgoer sees a change in the status of the film-world, and these subtle reconfigurations make us rethink our relationship to our own world, and offer the most profound ground for this new image. Now fantasy is as achievable, as available as any other image form, how interesting an image is will not be measurable simply by how adventurous it seems. Fluid film-thinking could possibly propose a new knowledge of thought – something like the prediction of Roy Huss: 'film will no doubt continue to use a host of special effects that will markedly depart from naturalism to map out a "chamber nautilus" of the mind'.[6] Looking at film using not just an 'idea' of thinking, but the template of creative, poetic intention, film opens up to reveal more than we had maybe anticipated (but perhaps always subconsciously enjoyed).

Colour

With the image is always colour and shade, and some of the most thoughtful moods of film are felt through colour. Simply put, the filmind can feel the drama to *be* a certain colour (or perhaps a movement from one colour to another), and the filmgoer can then understand film colour as *originating* from the film story; as *being with* the film story. The filmind here has the thoughtful freedom to enter into any colour – has its own *will* as regards colour use – and can give a scene any hue. The film may feel (show) the love between two characters through soft red glows, or may bruise a hate-filled film with reds and purples. Filmosophy is less concerned with the meaning of colours than with the way in which film *has* colour, *uses* colour, and how we should *approach* that use in talk about film. A writer might use the rhetoric of 'the director used this colour here, on these people, to say this, or to mean that', and their interpretations can certainly get the film's meaning, to an extent. What an analysis of this sort lacks is fluency of expression, and thus a certain communication of interest and importance – films can create their own colour meanings and references.

Hugo Münsterberg felt that colour would affect the filmgoer's 'consciousness of unreality',[7] while Gerard Fort Buckle saw that this new photography 'is undoubtedly the greatest power that the screen holds', 'should one tint the scene of a murder committed in the soft moonlight, true to nature, or should one assist the mind of the viewer by tinting the scene with a cold atmosphere which gives the viewer a shudder to behold?'.[8] Only realistic colour has meaningful force for V. F. Perkins (realistic in the sense that it comes from *within* the film-world), while the analytic formalist Edward Branigan merely collates colour forms, and can only ask us to understand colour through 'systems' or 'strategies'.[9] But Eisenstein understood that colour should be seen and used as a dramatic factor, and argued that it can encompass and elucidate a situation almost on its own.

Yet colourism can just as well be found in the varying shades of black and white – though modern film studies continues to merely find 'cultural' meaning in the decision not to film in colour. For Perkins the orthochrome black and white of Godard's *Les Carabiniers* was significant because of what it rejected: a modern colour image. But these images have a feeling (hold a thinking) before and under any possible cultural interpretation. The thinking, the shading, of black and white can behave exactly like colours, where shade is actively used to give an *immediacy* of meaning in and around characters and events. Deleuze called black and white Expressionism 'the precursor of real colourism in the cinema', and Eisenstein knew the power of utilising 'the outlines and tonal "sounds" of grey photography'.[10] For example, shadow and light can enable the film to think relations between people: film may feel the darkness within a character, or the darkness framing a scene of death or suffering; or it may feel lightness as love or revelation, as relief or happiness or safety. In other words, the filmind may dramatically think events through light.

Darkness, say in the case of some film noirs, might be a thinking of the ignorance of the fall-guy hard-boiled detective, or the trapped feeling of his predicament, or the site of mysterious terrifying unknown. The film thinks this blackness (which the filmgoer understands almost directly – much as we know and feel darkness in our own lives). Darkness offers its own multitude of thoughts; sometimes feeling the concentration or exclusion in the mind of a character – perhaps closing in around a character as they remember a time gone by. Sometimes the filmind almost becomes the clouded darkened mind of a character – thinking their inner emotions through image. Sometimes the filmind gives its 'own' feeling to a scene (leads us to understand the scene in a certain way), perhaps constricting and closing in on a character using darkness.

Perhaps like music, a film can think certain colours for the presence of danger or evil. It can also simply understand a scene or vista with respect and humility. The filmind may feel different colours for different characters – which could be the film helping us to understand their personality, or the film feeling their mood or thoughts. In the moment in *Vertigo* when Scottie completes his transformation of Judy and she is bathed in a mist of green light, the film might be thinking in many possible ways: perhaps either feeling (interpreting) his loving, emotive gaze, or showing us how self-deluding his actions are, or thinking her as a ghostly return of the dead (or maybe all or more are being thought).

As mentioned in the previous section, the image can hold a basic level of colour – a mode of thinking that holds and keeps the world we experience at a certain tone. This tonal thinking may allow only certain colours to show, may favour other colours, or may deepen and blush all (perhaps a low colour level is thought such that significant colourful moments will stand out). *Basic Instinct* gives us its idea of an amoral world, perhaps drained, as if on the point of death, and almost transparent in its steely greyness. *The Matrix* thinks a brittle, chrome, almost sickly-green false world, perhaps feeling the cold and manipulative thinking of the Artificial Intelligence that provides it; while the real world is similarly cold in tone, this time in cool blue. (These are films, that, in very different ways, foresee a future almost without colour – even transparent, like glass.) But every single film has some colour-image level of thinking going on – *Starship Troopers* looks 'normal', but its sharp, clear, proud images are perhaps *thinking* the optimism and wide-eyed naïveté of the characters and the bright, solid ideology that they are being sacrificed for.

A film may think its colours historically – in Sally Potter's *Orlando*, as the film moves through different ages, so the film thinks these times according to their cinematic style, moving from soft romantic periods to sharp modern images. *GoodFellas* thinks (becomes) the *encounter* between Henry Hill and the mob – the film understands its beginning as romance, flushing and softening all colours into oranges and browns, and the ending with images as sharp and quick as the rush of cocaine. Kieslowski's *A Short Film About Killing* almost becomes the clouded, dark mind of the young murderer, sick with his world, and looking for a victim. In *Blind Chance* the film gives us the memory of a young man's stay in hospital, and thinks his perception of that time with a pained green similar to the one in *Vertigo*. *The Double Life of Véronique* feels her inner pain through a dark-edged thinking of the image, while in *Three Colours: Blue* it is the power of Julie's memories that the film feels through colour, blushing blue with her as the past surges up to the present.

When a single film brings both colour *and* black and white to the image it can either be a fruitful or clichéd meeting. The latter usually when memory or past is given without colour, or when the film perhaps wants to make serious an event or scene. A film such as *Natural Born Killers* conceives its drama in both, though with no necessary logic behind it. Compare this with Lars von Trier's *Europa*, whose black and white is complicated by colour (love, death) – the film feeling the emotions and attentions of the characters *through* colour. Somewhere between are films such as Tarkovsky's *Stalker* that seem to feel tones beyond black and white, and digital technology now has the image mapped and completely changeable, such that films can now think any *part* of the image in any colour or shade, and the future holds many possible thinkings for those that go there.[11]

Sound

Like focusing, or colour, or any element, the filmind steers the sound of the film. A general analysis of sound in a film may be perceptive about its use, and how certain sounds 'relate' to the action or characters. The possible lack here, again, is that the analysis is not *integrated* into the whole film. Sound is often left as an addendum, talked about only when it is ostensible, 'active'. Where a general study may find some sounds to be a metaphor for the danger a character is in, filmosophy finds a thinking *of* that danger, a feeling, through sound, of danger – either thinking the character's emotions or thinking its own knowledge (as when the character does not know he or she is in danger).

Sound can think similarly to montage or a layered image, but effect an even less conscious reaction. The filmind simply feels an added level to the images, and sounds are as good as additional 'pictures' in the filmgoer's mind. André Bazin may have argued that the primacy of the image is only a technical accident of history, but films still think more through the image side of the image-sound whole.[12] The concept of the filmind brings sound back into the life of film, making it *constantly* thoughtful and *integral* with other film forms. The sound-thinking of films is continuous: the filmind may think a regular conversation as abrasive and sharp, while making other characters' voices soft and warm. A great thoughtful use of sound is the selective, perceptive thinking of a character's subjectivity. In Hitchcock's *Blackmail* the film feels the girl's concentration, hearing only the word 'knife' in the neighbour's gossip. In Louis Malle's *Damage* the film feels the man's romantic concentration on the young woman, this time by drowning-out others' words with music. This sound masking is the focusing of audio – an intention of the ear for Stanley Cavell – and is a simple indication of the thoughtfulness of film.

Films can think via music as much as noise affects, and each choice powerfully reconfigures the images – and the names are there if you want to make an extended, cultural discussion of a movie: Béla Bartók's *Music for Strings, Percussion and Celesta* almost controlling the edit shifts of *The Shining*; Arvo Pärt's *Fratres* and *Tabula Rasa* bringing a heavy heart to *Little Odessa*; Leos Janáček's first two String Quartets feeling the love in *The Unbearable Lightness of Being*. The film can also think against the image using music. This asynchronous thinking arrives when the filmind decides to obviously undercut or counteract the images presented – realising film sound as another formal thought ties it to the film. In *8mm* our hero goes into the underworld of snuff movies, and the film feels the journey into another world through music from another place (in this case North African mesmeric beats and chants) – the music is not (just) a metaphor, not least because the filmgoer normally *feels* music first. The whole film (hot images and 'foreign' sounds) thinks the hero's out-of-sorts passage. A film may surround someone's speech with sympathetic music, or hound it with clattering percussion: the end of *Code Unknown* compounds and enlarges the simple confusion of a person locked out of their apartment (because of an unknown door code) by rattling the image with a marathon drum performance by a group of hard-of-hearing children. The sound-thinking indicates, almost make us *feel*, a larger meaning.

Silence is the darkness of sound. When the filmind decides to relegate sound, to suck any and all sounds from its thinking, silence can become a powerful feeling. This choice by the film can be thought for many uses: to let us see what might have been clouded in music; to let us hear our own heartbeat; to concentrate our perceptions. Or perhaps it is brought in to accentuate creaking, or prepare us for explosions. *Lost Highway* feels its sounds inside-out, sometimes even those sounds we hear, physically, inside our heads. The film creates a vacuum, leaving an absence we feel loudly. Like an awkward silence unnaturally extended the film begins with only breath and footsteps, and develops into the pure intention of the main male character. When he meets a man at a party the film reveals (more than a person could possibly experience) the silence the party becomes in the presence of their words. In *Lost Highway*, sound *emerges* from darkness.

For a writer such as V. F. Perkins sounds should be kept within the film's story; i.e. they should only come from sources in the film-world: record players, radios, and so on: 'The demand, on allegedly artistic grounds, for "a more cinematic use of sound" is most often a request for the introduction of noise divorced from its source, a decorative addition to the narrative rather than an organisation of its elements: mixture as against synthesis.'[13] For someone like Deleuze, 'out-of-field' sounds are no longer that, but add to the image (like sugar and water) to become a new image. *The filmind simply thinks a whole of image and sound*. Nowadays digital multiphonic auditoriums blast us with crisply interfering offscreen noises, and films can be awash with sound thinking. *Seven* thinks as much through noise as through images, the film feeling the horror by sometimes surrounding the characters with low but abrasive sounds.

Focus

There may not appear to be much thinking in a normally focused, sharp clear film, but it is still a decision by the filmind to have as much as possible of the image in focus, a thinking of inclusion and naturalness – but clarity only provides one line of meaning possibilities (centred around dramatic meaning). Focusing can definitely have phenomenological qualities in these films, the film thinking the changing attention of any of its characters. Cavell recognises that when only a small sliver of the image is in focus the film is making a choice, of what to make clear and what to exclude. Buckle talks of the subconscious and the conscious focus – the former being natural, infinity focus, where most of the image is sharp, the latter being a deliberate attention to something. Eisenstein realised much of this through his concept of tonal montage, and the emotional 'resonance' of particular shots. Even in 1912 Yhcam acknowledged that variations of focusing can indicate differing types of thinking.

Sharpness is not so much intended as needed in a normal film, but sharpness perhaps becomes more thoughtful when it is in obvious contrast to the *un*focused (for our theoretical needs here, a part of the image is unfocused when the attention of the film is on the focused, as in the scenes going on behind a conversation; it is *de*focused when the attention is actually on that which is blurred, or was focused – again these technicist terms should eventually give way to more thoughtful poeticisms).

Raise the Red Lantern and *The Draughtsman's Contract* both think their precision in relation to that which is ill-defined, and raise the thoughtfulness of the drama in doing so (thinking, through image, the precision of the Chinese household and the rationality of the draughtsman). In *Vigil* the film thinks through beautiful relations of blur and edge, near and far – film-thinking becoming the creative, naïve attention of the youthful protagonist.

Significant to this kind of film-thinking is the way film can be more than our thinking, keeping near and far sharp to our attention. Which leads on to why certain films think an image of depth, an active image with levels of action, alongside a usually motionless frame. (On the rarer other hand, 3D, or stereoscopic film, forces a depth of field where we may have chosen a different one.) Film does not match our own visual attention, as concentrating on a far object with a near object apparent, the near object is not only indefinite, but significantly 'doubled' (recently visualised in a moment in, of all films, *Patch Adams*, where a mental patient holds up four fingers and our hero focuses on the patient's face beyond the hand, revealing eight blurred fingers; Robin Williams, playing the hero here, also played a actor who *becomes* out-of-focus, and thus unable to shoot his film in *Deconstructing Harry*).

The first unrealised beauty of the photographed image was the defocused.[14] Where the unfocused makes us realise the thoughtful primacy of subjects and objects in normal films – blur putting into relief the sharpness we had taken for granted – the defocused, the willed intended blur, is a pure example of film's neothoughtfulness, creating images that we could not ourselves generate. On seeing the 1921 film *El Dorado* by Marcel L'Herbier, Jean Epstein wrote of a fandango scene: 'By means of soft focus which becomes progressively intensified, the dancers gradually lose their differentiations, cease to be recognisable as individuals, *become merged in a common visual term*: the dancer.'[15] *Vacas* brings us the wood where most of the magical events takes place by thinking its *whole* colour, that is, by pulling back such that the many greens and browns merge as a single freckled hue – the wood itself from a magical thought. Two films, *Three Colours: Blue* and *The Scent of Green Papaya*, profoundly explore the thoughtful feeling of an image beyond definition. And unlike experimental films which may explore such images (usually imitating a painterly aesthetic), placing such 'experimentation' within a story is much more difficult and much more fruitful if successful. *Three Colours: Blue* feels (thinks) both the emotional strain on the widow, and perhaps the de-realising power of music, when she finally starts completing her late-husband's requiem, collapsing the room into a haze. Music is here thought as fuelling the most powerful sense, depriving sight of any useful role. And *The Scent of Green Papaya* seems to feel the merging souls of the two lovers, ending the film by blurring their environment of luscious green foliage.

Speed

The thoughtful intensification of time is commonplace in cinema, and is usually used either for phenomenological or poetic effect. Within filmosophy it is seen to issue from the heart of the filmind, and essentially this thinking beyond our thinking allows us into perceptions we can never reproduce ourselves.[16] But before slowness there is zero speed, stillness, where the film locks so wantonly onto a moment that cinema ends and the love of the image is rediscovered. A 'film' such as *La Jetée* thoughtfully, finally, opens (our) eyes to what we forget we can experience everyday: movement. *Butch Cassidy and the Sundance Kid* and *The 400 Blows* differently end on still-thoughts: one possibly thinking, retaining, their proud courageous memory in an act of immediate immortality, the other thinking a moment of freedom, one resounding with the future. And then there is the accelerated image, rarer in cinema than skiing mice (though I write this before the much-anticipated release of *Stuart Little 4*), thinking a certain urgency or madness perhaps. The funeral procession in *À Propos de Nice* shakes with speed, and, as Cavell reports: 'The point of the device here – cited explicitly, at the screening of the film I attended, by the film's cameraman, Boris Kaufman – is to comment on the desire, at fashionable seaside resorts, to hurry death out of sight.'[17] Speeded time in *Koyaanisqatsi* may rethink humanity as a large machine, but films such as *Mauvais Sang* and *The Element of Crime* think a certain existential escape (respectively, Anna at the end at the aerodrome, and Fisher fleeing a scene in a beat-up VW Beetle).

But slowed events and actions predominate (belying cinema's schizophrenic preoccupation with spectacle and poetry), and seeing this slowedness as the thoughtful dramatisation of a filmind, thickening and delaying time, allows for more fluid interpretations. But perhaps the first port of call of the slowed is that which we wish lasted longer – a film may feel the incredibleness of a scene and give it more time, and our filmgoer is served with moments beyond their ken.[18] Gerard Fort Buckle had an interesting take on this experience of the filmgoer: that as we watch slow-motion film, 'the mind (thought) is completely different. It is working slowly ... the mind has become almost disinterested ... because thought is being replaced by vision'.[19] And perhaps film is thinking like this sometimes, replacing the information of film events with scenes so slow that after we have understood the image, after we have gathered the information, we are left with pure image. But this is only one kind of film-thinking, and the slowed image offers almost endless power. Distinct from that interpretation is the feeling that a slowed image *increases* the amount of 'information' to be gathered – that slow-motion is a thinking of utter importance, brought in when a significant moment has the power to extend itself, prolong itself (filmind and 'event shown' being, conceptually, one and the same thing). Slowed scenes can become a thinking of importance or beauty for a character – as in Hitchcock's *Strangers on a Train* when our hero enters the house of his appointed murderee, and is met by a dog that licks his hand: the film feels the importance of this moment for him, the importance the moment should have for him, extending it, understanding the jump back to reality this tactile moment forces on the protagonist. Slowness becomes a willful reorganisation of film's time, and the most immediate and understandable instance of film-thinking.

Framing

Framing is a position of thinking. Just a scene of two people talking can be framed, and thought, in many different ways. Showing both or one at a time; giving space to their environment; framing from behind objects; it can even be responsive to them, or almost ignore them – letting them walk into and out of the frame. Many types of framing have of course been noted at some time or another by writers on film, but realising framing as resulting from the knowledge the film has of its whole, and reconfiguring it as the film thinking the drama of the story through framing, opens up the possibilities of meaning produced by even slight inflections of the frame.

Looking at the frame itself – squarish, or thin and wide, and many variations in-between – the film can start thinking almost before it shows anything. As Cavell writes, 'shape *pervades*, like gravity, or energy, or air';[20] the frame of cinema is steering our thinking before we realise it. A wide-framed image can give many different feelings to a film – used most obviously to capture open space, nowadays it has more complex uses. What it can do is give an opportunity for the filmind to think relationships between characters, spacing them apart, putting them 'on the edge' (thinkings we understand affectively rather than metaphorically). The wide frame can be a thinking of grandeur (in the 1920s it was actually referred to as the 'grandeur screen'), or a thinking of the equal importance or relationship of multiple events. Multiframed films, such as Brian De Palma's *Snake Eyes*, Norman Jewison's *The Thomas Crown Affair*, or Vincent Gallo's *Buffalo 66*, serve to increase information, or like edit shifts, become a thinking that equalises or compares moments. And the squarish frame doesn't preclude this thoughtful image (Kubrick made only one widescreen film, *2001: A Space Odyssey*, and Kieslowski found a wealth of ideas in his basic frame). By 'choosing' the tight square frame the film is already giving feeling (meaning) to its events, however slight that feeling may be (compare the 'regular' image of *My Name is Joe* to a film with a similar gritty setting, but thought via a grand wide image, *The War Zone*). Our eyes in normal perception naturally see a wider than high visual field, yet we understand the squarish image as more realistic – or rather the wide image is more often used with more aesthetic intent, and we receive more reality through the televisual frame.

Film can think any vantage point in a single room, and a conversation between two people can be immeasurably inflected or revealed by the will of film framing. Think of ten people looking at a scene – each will not only see the scene differently, but will also frame it personally. If I am listening to two people talking I may have more interest in something behind them, and so 'frame' them accordingly; film can think this intention, and more. These analogies give a reason for why different framings are used, but also lead us to understand why interpreting framing as thinking reveals so much. For example, in *Light Sleeper* the hero and his girlfriend are talking at a table, and the film frames them with a concrete block between them – here the filmind reveals (and instinctively makes us feel) their separation. *Vertigo* thinks similarly – framing and shifting between characters either side of a lamp, or pot of paint brushes, thinking their proximity, either near or far. In *North by Northwest*, Thornhill and Eve Kendall, the woman he has recently met and flirted with, are in a train station, and the film thinks their increasing familiarity by gradually shifting from images that frame them in the larger scene of the station to ones that are close and intimate. The concept of film-thinking brings meaning and form together, and the gap that can appear in some film interpretation (low angle – maybe 'means' this) is collapsed. Again in *North by Northwest*, think of the framing when our hero flees a murder at the UN and we see him from an enormous height: the film creatively, dramatically *feels* his vulnerable position – the film thinking a way of understanding his present situation. The extent of the frame's thinkings are wide and varied. Inclusion of all dramatic elements in one frame can be a thinking of real danger (man and lion, Keaton and cannon) or real connection (Nanook and hole and seal). For some the frame masks a larger reality, and the filmind is here possibly thinking a sense of concealment, teasing us with what is offscreen – but the 'edge' of the film (of the film-thought) can just as well be a thinking of limit as it can be one that indicates an unseeable excess – it has no one definition.

Framing the view of a character, as we saw in chapter five, is an ever-popular way of leading the filmgoer through a drama. George Wilson understands point of view to be when the actions of a film

> are used to depict or symbolise or reflect aspects of the way in which the character perceives and responds to his or her immediate environment ... to let properties of the way in which the fictional world looks to us on the screen stand in for properties of the way in which that world is experienced by the character.[21]

Here Wilson is extending the definition to cover symbols and 'properties' in the image, allowing for more filmic events to be covered by the term. But, as I have argued, *the film is still thinking its own interpretation of a character's subjective viewpoint*, and extending 'subjectivity' across more and more of film, as Wilson is suggesting, only confuses by narrowing a film's rhetoric – to that of just either subjective point of view, or those objective, neutral scenes which made Wilson seek a '*grand imagier*'. The film makes a decision to think as if the character, and by thinking 'as' a character the filmind can alter the film in any way it wishes to give us an idea of the motive or feelings of the character. Thus what we are concerned with here is how seeing point of view in this way might alter and help our interpretations of these kind of moments in film.[22] The idea of the 'point of view shot' can at times be so crude as to be misleading – there are a multitude of ways that film can think with, for or around a character. We might see a scene from one character's stand-point, but the film could still be thinking *for* a different character (the first character might say: 'I don't see what you obviously can', while the filmind gives us the type of view he says he cannot see).

Cavell indicates this parasubjectivity when he writes, 'if we have been given the idea that the camera is placed so that what we see is what the character sees *as he sees it*, then what is shown to us is not just something seen but a specific *mood* in which it is seen'.[23] Film can think for, with and around any character, can bring us to an understanding of how a character is perceiving (feeling) what they see. In the end, when a film decides to show us something from a character's viewpoint, the impact and meaning of the *decision* is just as important as what we then see. It is most often a thinking of the importance of a particular moment for a character – the filmind gives a sense of their viewpoint when it feels the moment will give the filmgoer a better sense of the drama, or perhaps when it feels the character has invested a lot in the situation.

But the real beauty of framing is laid open with the close-up. Jean Epstein put it best: 'The close-up is the soul of the cinema.'[24] A special, high attention thought, it magnifies feelings, and so transforms cinema into intimate importance. For Münsterberg the close-up is more simply the filmic equivalent of our modes of 'attention', and can give us that which deserves our attention: 'Suddenly we see not Booth himself a he seeks to assassinate the president, but only his hand holding the revolver and the play of his excited fingers filling the whole field of vision.'[25] But the close film-thought is more complex, and certainly not simply phenomenological. The thoughtfulness of the *decision* to move in close is what fuels the thinking of the close-up itself. The large close-up Germaine Dulac calls the psychological shot, 'the very thought of the character projected onto the screen. It is his soul, his desire … inner life made perceptible by images'.[26]

Seeing it as the thoughtful intention of a filmind allows us to understand many more of its uses and meanings. It becomes affectionate, intrusive, questioning, loving, inhibiting, voyeuristic. On objects it can bestow significance and importance (think of door handles in thrillers). In fact, in the history of cinema the close-up has become more prevalent, recently encouraged by video transference where the small television screen is happier with larger objects and characters. And when the film decides to bring us the face, again the thoughtfulness of the decision (coming after an act of violence; a devotion of love) is what fuels the thinking of the close-up itself. The filmind wants us to know how important the preceding moment is for the character involved, or wants to make us ask ourselves what it means for another, seemingly peripheral character. Plus, in the context (within the shifts) of a film's thinking, a close image is as suited to feeling tenderness as it is to fuelling calculation.[27] Add to the framing the dimension of time and the thinking of the close-up grows in power – such as the moment in *Philadelphia* when the protagonist exits another lawyer's office, having failed to enlist their help: the film tenderly closes in on his face amongst the busy street, and holds, understandingly, feeling his powerlessness. The thoughtful lingering on faces can thus develop their own internal tension.

The possibilities of thought being felt through framing extends from here. It is tempting to talk of 'deframings' as we talked of defocusing, but that would necessitate defining 'normal' framing (we *can* acknowledge when something is focused and not focused), and the point of the filmind is to bring all kinds of forms together in one organic picture of film-thinking. But importantly, these kinds of (de)framings should not be viewed as excess to other (more normal) kinds of framing, but integral and understandable. In order to fully integrate 'style', and help ward off those who can only refer to 'excessively stylised' filmmaking, we must use the idea of film-thinking and the filmind to ground these forms. Studying a film such as *U Turn* and offering thoughtful reason for some of its framings does not mean the film cannot still be criticised for being overwrought with style, or that there is not a kind of aesthetic undecidability, but it may temper those arguments. *U Turn* offers both kinetically exhilarated and morally disturbing thinkings, framings that feel the confusion or viewpoint of our hero, and framings that feel the moral 'un-levelness' of the town he arrives in. In such as film as *Frenzy* violence is thought directly through the frame, destabilised and sickening (like watching the horizon in a storm-tossed boat). In *Tierra* framing thinks like an existential force: at one time our hero is knocked out in a field – as he falls the film falls with him to the right, framing his head sideways on (his head on the right, sky on the left); as he loses consciousness the film feels this (and perhaps more thinkings) and moves to now frame his head against the earth (head on left, right half now filled with soil).

Movement

In his imaginative biography and diary of the German filmmaker Friedrich Wilhelm Murnau,[28] Jim Shepard lovingly details Murnau's inventive moving of the camera – using bicycles, overhead cabling, even strapping the camera to the front of the cameraman in *The Last Laugh* – and traces how his stint of flying during the Great War brought Murnau to the realisation that film needed to be truly mobile. Shepard's book, though small, ultimately stands as an archaeology of the inspiration behind the birth of real movement and fluidity in the cinema:

> What Murnau dreams of, when he lays his sleepless head to his pillow at night, is the camera that at any moment can go anywhere, at any speed. The camera that out-strips present film technique and fulfils the cinema's ultimate artistic goal. The first difference between cinema and photography has to be that the viewpoint can be mobile, can share the speed of moving objects. He wants, viewed through mobile space, the encounter of surfaces; stimulation and its opposite, calm; a symphony made of the harmony of bodies and the rhythm of space; the play of pure move-ment, vigorous and abundant. He wants new modes of expression corresponding to the art of the image machine, and he seeks them with the utmost perseverance. He wants the camera to be both participant and observer, like the dreamer who acts and watches himself doing so. He wants to move from the geometry of the one-dimensional surface to the geometry that applies in depth.[29]

Film is a thinking in space, a spatial reasoning that can describe and understand and transfigure the objects and people within it – even Bazin can admire 'the astonish-ingly perspicacious mobility of the camera' in a film such as *Les Parents terribles*.[30] Like many theorists, Yvette Biró at first sees only subjectivity in cinematic movement, but then realises that is not enough: 'in the rhythms of the camera's movements, in its circling, bending and turning, crossing and surrounding movements, in its slower or faster pace, there lies a hidden poetic ideal, *a comprehensive thought independent of the story line*'.[31] This independent thought, like the filmind, allows for wider inter-pretations, and dramatises form in order to enhance or contrast with the story – Biró subsequently comes to see movement as thoughtfully articulative and interpretive. She looks at *Last Year in Marienbad*, and attempts to capture some of its power:

> the camera brought to life a separate universe … it simply dissolved and eliminated the reality of space … we felt that in this place everything had become relative, any object or event might be replaced by another, one just as fleeting and intangible

as any other … showing us how inextricably physical and symbolic space-realities are intertwined.[32]

Where this brings us to is a recognition that the moving of the frame is also a moving of (new) thought, and that conceiving of movement in this way may help someone such as Seymour Chatman, who finds a camera which 'seems to be conducting its own inquiry' at the end of *The Passenger* (when the film leaves the hotel room and travels and surveys the street outside).[33]

Again, the technicist rhetoric will need to be re-routed – what, for example, are we meant to *gain* from seeing 'tracking shots' all over the place?[34] The film may well 'track' a character, but that is only one way of describing that movement in cinema. So it is simple: use a different term for each occasion – the realm of 'thinking' offers so many. They were referred to as 'Cabiria Movements' in early Hollywood, after Giovanni Pastrone's 1914 film *Cabiria*, which dwelled and delighted in them.[35] Nowadays a filmmaker such as Jean-Luc Godard speaks of the 'dolly shot' as being a moral judgement, and film-artists such as Jane and Louise Wilson make films that describe space, tracing it with movements, becoming the space it inhabits, ultimately feeling the elements that reveal an institution. Another kind of movement-thinking is the 'shaky' image, found in the television series *NYPD Blue* (but also in later Woody Allen films), which perhaps feels a certain kind of participation, a certain kind of fidgety attention, thinking the minds of the policemen and women always alert to details, and never at rest in a vibrant city. The obverse of this is a kind of subtle movement – Parker Tyler notes that Andy Warhol's films function simplistically like robots, and are thus anti-cinematic. But small inflections of movement can be as thoughtful as grand sweeps and glides. Cavell cites the 'reticence' of Renoir's camera in *La Grande Illusion*,[36] and looking at such a filmmaker as Ken Loach we can again see such a respectful and subtle film-thinking.

Thus we have seen that when the film decides to move, to glide and glance at its subjects and scenes, it can possibly introduce a descriptive and inquisitive thinking. *Every movement of the frame is already thoughtful, in the sense that it is a decision by the film, at that moment, to move.* The film may simply be following characters, but that is still a decision among others (e.g. to hold and view the characters coming, or going). A film such as *Terminator 2* may have almost constant movements, perhaps reversing the significance of 'movement' within that film, and illustrating that a thoughtful film is not necessarily one with active movements. But some movements can think very dramatically: especially when the film shows its knowledge and perhaps glides in on a character's face, forcing and reflecting a 'realisation' that the character is about to come to. The encroaching thought, the move-in on characters and scenes, is a common but significant movement. In *Smoke* the film perhaps thinks the growing attention of the listeners and closes-in on the characters' faces as they relate their stories. Similarly thoughtful is the float upwards, thinking perhaps a relationship of the events left below to a larger, broader picture. In *Distant Voices, Still Lives* the film glides 'backwards' (for our right/forward Western sensibility) as it surveys the terrace houses, and narratively into the past. The film also thoughtfully connects the elements of the boy's life, feeling the link between church and cinema – perhaps feeling how similarly the boy experiences both, as a flow from above (spirituality/projection). The movement of filmosophy is away from seeing film form as abstractly relating to meaning, to seeing film form *as* the drama of the film: the film does not carry or mean confusion, it *becomes* confusion, it inhabits the affects and emotions and concepts we receive in the filmgoing experience. Thus movements become possible emotions and conjunctions – the regal glide, the fluid description, the illuminating flight. The moving frame of cinema, the thinking of movement, can be both kinetic and conceptual; giving life to film and tracing lines of life in film.

Shifts

The filmind (the film) creates and colours and orders itself, and within this conception image shifts become another kind of movement, a decision to go somewhere else, to show a different view of an event in progress. The filmind can decide to show us another country or another moment. The reasons for shifts can then be re-thought as thoughtful feeling and intention. The meaning possibilities of shifts are enlivened by viewing them as acts of the filmind: a simple shift from one person to another becomes a considered, motivated, dramatic 'choice'. Seeing all film shifts like this raises the level of filmgoing: all shifts in image are thought, all shifts are interpretable. We begin to ask why shifts occur at the moments they do, and to ask what kind of thinking those shifts become.

Most film shifts revolve around characters – the filmind gives us different views of two people talking, or gives us a face, and then what it is looking at, etc. The film may be thinking that one person's reaction is more important than another's, or directing us (willing us) to understand the relationship of the speaker to some other situation or event (shifting from speaker to someone asleep in the corner, for instance). Through shifts the filmind can begin to 'inhabit' concepts – of 'disgust' perhaps, or magnetic passion. The organicism of the filmind reveals cuts, edits – shifts in images – as the active thought of the whole film. These shifts of concern, of importance, are simply driven by the imagistic reasoning of the filmind. To see that, to show this, to relate this to that, to contrast, to move ahead. Thus, a shift is the thought of the transition from one thought to another: the filmind deciding to think another image, another place. By shifting images, by deciding that another scene is needed, the filmind provides a dramatic analysis of its own action. This geography of images clearly reveals the thoughtful decision-making powers of the filmind. The shift is the thinking. This is why we can thus see shifting as a feeling of the filmind. Even action-movies can find thoughtful ways of using shifts – perhaps by staying with the characters during special effects or big explosions, rather than leaving them behind for the 'money-shots'.

Rhetorically, within film writings, these moments are better read as transitions, changes: 'shifts'. A term such as editing is too technical; montage is only one kind of shift; and talking solely in terms of cuts may not be responsive to the *flow* possible in film shifts. Again, as we shall see in the next chapter, the simple act of reconfiguring the rhetoric of such descriptions allows for a greater range of meaning possibilities. By thinking of editing as 'shifts' we might now envisage different aesthetics – such as those slight shifts where the minor reframing of a character is technically an edit, but needs a less brash description. Other technicist terms need to be rethought: for example, just identifying 'jump cuts' in a film is not enough. For a film's possible power to be understood we must recognise these moments as thoughtful: for example, perhaps *À Bout de souffle* feels the youthful (in)attention of its characters, or thinks a transcendent thinking by cinema – an ability to comprehend actions from without. This approach to 'editing' advances filmgoers' understanding of film by organicising the appearance of shifts in a film – that is, it melds the shifts to the whole film. 'Edits' are usually theorised as cold events, and their aesthetic development has been noticeable for its dialectical direction (*JFK*, *October*). Rethinking film shifts as a thoughtful intention allows more to be seen in less 'active' filmmaking. For example, *Funny Games* feels a definite phenomenological sense of fear and violence, shifting only rarely from each scene, perhaps feeling the trance-like state of the mother and father. The film thinks its violence through its shifts, and, through the strain on the filmgoer (perhaps unused to an unaltering image), *becomes* its violence.

And there are different types of shifts – Buckle thought the fade was like 'the closing of the eye in the human being,'[37] but it is more than analogous, almost thinking a goodbye that begs us to think again about the image we are leaving; perhaps a thoughtful invitation to replay in our minds the work of the film so far. Its cousin, the superimposition, the doubled thought, can be a place of dense and beautiful thinking. For Gilbert-Lecomte soft-focus, fades and superimposition, 'can reproduce paranoiac transmutation which the mind imposes on objects when it suddenly discovers their secret hallucinatory horror.'[38] Within filmosophy, overlaying can be reconfigured as the film thinking an instant relationship between events, mixing possible meanings. Tyler notes a thought of comparison in Fellini's *Satyricon*, the film merging the still young Encolpius 'into the image of him painted on a decaying wall as if he were a surviving fresco ... it is a way of conceiving cinema as a mode of mythical magic'.[39] These overlapping thinkings, where one image emerges through another, give us time to feel connections. In *Seven* Somerset is researching the deadly sins in a library and the film merges his face with the images of death and depravity in the classical works he is looking at. As Richard Dyer notes in the DVD commentary, the film is *dissolving him into the sins*, feeling their seductiveness and the way that it is hard to escape their power (just as the film itself is ugly yet beautiful).

But in most films shifts are there to activate a story, to give multiple, logical views in a situation, and to take us from one situation to another. The filmind orders and controls, drawing our attention to some events, and leaving others behind. Shifting between two people talking, or from the inside of a house to the outside as someone walks through a door, are base thinkings of easy understanding and uninterrupted story. Beyond this, beyond 'continuity', are thinkings of the relations of characters and scenes. When a film feels a relationship between two characters it may 'decide' to show that through transitions of images. When *Touch of Evil* gives us Menzies and Susan Vargas on opposing sides of the image, in two different places, it is *feeling* their distance, perhaps the distance of Susan from any rescue, or perhaps the similarity of their situations. Either way, the film (the filmind) reveals its *understanding* of her position. For V. F. Perkins editing 'is important in the first place for what it *allows*', giving film 'the wild liberty of a mental process – of thought, imagination and dream'.[40] A theorist such as Vsevolod Pudovkin saw editing as equal to the shifting attention of the ideal viewer – what would they want to see?; how fast would they leave a scene? Similarly Karel Reisz advocates invisible editing – shifts that would match an interested spectator if that spectator could fly around gaining the most telling points of view.[41] All shifts are 'felt' by the filmgoer – they feel the meaning of the shift (before any 'interpretive' thinking) – and no more so than in larger sequences (or whole films) of shifts. As mentioned previously, towards its end *GoodFellas* feels the flitting, cocaine-fuelled mind of Henry Hill, shifting within and between scenes with increasing speed. This is a decision by the filmind – *to empathise, to become, where it could have observed and judged*. The fast-shifting film might also be thinking a certain impatience, or maybe it is a thinking of multiple associations.

The filmind may also prioritise the image over the shift, and the relative impact of unbroken images over multiple shifts is *the* film debate of the last century. For André Bazin the 'long depth take' (found in F. W. Murnau, Erich von Stroheim, Robert Flaherty) has uncertainty of interpretation built into the image, it allows more thinking

by the filmgoer and gives the filmgoer choice and meaning creation, it is emotionally satisfying, and will 'reveal the hidden meanings in people and things without
disturbing the unity natural to them'.[42] He cites the example of the lioness, cub, child
and worried parents all in one long shot in *Where No Vultures Fly*. (Though just because the long shot *may* be better here, this does not mean it should always be used
over and above shifts.) For Bazin the long-depth take is based on a respect for the
duration and inherent composition of a dramatic scene, which positively creates an
artistic ambiguity (the filmgoer is free to choose meaning). Montage abstractly creates meaning, and is more literary in comparison to the essential cinema of images.
Montage here is found to deny the image, collapsing it into just an element to be
'used' by editing.

But though montage techniques certainly swayed early filmmakers away from
the power of the single image, and came to be used in increasingly turgid ways, it is
certainly a pure form of film-thinking, and not unambiguous in meaning – though
the concepts it gives rise to are perhaps undercut by our relationship to its thinking:
filmgoers may not always take to being lectured by images. And yes our lives may
be technically one long take, but sometimes life is cut about and episodic. Short and
long takes seem to be more in harmony in modern cinema: some kinds of thoughts
are long and some involve more shifts. Bazin may prefer the long-depth take, but
he can also appreciate a film such as Orson Welles' *Othello*, which shifts around a
fair amount. For Deleuze it is mainly montage (collision, shock, 'the intellectual process' itself[43]) that is doing the thinking of cinema. While montage techniques have
changed since early forms – for Godard montage is now really mixing, with fades,
blends and superimpositions at the forefront – for many, such as the philosopher
Giorgio Agamben, it still gives cinema its 'specific character'.[44]

For Eisenstein the image of thought is found in the construction of a dialectic
image affecting the spectator's body as much as brain. He sought thinking through
the fight of images. He presents films that are upfront with thinking, and spoke of
the creation of concepts in montage. But, as Eisenstein found, it is *in* the shift, inside
the shift (the interstice), that we find its thinking. A theorist such as Colin MacCabe
would see montage in terms of conflicting discourses,[45] and during montage sequences we can see that the filmind is expansive in its realm of reference. Obviously
metaphoric in places, the real interest of this thinking is the conception of how the
thinking is produced: the film becomes a world of image-ideas (iconographic image-
ideas for Godard), remembering some from earlier in the film, bringing in some from
other films or arts. The film constantly feels connections and links, and does not mess
about in showing them. Classic uses such as the Kuleshov effect (face then bread
equals hunger, same face then coffin equals mourning) can be seen here as an active

willing of meaning, the filmind attempting to manipulate and predict the outcome of the filmgoer's thoughts based on our need for context.

Here film becomes a thinking of analogy, comparison, contrast, causality, generalisation; and in montage this is done explicitly, brashly. Film cannot make explicitly definite propositions, but it can think propositionally, and the propositional shifts of Eisenstein have been replaced by an infinitely more subtle realm of the complete thinking film. The 'alogical' intellectual dynamisation *religions-montage* of *October* is 'effective' – as is the women/clucking chickens in Fritz Lang's *Fury* – but as a kind of film-thinking it is basic. A good example of Eisenstein's emotional dynamism (slaughter of workers and cow intercut) can be found in the killings at the end of *Apocalypse Now* (Kurtz and bull). (What would have been interesting is a *Ulysses* by Eisenstein, where we might have seen shifts like a *freed* mind.) Alan Spiegel recognised the thinking of montage in his 1976 book *Fiction and the Camera Eye* – it is montage

> that always reminds us of the associational structure of a rapid mental process ... each picture in a film shows us not only a physical reality but a mental reality as well, a point of view – either that of the character or of the director himself – and that the instantaneous movements from one point of view to the next ... find their affinities in the speed, flexibility and transforming power of human thought and feeling.[46]

Seeing shifts as thoughtful makes montage techniques more understandable, and further equalises these 'active' forms with more subtle shifts. In a sense, filmosophy here reduces the power of montage by highlighting the possible power of other less obvious or active forms of editing. As film-thinking montage has a very suitable home, one which allows it to be understood alongside other kinds of shifts. A film that suddenly introduces a 'montage sequence' is often seen to be confusing and mixing its styles – but within the filmind one can integrate those sequences; because the rest of the film's shifts are also kinds of thinking.

Shifts can also expand and collapse a sense of space for the filmgoer. Ricciotto Canudo (1879–1923) prefigured Paul Virilio in speaking of the 'speed' of cinema, how film transports us (at the speed of light) to places and scenes, and how it is the culmination of modern life's love affair with faster and faster movement. The filmind can move from one 'place' to another without apparent hindrance. Münsterberg recognised the powerful nature of film shifts: 'Not more than one sixteenth of a second is needed to carry us from one corner of the globe to the other, from a jubilant setting to a mourning scene.'[47] We must understand that the filmind is possibly everywhere all at once – it has no boundaries of thought. It is less a question of 'transporting you instantaneously' to somewhere else, but a simple thinking of another space (like a comic strip). During the length of a film the number of major shifts in location or time are actually very small, and the filmgoer is used to that amount. So a film such as *Lost Highway* – which seems to almost reverse those numbers – thinks in a very different way, feeling links between places as much as between characters, shifting temporally as much as spatially.

Film breaths time. Even in 1916 Münsterberg felt the transcendence of film: 'the photoplay can overcome the interval of the future as well as the interval of the past and slip the day twenty years hence between this minute and the next'.[48] Deleuze carried this on, profoundly, finding a direct (filmic) representation of time in some modern cinema. The filmind gives us images and situations with knowledge of the whole film, allowing it to think a 'time' in relation to any character or any action or event. There is no 'presentness', only the film-time that meanders where it pleases. Action that we might denote as present could turn out to be 'long in the past' or 'way in the future' later on in the film. When we reach the end of the film only then might we feel we can allocate parts as film-past, film-present or film-future (think simply of *Pulp Fiction*). Shifting images can also think in a similar way to slowed images, extending and emphasising a moment (the rising bridges in *October*, Benjamin Braddock's first sight of a naked Mrs Robinson, or any big dangerous stunt by Jackie Chan) – the film here feeling the importance of that moment through time shifts. And when the film gives us concurrent events it is not only a simple example of its 'omniscience', but a thinking of dual importance and more.

Shifts can also mark a move into memory, fantasy, dream or hallucination – all are given and *inflected* by the filmind, with or without the blurred, warped or watery image that usually signals the transition. Filmmakers such as Resnais and Godard are as much editors as film directors. For Cavell, Resnais' *La Guerre est finie* gives us 'an idea of the simultaneous gravity and weightlessness of the past, as though our present is merely a shifting orbiting of our memories'.[49] When considering the filmind as having the whole of the film in its grasp, flashbacks and flashforwards become more intelligible – the latter for Münsterberg echoing with 'expectation' or 'imagination'.[50] As regards 'flashbacks' film thinks (its own interpretation of) a character's memory, usually then just merging this initial subjective-memory thinking into a general thinking of that past situation. The 'flashbacks' of *The Usual Suspects* illustrate why point of view and other character-centred images need to be reconfigured through ideas of a uniquely intentional filmind. All films think their own (minimally or maximally altered) version of character perception, not that we should always be sceptical of flashbacks etc., but understand that film is a creative force, able to conceive of anything. *The Usual Suspects* creates the recounted, remembered story given at the police station, leading us to believe that the film is simply, understandably, giving us earlier scenes from a greater story – but the filmind is actually 'creating' the story told by 'Keyser Soze'. (Though this may sound strange, it is no more so than when a film creates the situations surrounding a character's normal recollections.) In this kind of completely false flashback the relation to 'actual' film-story events becomes so slim that there is almost no memory, no time relations – only film-time and film-thought. The concept of the filmind thus creates a critical mode of attention, because at base it makes us understand that every image of film is intended *from a certain perspective*. So, when we realise that the 'flashbacks' of *The Usual Suspects* are actually the invention of the teller, we can better understand how we came to 'see' those images and events. The images of the tale being told are imaginative and 'pure' film-thinkings. The filmind is here illustrating not only its ever-presence, but gives an example of its capability, in showing somewhat 'supra-original' characters and events – almost 'playing along' with the master criminal in 'showing' his story.

More interesting for illustrating the possibilities of filmind's shifts is *Pulp Fiction* – in that the question here is *why* the film shows us these events in the non-linear order it does. Having the whole film in its knowledge *Pulp Fiction* can choose how to order its events – and what it does is rethink cause and effect, feeling the importance of the events and their outcomes. *Pulp Fiction* plays with these possibilities more than many, the film creating its own time-relationships. Much has been made of its time-jumping, going from an evening scene with one set of characters to (what we later realise to be) an earlier afternoon scene with another set of characters. This perhaps gives a pleasure of transcendence, of feeling the power of film in being able to manipulate time. The whole film understands the relationships between all the characters and decides to bring the cause and effect relations to the fore. It adds a dessert to the film – the filmgoer may come out and spend more time analysing the causal relations than if they had been presented in a normal linear way. Differently, in *Lone Star*, the film feels a certain continuity between past and present, and thinks this through an uninterrupted image taking us back to previous events – the film will glide over bar tables, filling their seats with the fathers and younger selves of the people at the beginning of the movement.

Finally, Deleuze's time-image marks a kind of film-thinking that reveals time through various non-linear relations. For Deleuze editing holds the key to understanding time, and modern cinema (especially Antonioni, and we should certainly add Angelopoulos) 'shows time through its tiredness and waitings'.[51] This aspect of his time-image reveals time through our relation to expected (movie) time – lingering, pushing, enveloping time through heightened moments, making time visible almost. When Deleuze talks about another aspect of the time-image, irrational cuts, he is referring to shifts that not only tear us away from a classical mode of construction, but more importantly enact a thinking of pure relationality (not that this pure relationality is always pleasurable or aesthetically pleasing). It is pure because it relies on nothing but its instant of collision – the moment that movement is stopped by stillness, that time is flicked forward a few seconds – making visible 'a coexistence of distinct durations ... which can only appear in a creation of the image'.[52]

In this cinema, time appears as itself – as Richard Dienst attempts to explain, 'the time-image multiplies [film] dimensions and layers in order to liberate time from the movements that occupy it and to allow time to form more complex figural "thoughts"'.[53] But Münsterberg reviews Deleuze better than us all: 'with the whole mobility of our association of ideas, pictures of the past flit through the scenes of the present. Time is left behind ... The freedom of the mind has triumphed over the unalterable law of the outer world.'[54] Theorists have been swayed by montage into thinking that most shifts enact a thinking of 'relation', of this to that, but seeing them through a filmind – as multiplied emotions or questioning spaces – allows for more varied interpretations. Our filmind conceives of *all* associations, practices *any* collision, feels *any* change of thought. In the filmind it is not only modern cinema and irrational cuts that hold thinking, but all (simpler) forms of shifting. Just the shift from one face to another can feel (through speed or fade or timing) so many emotions or ideas – whether of their relationship, or about the relationship the film feels towards its characters.

Film examples

To end this chapter let us look at some extended film examples using the concepts of filmosophy – a couple of films by the Hungarian director Béla Tarr, five films by the Austrian Michael Haneke, and four films by the Belgian filmmaking brothers Jean-Pierre and Luc Dardenne.

Damnation features a love triangle, and is set in a small Hungarian town where the people seem stuck, and drenched under incessant rain. The film feels the repetitive world of its characters from the start, drifting slowly back from the drone of endless mine carts swinging their way up a hill. The film backs through a window to reveal its central character, Karrer, watching the scene, providing a reason for the film's concentration on the carts, and an impetus for the film's overall attention. It is his experience that seems to fuel the image-thinking of the film. The industrial town where this story takes place is shown in empty frosted greys. Some films think in colour, some films believe that their characters lead lives without colour; not so much black and white as light grey and dark grey. The fog becomes the sadness of the town, all-pervading, and not even sex can seem to relieve the gloom (even the privacy of the home cannot escape the setting, the repetition). The film returns to spaces like a film-loop, glued by ambient tones (and the sniffles of scavenging dogs). And it is quite beautiful: pulling back from the mine carts in a later moment, the film slides through the window slats to find Karrer, this time not staring, but making love to the woman he has pursued.

At London's National Film Theatre, in an on-stage interview with Jonathan Romney, the director, Béla Tarr, talked of his aim to get away from 'story', to reveal the way that locations 'have their own faces' – there being a 'logic' in a 'certain kind of space'. This is in line with his belief that film should reveal 'presence' (rather than pat meanings through allegories or symbols, which are 'so far from the genre of film'). For Tarr film is a simple, concrete, primitive, limited, definite language (this 'definiteness' recalling Godard's words that we should replace vague ideas with clear images), and the filmgoer is a 'more mature partner' of the film, who Tarr hopes will leave the cinema a 'different person'.

Another film directed by Tarr, *Werckmeister Harmonies*, might be said to attempt 'political images' (political thinking in images) via the moving, gliding, linking image. The film virtually consists of these long gliding thoughts ('long takes', or 'sequence-shots' in traditional, technicist film language) that travel the length of streets, or caress interiors like a supernatural cat (we may even imagine the edit shifts ourselves: remembering a scene we feel sure there must have been some sort of shift cut – but there was not, we are just so used to having them). Time, its direct image, is given again and again.

First of all these lengthy thoughts seem to want to reveal and think a phenomenology, or a truer humanism. These are no longer 'long takes', but thinkings of the human 'gaplessness' of experience – we do not edit experience and the film wants to show this: following the lead character Janos as he surveys the whale, or keeping endless pace with Mr Eszter and Janos as they walk side by side (their faces bobbing in front of us for a relative eternity). But most interestingly, this kind of thinking physicalises relationships between characters (the film wants us to *feel* this physicality). The most beautiful example in *Werckmeister Harmonies* occurs in the main square of the town, where visiting showmen have brought an enormous stuffed whale. The townsmen (seemingly *all* the men of the town) stand around in loose groups, perhaps waiting for work, or simply there to keep warm by fires. At this point the film begins to tour the faces of the men, tenaciously, almost impertinently, gliding from one cold furrowed brow to another: here the film seems to be asking the men something, demanding a response, forcing a realisation perhaps. Each time the film settles on another face, the pause seems to reveal a 'questioning' nature to the film's thinking. Thus the film not only connects each man to the other, but politicises this linkage – the film is joining the men together and asking something of them (to wake up, to revolt, to *move*). And so later the film is able to lead (floating at the front) the silent and powerful sight of hundreds of townsmen marching on the hospital to vent their anger – an anger perhaps even released by the catalyst of the unmoving whale. The innocent are driven mad ('nothing matters, nothing counts' we hear), and so, wordlessly (leaving their actions to images), they trash each hospital room, only to reach a melancholic recognition of futility.

In comparison, *Damnation* might also be seen as a thinking of stasis and movement (or growth), a film that thinks through these 'ideas' with images. This can be the political stasis of the town (and, again, especially its men) and the movement that the film brings to it (surveys it with). It can be the head that stares and the film which investigates. It can be the seated Karrer and Sebestyen and the dancing townsfolk – where the cloakroom woman talks of dance, and 'the way that movements speak'. That melancholy breeds boredom which breeds non-movement is actualised by the movement-thinking of the film. While characters sit and drink the film is almost always restless. Even small changes in angles force the filmgoer to actively keep a character in the centre of their sight. The film simply, subtly, makes us see the stasis all the more *because* of this movement. The still is revealed by 'our' forced movement. (The film does hold still sometimes, especially on the woman at the centre of the love triangle – holds still like the attentions of her lovers.)

Importantly, the film thinks a pure relationship between the town and the characters. Karrer's scenes are almost always begun without him: the film will slide in from an industrial setting, or even from close to a building, to 'introduce' him. The link is not made graphically, but *affectively*, through the movement of film and the movement of our memory (seeing him after some setting, we 'remember' the setting while now following him – the setting and the man become mixed). In fact the film holds itself very close to the buildings of the town, often caressing their rough concrete like a forced love affair – the film tries to find beauty *within* the town. The image of rain washing over this concrete at the film's close comes near to 'becoming' this industrial beauty. At the end all may be summed-up in dog-eared and earth-bound metaphors of damnation, but the questions and ideas of the film are not reduced to or closed-off by these ends. By turns boring and mesmeric, *Damnation* may frighten some with its drifting narrative – you may either lose yourself in its 'time' or become simply impatient – but it is, at least, thoughtful.

Funny Games, *Code Unknown*, *The Piano Teacher*, *Time of the Wolf*, *Hidden*. These films directed by Michael Haneke are a shock to thought. This is filmosophical cinema, asking questions of us, revealing new linkages between worlds and ideas.

This is aesthetically powerful cinema – it is the images and sounds themselves which affect us, before and around their themes. The filmosophical ideas are memorable and impactful because this cinema is also striking and beautiful: the winking killer of *Funny Games*; Marie lost in dust in *Code Unknown*; the scene of Erika's final gesture in *The Piano Teacher*; the walk through grey morning mist in *Time of the Wolf*; the sudden death in *Hidden*. Here I shall try to outline some areas and types of film-thinking in these works.

Funny Games polemically presents us with a fictional universe invading a 'real world' – a typical bourgeois family home (the film shows us golf clubs, slippers, a full fridge). But the film initially softens the killer's voices when we first meet them and frames them undramatically – seeing them how the family initially sees them: as unthreatening. Then the film shades Paul in darkness when he is shown up close – making us feel the darkness of the moment when he picks up a golf club. (Later he is again thought in half-darkness – a dark head and a light mouth; dark thoughts, but with a gameshow presenter's chatter.)

But it is a certain smoothness that pervades the film's thinking – we are calmed and seduced and made to feel this decadent life (whose classical soundtrack is interrupted by a screaming mess of chaotic sounds). The calmness of the film is also the calmness of Peter making a sandwich while Paul shoots the boy. It is then that the film gives us the room and allows the horror to seep through the image – the film seemingly feeling the shocked stillness of the parents. The film holds on to its characters, making us feel the repercussions of violence; the violence is as much to our normal viewing experience – we are held to these events and are unable to change our perspective. This image-violence is a shock to thought, to realisation, to new belief.

The killers act as if they are omniscient gods, calmly controlling the family. They do not strain or tire, but play out the scenario with unstoppable blankness. Peter almost seems to be Paul's creation – he cries when Paul gives him a deprived and abused background, then smiles thankfully when he is given a privileged back story. But looking at the film itself, the killers are almost part of the filmind: the film is in collusion with the killers, and the killers know they have an audience and gesture to them with winks and asides. In a sense the killers control the film, the film is the mind of Paul. With the boy held by Paul, the film frames the father straight on, such that he asks Paul (as 'the film') to 'let him go'. This is a mind (Paul/filmind) which calmly watches the boy attempt to escape – he/it knows his fate. Both the film and the killers know the end and the beginning of the film (as well as its optimum length).

In effect *Funny Games* confronts the filmgoer as a consumer of explicit unrealistic guilt-free violence. Typical fictional horror is a game, played out for our enjoyment, and as filmgoers we are perhaps degraded by these fictions, by these lies about how people die. *Funny Games* denies us this game-like fiction – in fact it taunts us with our desire to have a typically constructed fiction: 'But you want a real ending, with plausible plot development, don't you?', Paul/the film asks of us, implicating us in the horror – 'Don't forget the entertainment value' says Peter later. But the family here, like bland typical eggs, are killed for no reason: reality is more meaningless than typical fictional representations.

Code Unknown also thinks before and around and inside 'violence' (represented, acted, or 'real'); thinking *against* fictional violence games. The social and ethnic violence here is too large to represent – reality is chaotic, confusing, random, unbroken, continuous, and these films show us a much less mediated reality/ representation. In *Code Unknown* time is unbroken where possible; or fragments of reality are cut short, indicating the impossibility of revealing true reality on film. Instead these films reveal and force out the rough humanity that lies dormant beneath the staged 'reality'.

At one point in *Hidden* the film holds on the television showing violence in the Middle East, while Georges and Anne, in their emotionless home, fuss over the whereabouts of Pierrot. The images are now taken for granted and offer no new information. We are used to the representation of war, to the design of television reportage that holds the effects of a war in check – that muffles and subverts the reality it can never show. *Funny Games* is also after 'the truth', the truth beneath the fiction, the emotional truth beneath the bourgeois exterior (fear and suffering?). In *Code Unknown* Anne 'creates' terror in an audition for a clichéd horror film. But then, like the killers of *Funny Games*, the voice asks to see her true face – the truth of violence rather than its representation.

All of these films think an image of time that holds and studies and tries to understand their characters and events. The filmind of *Code Unknown* allows time to unfold itself, rather than being constructed through multiple shifts – this allows us to feel a, possibly infinite, affinity with the characters. Time is given uninflected in this cinema: time for a supermarket argument to breed and unfold and then melt away; time for whole stories to be told; time for abuse to begin and end on a metro train (time for us to work out, in social terms, why that abuse began and how it might be ended); time for a mother's grief to be given directly, not reflected in another's reactions; time for a woman to hear and then forget a neighbour's violence. We watch them as we would almost do in reality – we accompany Anne and Jean as they walk and talk; we then feel the realness of their subsequent drama, and the interconnectedness of their lives. This time-image links events and equalises characters. The film does not bring in characters from 'elsewhere' by shifts – characters appear in the same space as each other. The filmgoer phenomenologically feels them to be from the same place. Time is given directly to emphasise the film's *belief* in what it shows: the filmgoer *feels* this time; we *feel* the time it takes for a woman to find a place to start begging. The film 'holds' us to these events – questions our response and our understanding.

But *Code Unknown* also thinks by shifting suddenly to black intervals, creating fractured scenes that shock us to thinking – thinking their relations, their emotions. These black-shifts often cut into stories being told – the film thinks in fragments, parts of a whole (reality) that could never be represented, and so should never be attempted. These fragments also make us feel the miscommunication between people and groups and countries and ethnicities – they make us feel the separateness of these worlds.

Frame and image thinking also informs two later films. *The Piano Teacher* knows Erika's tightness, her structured life, and reveals it through thinking a certain precision, order, repetition and tautness (like the image of the piano itself, bisecting the image with its keys). The film most often simply observes Erika, front on, watching her, listening to her face. At Walter's entrance examination the film shifts ever closer, revealing her feelings even if her expression does not. The film thinks a kind of detached framing to make us feel the isolation and separateness of Erika: the film often frames her from behind, such as when she is about to put broken glass in the coat pocket of her student. The film also makes us feel the coldness of its central character by always returning to cold white images in its thinking: the window in her classroom; the bathroom where her and Walter finally come together; the ice rink that she totters across; her emotionless bedroom. And then at the end, as she begins to receive her desire, we see her against blackness for the first time – a feeling of some sort of death inside.

In *Time of the Wolf* the world rejects man by depriving him of fuel and water, forcing all to fend for themselves. The film reveals this new equality through its thoughtful image of darkness: the film makes us feel this new state of man. The film thinks an indistinguishability through a dark grey image, one that merges the mother and her children into the world. We see them through and in this greyness, this darkness that devours them. Then later, the various groups of the station room are indistinguishable from each other, all becoming a grey haze of heads and bodies. *Time of the Wolf* thinks a true darkness (similar to *Pola X*), a darkness before mankind, a darkness that is truly unsettling (for both the characters and for the filmgoer). The image here is itself pre-technological. It is confusing; it is ill-defined; and it leaves us searching the image for some definition, some logic (some new rules for living). That definition to the image can only come through fire (either from the sun in the day or from fires made at night), and it is fire that eventually gives definition to the boy – makes us see naked humanity, the possibility of humanity; bringing humanity to those who want to kill and ask questions later.

The concepts of filmosophy can also perhaps help us handle the way *Hidden* moves between and through its recorded and immanent film-worlds. As *Funny Games* reminds us, the filmind inhabits the film, and in doing so it can create an objective or subjective or transsubjective viewpoint. The opening image of *Hidden* seems objective – a view of a street – but then is revealed to be subjective (in being the viewpoint of an actual observer who has recorded the street on video). The filmgoer receives a very simple and direct shock to thought – the rewound video immediately alters our perception of the street. From being a relatively meaningless establishing image, of location and time, to being a scoped and intended image (the gaze of an other). *Hidden* thus shocks us into realising that perhaps all images are thought, are intended and directed. Subsequently, the film takes on an added intention. The film that follows Anne and Georges from lounge to kitchen suddenly feels watchful and subjective.

The film also reveals Georges' memory after seeing the drawing of the bloody-mouthed boy – providing the filmgoer an image of the young Majid, wiping blood from his mouth. The filmind almost picks open Georges' memory at that point, cutting into his mind, his memory cache. And in giving us Majid for only a second the film makes us realise how hidden this memory is, how repressed and locked away it is. At another moment (the end of one of Georges' literary programmes) the film moves from the subjective television image to the transsubjective film image – transsubjective because the objective-like image (simply following Georges as he takes a phone call) is infused with the subjective (from the link with the television image, and from the idea that Georges is being watched). What *Hidden*'s film-thinking presents us with is unwavering attention, the attention of history, of time itself on the events of now. It is the film itself, as past rising up to the present, that accuses Georges – the image almost hums with intention. And as in *Time of the Wolf* it is the children who must take responsibility – who must make up for their parents' mistakes.

Bourgeois society hides its fears, its memories, its humanity. These five films filmically fracture and force open that society to reveal what is hidden. These films also reveal media representations as intended – they are choices, beliefs, judgements about the world. In moving from omniscience to subjectivity *Hidden* especially makes us understand how all images are created – that media images hide as much truth as they reveal. They are not reality but a kind of 'model' of reality (as Haneke has said in interviews). We are consumed by representations, and think them to be as good as reality, but these films show moving images to be ordered and thought – exactly by confusing us about what is 'reality' and what is its facile representation.

Our final examples come from the Belgian filmmaking brothers Jean-Pierre and Luc Dardenne, who have bled their documentary foundations into a mesmerically pure fiction style. Their films absorb us in a recognisable world that nevertheless shows us ordinary things in a *new* way, makes us look again at what we thought we understood. Their four most recent films – *The Promise*, *Rosetta*, *The Son* and *The Child* – almost entirely reject some key conventions of fiction filmmaking (shot/reverse-shot, point of view shots, establishing shots, and so on) in favour of a close and empathetic form of film-thinking. These films use images to think about (and for) their characters – thinkings which steer the emotions of the filmgoer. Here I shall sketch out a few areas of film-thinking in the four films: action/space, ellipsis, empathy, questioning, transsubjectivity.

The films ask us to understand action more than words (images more than dialogue). Physicality is a theme across all these films: most are based around work and labour; and all include forced contact, some sort of fight or wrestle between the main characters (for example, Bruno and Sonia in the apartment after he has sold and then bought back the child). But, moreover, each concerns the meaning of physical being. In *The Promise* the father makes of his son a work mate (a father who does not want to be a father, but 'Roger', a friend, a colleague); in *The Child* the young man endlessly traipses around town selling 'stuff'; in *Rosetta* the girl is addicted to work (as an escape from, a reaction to, her mother's sloth); and in *The Son* man and boy attempt to get closer via work – indeed, the boy copies him, mimicking his actions (airblowing sawdust from his clothes, ordering the same food). But action in the images is enriched by the action *of* the images. In *The Promise* the film gives us repeated images of Igor racing around dusty industrial streets on his moped, the background a blur – the filmgoer receives a sense of a fast-moving life, a speeding image of a boy growing up too fast, beyond his years. (Later, when Igor has been calmed by the responsibility of the promise, the film gives us his less frantic movement, standing quietly in a bus.) It is the films' forms that think a physicality that the filmgoer affectively, directly, *feels*: the rough shift cuts, the always active movement, the grainy grey image. If *The Son* thinks about distance and physical/ emotional space, it is about the *closing* of distance: of presumption when far away, of understanding when closer, of knowledge on contact. The films think a certain relationship to their stories, enhancing them, allowing the filmgoer to *receive* the meaning of the dramas as much as they do by *interpreting* the events.

The four films are ostensibly straightforward narratives, almost played out in real time, but with significant shift-ellipses, jumping forward after each scene, often right into the middle of an ongoing action. As when we are thrown into the father's attempted beating of Igor in *The Promise*, or when *The Son* suddenly shifts from a calm image to one of the father running down some stairs. Indeed *The Child* begins with Sonia already halfway up some stairs, and *Rosetta* plunges us straight into her violent refusal to leave a job. These shift-ellipses make for a brisk pace that draws us in, *absorbs* us – the filmgoer is left no time to assess situations or reflect too much on character actions. This is crucial to the thinkings of the films: we are held by the films, and the films do not want us to dwell. To be is to do; we must understand the characters by their actions; we should feel meanings directly without undue reflection (until the film is over).

Each film, with its close images and following movements, makes us feel that the characters really are being understood by a filmind, a metaphysical film-being that watches them without their knowledge. Many images resemble furtive, almost angelic surveillance, with most frames being half-obscured by the corner of buildings or walls. Of course any film can be said to be 'watching' its characters, but these films show a concern, an *empathy* for the characters that belies a new kind of film-thinking. This 'thinking' style is responsive, reactive, inquisitive, yet knowing. The filmind has knowledge of the whole story, knows the relationships between its characters. In *The Son* it is the film (by way of a linking movement) that makes the first connection between man and boy, while the father's back is turned. The filmind reveals its knowledge of the situation – it *knows* which boy the father has been looking for.

But we do not receive the thinking of the father through the thinking of the film images. We receive a *feeling* of his thinking. The film aligns us with his thoughts without ever presuming to more directly *express* them through image design. The film shows us him in a way that helps our understanding of him, but does not presume to reveal his 'actual' thoughts. *The Promise* (its filmind) *wants* us to understand its young protagonist. The filmgoer feels this presence from the beginning, when the film follows Igor after he steals a purse: the film *looks* at the boy (it does not just *show* him, it *thinks* him), not so much confronting him, as wanting to understand, wanting to work out why he makes the decisions he makes. *The Child* (perhaps their simplest film to date) similarly thinks about Bruno, always facing him, attempting to work him out. *The Child* is a film that tries to understand Bruno, why he does what he does, how he comes to make the decisions he does.

Perhaps most significant about these four films is their movement away from 'classical' filmmaking forms, especially as regards point of view images and the traditional shot/reverse-shot. In *The Son* the father tries to see into an office where details important to him are being discussed – the film aligns itself with him, squeezes a look at what he sees (half a desk, a hand, a pen), but without shifting to a point of view shot that denotes his *actual* seeing-point, his 'actual' thinking. What we get is a thinking of his half-knowledge, through an obscured, fractured, half-information image. What this means is that the four films do not break into their stories to try to replace their characters; they do not remove them from the film (by replacing them with a 'view-point'). Importantly, we might say that the films do not presume to *become* their characters.

At the very beginning of *The Son* the film, the moving sound-image, *emerges* from behind the father (moving up from darkness to reveal the back and then the neck and head of the father). We feel that the film derives itself from him, has lived with him, will live with him. The film thinks this close affinity, thinks (through framing and movement) this empathetic emotion. The film clings close to the father, tracing his neck and back and profile more than his face or locale. There is almost no space, no measurable distance between filmgoer/film and father. The film thinks an intense bond, creating a *pure relationship* between character and filmgoer. We begin to feel what he feels: tension, half-knowledge, anticipation. The film's thinking does not create an identification so much as an allegiance, a *being-with*. Through this closeness the films also enact a questioning thinking. The films watch Igor and Rosetta and Olivier and Bruno think, watch them make decisions, almost hears them decide. All of the films at some point 'hold' on each of them, studying their faces, questioning them, asking them 'what are you going to do?' The responsibility and conscience in both *The Promise* and *The Child*; the betrayal and enduring affection of the boy in *Rosetta*; the closing of distance between man and boy in *The Son* – each is unexpected for the protagonist. These are people who are unprepared for the humanity that will not let them go.

In the cinema of Jean-Pierre and Luc Dardenne the characters are accompanied, are followed and watched, by another consciousness, a new-consciousness, a filmind. This thinking is at one and the same time subjective and objective (it acts like another character, yet can occupy multiple spaces and shift from one time to another), in films that absorb the physical through (and into) the metaphysical. The 'filmosophical' thinking of these films is distinguished by their refusal to even attempt to 'become' the characters. The Dardennes resist these conventions of classical fiction filmmaking, and in doing so the films think with humility and respect. One person's actions are never completely understandable; we can never become them to understand them, we must learn from what they do. Ethics resolves into a question of action: what do we do? Each of the four films presents us with a filmind that is asking that for us, of a person, from a point of view we can never have: an omniscient, invisible, free mode of thinking.

eight | filmgoer

Let's go into a cinema where the perforated celluloid is purring in the darkness. On entering, our gaze is guided by the luminous ray to the screen where for two hours it will remain fixed. Life in the street outside no longer exists. Our problems evaporate, our neighbours disappear. Our body itself submits to a sort of temporary depersonalisation which takes away the feeling of its own existence. We are nothing but two eyes riveted to ten square metres of white sheet.

– Jean Goudal (1925)[1]

Watching a film is like having a daydream. It operates on portions of your mind that are only reached by dreams or dramas, and there you can explore things without any responsibility of conscious ego or conscience.

– Stanley Kubrick (1971)[2]

In this artificial solitude a part of us is porous to the effects of meaning without ever being able to be born into signification through language.

– Jean Louis Schefer (1981)[3]

In this chapter I will discuss how the concepts of the filmind and film-thinking might reconfigure our understanding of the encounter between film and filmgoer,[4] and look at how the language and rhetoric of the concepts can shape the experience of the filmgoer. Because this chapter is devoted to a philosophical investigation of the encounter between film and filmgoer, its usefulness lies somewhat *before* more 'interpretive' theories of the 'spectator'. For a start, many of those theories concentrate on our connection (emotional, imaginative) with characters within the film, and are less concerned with the power of the 'purer', formal image. In a sense we need to understand the basic encounter before we can confidently talk about, say, voyeurism or identification or desire or pleasure (and other undeniable facets of filmgoing). Though at points in the chapter I will relate my finding to these ideas and concerns, the attentions here will mainly be of *assistance* to those interested in theorising such filmgoer positions. So what I shall not be attempting is an understanding of every possible (careless; attentive; sloppy; academic; open; blind; dumb; intelligent; trainspotter; passive; romantic; lustful) filmgoer. Thus I shall not be discussing any hypothetical 'weak' filmgoers, nor when a filmgoer is removed from the film, for instance when they suddenly realise they are watching actors and sets. How can a person who experiences a film be any less than people we all know: complex, active, passionate, but also melancholic, romantic, swamped by sounds and images. After outlining the basic, personal and cognitivist experiences of filmgoing, I shall start to discuss how understanding film as thinking reveals an intimate relationship between film and filmgoer. My philosophy of the filmgoer leads us to a phenomenological 'mix' of thinkings: the film and filmgoer join in thought, and the process of that encounter provides immediate meaning and knowledge.

Filmosophy is about proposing a new way of understanding and experiencing film, and in the next chapter I will attempt to argue that the concept of film-thinking provides a better language of description, and thus secures a much more suitable encounter between film and filmgoer. The filmgoer who experiences a film with this language in their knowledge, with this more organic linguistic backbone, will have a more suitable *mode of attention*, and thus *experience more*, and thus have *more meaning possibilities* to steer their interpretations. The experience of film becomes in some sense 'organic' because style is tied to meaning with natural, thoughtful, humanistic terms of intention (by the filmind). This is the makeup of a filmosophical filmgoer.

But first, to understand how filmgoers experience film we must note what normal experience is marked by. Experience, through sight and hearing, is a mode of thought, filtered through context and personality and language (and probably much more). And we all experience things differently – do the clouds waft past the moon or does the moon glide through the clouds? We gain a coherent representation of the world from partial views, and we cope with this because we are in control, and because we are continually, naturally, giving ourselves longer establishing views – 'master shots' as it were. But the (natural or active) choices we make in attending to things is crucial. Simple experience is always a thinking action – picking out images, seeking recognisable sounds from a noise, watching one person while listening to another. Then we put our 'experiencing' in front of films. V. F. Perkins called it a kind of 'public privacy',[5] that anonymity we feel during a (usually) communal experience. And the exact position for the experience is important – I first saw *A Short Film About Killing* at the London Film Festival in a seat at the front right-hand corner of the cinema. The screen appeared distorted and depth was to a certain extent flattened, adding especially to the experience of colour. The filmgoer can prefer to be right at the front, thus engulfing the field of vision so much that you might have to turn your head to see events at either side of the screen. Or sit at the back, putting the rest of the audience and the whole frame of the film in view. Personally, I like to sit a couple of rows from the front, allowing the film to pleasurably swamp my senses. I believe that to achieve a more aesthetic and truthful interpretation one must receive the meanings of a film in this fully *involved* position – sitting at the back to maximise your critical faculties can produce a mistaken and cold interpretation. *Experience the film, then interpret the meanings you felt.*

Cognitivism

Because films engage mental processes, cognitivist film theorists have looked to theories of normal human cognition and emotional response to help account for the experience of cinema. In what way do we experience film? Does it have an illusory effect? How do we understand actions and characters and emotions on film? What *kind* of emotions (horror, empathy) do we experience? Are they the same as or significantly different to our normal experiences? These cognitivists are also in part reacting to the dominant reading of the filmgoer by continental theory: that the resemblance films bear to everyday life confounds the filmgoer (that cinema produces an illusion of reality, and so the filmgoer is duped by what they see and hear, is passively tutored by the film); and further that the filmgoer engages in an irrational activity of attention. Thus cognitivists oppose their conscious rational filmgoer activity with the subconscious irrational activity of the continentals.[6] For cognitivists film is not a language (for Lacanian film theorists, the subconscious is structured like a language), and films should be understood using folk psychology and commonsense, not grand theory or subconscious operations. Within filmgoer cognitivism there are three main theses: the natural understanding thesis; the rational problem-solving thesis; and the commonsense interpretation thesis. In other words: the filmgoer uses real-world thought-processes to understand the film; the filmgoer is there to make sense of the film; and interpretation should rely on commonsense conclusions about the drama (as opposed to, for example, psychoanalytical readings). We looked at the rational and commonsense nature of narrative comprehension and interpretation in chapter six, so let us look at the first thesis.

According to the natural understanding thesis the filmgoer is a rational agent, using naturalistic processes of mental representation to understand film's drama and forms. Physiological and cognitive systems are 'hard-wired' within us – universal systems, prior to culture and personal identity, that allow us to understand the world (our three-dimensional world, how light falls on objects, and so on). For instance, Paul Messaris's book *Visual 'Literacy'* attempts to almost set in stone a language of film that can be taught – to solidify the 'communication'. Messaris simply accepts that a person's normal experience is sufficient to allow them to understand the compositional forms of film. (Perhaps a larger question might be whether a better film is one whose composition is normal-experience related, or completely, strangely, filmic?) Messaris argues that each filmic device 'can be said to acquire its meaning by approximating some feature of real-world experience'.[7]

On the one hand it seems perfectly fine to say that our ability to understand film is derived from hard-wired perceptual habits – but this is not much more than saying we experience film using the same brain that we use to experience reality. The interesting questions lie well beyond these points. Basically, the reason why a strict analogy between our thinking and film's thinking is unacceptable is the same reason why we should steer away from simply accepting that we understand film like we understand reality: film-thinking is not mappable by the terms of human thinking. As George Wilson notes, we do not see 'tracking or panning shots as corresponding to the continuous reorientation in space of the visual field of people such as ourselves … we do not see a straight cut, even within a scene, as representing the phenomenology of a shift in a perceiver's visual attention'.[8] Thus it seems somehow wrong to try and always equate film with real-life experience – the film experience is not strictly analogous to real-world audio-visual experience, and films are most certainly creating new ways of thinking and 'perceiving' above and beyond those of our real-life experiences. We understand film *fully*, not by 'likeness to real life', but by our adaptation to a new kind of thinking.

Film experience is presented by cognitivists as being totally understandable as a continuation of normal experience, and it does seem to be a form of communication we all understand – though perhaps not quite a 'visual Esperanto', as Stuart Liebman calls it.[9] V. F. Perkins argues that we make sense of cinema by relating it to real-world knowledge. Seems reasonable, but just what is this 'relating'? And just how much relating is going on, now that film creates its own unique worlds so often? It seems fine to say we understand film so easily because it is so similar to real life, but the bigger question is how *should* we understand film, how can we *advance* our understanding of film. Film experience is different to, but also draws on, our normal experience – in the cinema we are perhaps scanning *across* the view presented, whereas in life we perhaps scan *into* as much as across. If we are talking about the thinking film then it seems *we adapt* to its thinking, we adjust ourselves. The crux is that just because we can recognise images on film because they are almost identical to reality does not mean that we understand or relate to film exactly as we understand and relate to real events. We can easily feel we are 'there', *but that 'there' is not a copy of our world*. The very fact that we so easily understand (most) film relates to its powerful capacity to create meaning and knowledge. Film seems to have no delay in its understandability, in its *effect*. Interpretation may well come after a 'delay', but we seem to take-in film and feel meaning immediately.

In *The Philosophy of Horror*, Noël Carroll describes three theories of film experience: the illusion theory, the pretend theory and the 'thought' theory. Each of these theories respond to the 'paradox of emotional response to fiction': the problem of why and how we respond emotionally to fictional characters and events even though we (may – see illusion theory) know that the characters and events portrayed are not real. The question here is whether 'existence' beliefs are a necessary condition of emotional response?

Theorists such as Jean-Louis Baudry used the presumed illusionism of film to call for avant-garde and Brechtian filmmaking. If the filmgoer is fooled into thinking they see objects directly then realistic films could have no artistic power! Thus, following this through, we are fooled by films just as we are fooled by the world. There are no things in themselves – we have appearance, and theories of reality. Hugo Münsterberg writes: 'If the pictures are well taken and the projection is sharp and we sit at the right distance from the picture, we must have the same *impression* as if we looked through a glass plate into real space.'[10] For illusion theorists the film image is not a sign of an object or scene, but an analogue or double of the very object or scene itself – film transparently gives us an immediate perception of the world. Filmgoers entertain epistemically benign illusions, and themselves are basically passive, or at best, stimulus-response machines. Thus in illusion theory film reproduces reality, and we see the objects themselves. Or perhaps we watch film like we watch reality – the experience is the same. Or perhaps film just makes the filmgoer *think* they are seeing real present people and events. But there are a greater number of cognitivists who argue that film is *not* essentially illusory, representations do *not* cause us to believe that what they represent is real.

In the 'pretend' thesis it is not *literally* true that we fear cinematic monsters – it is only 'make-believedly' true that we fear them. What we actually experience in such cases are only 'quasi-emotions', emotions made by 'second-order' beliefs.[11] Can the filmgoer thus decide not to be scared by a film? Can we turn off and on our 'make-believe' emotions? Are our emotions not sometimes too strong to be simply make-believe? And just because we are not aware of playing a make-believe game, does that mean we cannot be in a subconsciously make-believe state? Carroll comments: 'Surely a game of make-believe requires the intention to pretend. But on the face of it, consumers of horror do not appear to have such an intention.'[12] And if it is make-believe, why am I sweating at the end of a dramatic scene? Our belief in the events, and our desires for certain things to happen or not to happen, do not seem to be pretend (imagined) beliefs and desires – they are part of a *new* relationship.

Similar to the 'pretend' theory is the 'counterpart' theory of emotional response to fiction. We cry at the end of the afternoon television movie because dramatic emotions displayed on the screen are often playing out scenarios that we have been in, or might one day find ourselves in (a loved-one dying, an emotional reunion). Our emotions are real (real tears) – because it makes us think of real-world emotional events. The fictional events have a *plausibility* that provokes our emotions. We might not believe a monster is actual and existing, but we think it is possible it might exist in the future (though would we say we 'believe' in a non-existent, 'possible' object?).

In the 'thought' theory of emotional response to fiction, Murray Smith and Noël Carroll argue that filmgoers can be moved emotionally by imaginatively entertaining thoughts, without necessarily believing in their truthfulness. They distinguish between thought and belief – for Carroll, we believe something when we 'entertain a proposition assertively', but in the cinema we can be moved by thoughts we do not necessarily believe, stating that 'thought contents we entertain without believing them can genuinely move us emotionally'.[13] For the analytical film philosopher Gregory Currie filmgoers use their imagination, at times, to fill in gaps, to see the unseen, to think about a character's actions. Imagining is part of the evolutionary adaptive functioning of the mind – filmgoers imagine beliefs, simulate terror, and so on. Currie finds no actual belief in the 'reality' of the events in films – yet while filmgoers may not actively believe that the events are real, they do believe that the baddie is very close to the good guy, and we want the good guy to get out of there, quick. (For Currie our experience of film is also mostly impersonal – the filmgoer does not feel as though they are 'in' the film, nor do they identify with the 'camera', or the point of view of the film.) We may believe that vampires do not exist, but in the cinema we may *allow ourselves* to think they exist (and scare and horrify). On arriving at our cinema seat we switch to a mode of thinking that is receptive to these fictional effects. This thesis begs the obvious question: how can a monster scare us if we do not believe in it? Are we merely frightened by (fictional) thoughts? Are we scared by our mental imaginings? Does this not take us back to square one? Why do we not say we are scared by the image? Karen Bardsley has recently argued that some cognitivists rely too heavily on the notion of the imagination. How do kids enjoy films so much when they are yet to develop the capacity to simulate beliefs in their imagination? For Bardsley, to say that a filmgoer constantly uses their imagination in order to understand film fiction seems to be stretching the concept of imagination too far.[14]

It would seem that, in following the narrative, the filmgoer does not *necessarily* need their conscious active imagination, only their audio-visual perceptual capacities. The filmgoer's experience seems primarily perceptual rather than imaginative. A film such as *Moulin Rouge* almost completely overwhelms the audience, leaving almost no time or space to imagine anything. Richard Allen talks of the way that films both exercise and limit our natural visual capacities. Perception is an ability, a capacity, not a material process, and, for Allen, the psychologist confuses this 'ability' with an investigation into mental processes. We do not see something, then recognise it, because as Allen writes: 'If visual perception was framed by schemata in the manner characterised by [cognitivists], then one could never step outside the schemata to match the template with data provided from the sensory array.'[15] We do not access schemata to recognise a bird, we simply see a bird. How could we first project a category of a bird before first seeing a bird? We must see a bird first, then maybe add its image as a category. Similarly, the film is 'in' the filmgoer's mind – there is not an image and then our mental representation of that image. There is not an emotion in the image, and then an emotion in the filmgoer's mind – they are one and the same. Though we mix 'two thinkings', our thinking with the film's thinking, there is only ever one mix. There is no 'intermediate' thought or imagination. In order to simply understand the film we do not need to divert it through our imagination.

What we might do is contrast the imaginative leap we take at the beginning of the filmgoing experience, with the then non-imaginative engagement with the film. Filmgoers very quickly assess their situation when they enter the cinema – they understand that the emotions displayed are of a fictional nature, but decide to *engage* the film on that level. The filmgoer normally then assesses the characters and events on that fictional level. For instance, we might see an actor expressing an emotion, but we would understand that it is a person crying – it is true for us that a person is crying and grieving 'in the fiction'. We know it is a film, but nevertheless we (wish to) experience it as a world.[16] Filmosophers want to believe the film, want to be swept into the film, want to engage with the drama as fully as possible. We *want* the horror to scare us, the comedy to make us laugh, the drama to make us cry. (In this sense filmosophers are closer to day-to-day filmgoers than many a film theorist.) This is the only sense in which I believe we might say that the filmgoer imaginatively engages the film – but the conscious imaginative switch happens at the beginning, and from then on we feel the emotions directly.

One problem of these cognitivist enquiries is their wish to understand the realism of film. These theses of illusion and make-believe and imagination are hampered by their reliance on film just showing real-looking people and objects, and we know that cinema does not do that all the time. In using realism as a touchstone they are blind to the possibility that film is the creation of a *whole new world*, a whole new 'realism'. Significant is the fact that cinema, especially modern cinema, is less and less based on 'reality'. Films that fluidly mix digital and real-like events are stretching our understanding of film drama. Notably, questions of what was actually recorded become redundant – half of *The Matrix* never actually took place in front of the camera; as Bazin wrote: 'The photographic image is the object itself, the object freed from the conditions of time and space that govern it.'[17]

What is significant about film is that it shows us a new reality, and thus engenders new thinking, new experiences, new emotions. It may be true our real-world thought-systems allow us basic entry into the film, but from then on we are thinking rather differently, modifying our thoughts and meeting the film in kind as it were. We still 'experience' feelings as we would in real life, but the experiences do not occur in the same places – being face to face with someone is a *different* experience to a film closing in, tightening in on a character's face. To rely on 'analogy' for all interpretation is mistaken and limiting. Films give us new emotions, new thoughts, *and engenders its own type of responses*. And by engaging with the film the filmgoer helps this engendering of new responses – we go to the cinema to see new things, learn about new things and get new experiences. For Heidegger, art suspends the viewer's 'usual doing and valuing, knowing and looking'[18] – films suspend our *normal* beliefs and desires, filmgoing becoming an ecstatic arrival into an openness, changing our view of the world. Cinema seems to engender a new kind of belief – we recognise its reality as being like ours, but we do not expect its reality to always act like ours (in fact we like it to differ quite a bit).

All this leads to the question of how we comprehend narratives (not just the understanding of 'film' *per se*), and whether we use our conscious or subconscious mind. For David Bordwell the filmgoer's experience of the film is actively constructive; narrative comprehension thus requires conscious thinking, working out, inference-making. But for Allen, Bordwell's theory is flawed in that he argues that the filmgoer is *active* in constructing the drama, but relies on a psychology which posits this activity as *subconscious*, not conscious.[19] Allen asks when exactly might the filmgoer become conscious of these subconscious processes? Therefore he denies that there are any subconscious inferential processes going on in comprehension of narrative – asserting that we do not necessarily *need* to 'make inferences' to understand films. For Allen, film comprehension is an effortless *conscious* understanding; we do not have to 'think', we immediately perceive and understand the drama. Does this then mean that the film holds the 'conventions' not the filmgoer? What is the filmgoer doing? How much story *do* we construct? And if we consciously understand film, what *is* our subconscious doing during the film experience?

To posit all film understanding at a conscious level does seem to ignore the wealth of information that film gives out – is our subconscious not taking some of that information in? And just because we are not consciously aware of constructing of the drama, it does not mean it is not 'active'. Thus this division between active and subconscious seems forced. Why can we not say that a filmgoer's mind will at times be both active in working out the film, and subconsciously receptive to the film? A filmgoer that is active in thinking with and against the film, but who is also open to the film, ready (conceptually) to receive its subtle thinkings in their subconscious. A filmgoer that thinks image and conventions and hypotheses as one, in each moment of perception and cognition. It also might seem quite reasonable to say that dialogue and events and action and gestures meet with the filmgoer's active consciousness, and movements and colours and edit shifts meet with their receptive subconsciousness. But it is not a simple division of thinking: 'content' is not solely handled by consciousness, and 'form' is not solely received by the subconscious. Gestures and actions can subtly affect our subconscious understanding of the drama, and colour and movement can easily catch our eye and ask of us to relate it consciously to the plot at hand.

Filmosophy is not only interested in one or the other; it is not just interested in the 'subconscious' feeling of film-thinking; not just interested in film-thinking that just affects our subconscious; as each concern would cut out much interesting film-thinking. Good film-thinking is not just that which affects our subconscious. Film-thinking can be obvious or subtle, loud or quiet, can speak to our conscious or subconscious mind. The most interesting film-thinking is that which affects both our consciousness and our subconscious. In order to remove this fluid division, we might talk simply of the filmgoer 'feeling' the thinking of the film – a feeling that might be subconscious or conscious, depending on the filmgoer (perhaps depending on what sorts of concepts they have at the back of their mind). A particular film-thinking (a movement or framing) will not reach the same part of the mind of each of the audience – not everyone will consciously see the same things.

Phenomenology

As we have seen, cognitivism sets out a constructivist, epistemologically idealist account of the filmgoer: we are confronted only with images and sounds and have to imaginatively 'construct' fictional entities and comprehend narratives through inference-making. But contrary to 'inference' theories of film comprehension, phenomenology holds that film is an object with *inherent* meanings, representations, and aesthetic features. For example, Allan Casebier in his 1991 book *Film and Phe-*

nomenology holds an epistemologically realist theory of cinematic representation (phenomenological realism, not stylistic realism), arguing that the filmgoer directly sees independent fictional entities. Film holds recognisable people and objects that exist independently of our mental operations. The fictional events of film exist independently – and thus there is no 'fabula' (story) or 'diegesis' (all fictional events), but an integrated whole film. Therefore narrative comprehension ought to be recognised as perceptually intuitive.

There are perhaps two areas for the phenomenological study of the filmgoer: the phenomenology of the cinema experience, and the phenomenology of the film experience. In the former, as was touched on in the introduction and at the beginning of this chapter, the whole of the filmgoing experience is open to investigation and interpretation: distance of filmgoer to screen, type of projection, amount of other people in the cinema, the brightness of the exit signs, and so on. For instance, Münsterberg wrote:

> if the eye falls upon a woman playing the piano directly below the picture, the illusion is destroyed. He sees on the screen enormous giants whose hands are as large as half the piano player, and the normal reactions which are the spring for the enjoyment of the play are suppressed.[20]

But here I shall be mostly concerned with the latter area of study, where phenomenology leads us to realise how mutual and organic the relationship between film and filmgoer is. In phenomenology subject and object are seen as inseparable, and meaning is always *experienced*. This does not entail a *transparent* theory of film experience, but rather a mediated cinematic realism – filmgoers see people and objects *via* the film's thinking. Filmgoers see people the way that the film wants them to be seen (as good or bad, up close or far away) – *the filmgoer feels this thinking in their experience of the film-person*. There is thus an immediacy of thinking and meaning (one in the other). As Merleau-Ponty wrote: 'The meaning of a film is incorporated into its rhythm just as the meaning of a gesture may immediately be read in that gesture: the film does not mean anything but itself ... A movie is not thought; it is perceived.'[21]

Film, because it is so closely related to our modes of thinking, becomes, not so much a mirror, but a companion, a cousin or *friend* of our thinking. For Artaud, 'the cinema is an amazing stimulant. It acts directly on the grey matter of the brain.'[22] The distance between film and filmgoer is eliminated for Artaud, and the film plugs straight into the filmgoer. When Deleuze notes that cinema's 'mental image' necessarily has a direct relationship with thought, he is indicating not only a 'relationship' that is internal to the image, but also active in relation to the filmgoer. But generally, our response to the visual is the most natural of all our mental reactions. Thus the meanings we gain from the visual can be more easily swayed by the formative, imprinting experiences of our youth. The case of the low-angle film-thought is normally understood via the similar human-thought, namely the role that it actually played in our 'learning from taller people' stage of life (*pace* Messaris). But, the film-thought has as many relationships as the human-thought – there is nothing wrong with this analogous application of meaning, but it could point to a limiting of our visual literacy – we should be learning new possibilities of the visual, not just subsuming film to human experience.

Coming back to Messaris, for him film is understood because it is built using normal perceptual skills. Again, this creates the possibility for the special 'direct link' between film and filmgoer. For Messaris film does not mean via its own conventions, rather we understand film via our normal experiences. Messaris finds that 'film and television conventions appear to be constructed on the basis of pre-existing cognitive principles for the perception of our physical and social environment'.[23] The 'constructed on' is the most important bit here – how is this movement, this constructing, developed? Messaris argues that we do not 'read' everything we see: 'images are *not* merely another form of arbitrary signification. Learning to understand images does not require the lengthy period of initiation characteristic of language learning, and permeability of cultural boundaries is much greater for images than it is for language.'[24] We easily grasp film because our basic perceptual capabilities allows us to grant the magic of film composition a realistic appearance. We may feel film directly, but a *fuller understanding* of film does not automatically come from normal experience. We can understand film *better* with a certain kind of knowledge (concepts) of film's actions, resulting in a certain type of linguistic direction (rhetoric).

When Merleau-Ponty says that a film 'is not thought; it is perceived', he is pointing out the immediacy with which we understand images. As filmgoers we do not have to 're-think' film, but immediately perceive and understand film. Understanding this direct link is thus the first stage in a consideration of the filmgoer. *Film attaches itself to our minds and refuses to let go*. The natural link between filmgoer and film turns into a pact, a mesh of 'minds'. We may initially understand film-thinking because it is so close to real-life situations, but that does not mean that film is not making us think new things. By the fact that we experience first-hand the decisions of the filmind, we are linked most closely to it. The filmind is *calling* out to the filmgoer directly, it is *trying* to talk to the filmgoer's mind. I say 'calling' and 'trying' because the link is not one that filmgoers are practised at recognising (that sense of coming out of the cinema having felt some 'meaning' without knowing how). The filmind's colours and movements and focusings are working *at the level* of natural (subconscious) thought, but that does not mean all filmgoers respond to or connect with or *encounter* them.

For Béla Balázs 'film art has a greater influence on the minds of the general public than any other art'[25] – and though this sounds like a sociological comment, his writings steer us to a more psychological interpretation. Eisenstein created films that almost force certain thoughts on filmgoers, and this 'influence', especially the measure of this influence, has been a preoccupation of film studies. Gerard Fort Buckle was concerned with the effect film has on our 'thought movement', and found cinema to be effecting 'a continual awakening and diverting of the thought waves', while only allowing the filmgoer 'a very small amount of retrospection'.[26] More ambiguously, Cavell finds that film has 'absolute control of our *attention*', and relates our differing relationships with the other arts:

> Music also exercises an absolute control of our attention; it justifies this by continuously rewarding it. Painting allows attention an absolute freedom; nothing will happen that is not before our eyes. The novel can neither command absolute control nor afford absolute freedom; it operates in the weave between them, as lives do. Its permanent responsibility is to the act of conversing with us.[27]

In the cinema are we completely removed from the real world? Does film not only provide relaxation and entertainment, but also an overcoming of the causal world? Thus, the question is how much film *replaces* our thinking. Does a bad film leave us no room for 'retrospection', or spark us no thought, and a good film shock us to thinking and meditation? Or the other way round – a bad film leaving our mind to wonder, perhaps critically back onto the film? The extreme is the idea that film overpowers our thought – George Duhamel put it brilliantly in 1930: 'I can no longer think what I want, the moving images are substituted for my own thoughts.'[28] This is like saying that the filmind covers our senses so well that there is no room left for *our* thought – that we need do no thinking, as the film is taking care of us, holding us close and relieving us of the bother of thought. For Artaud, above all, the cinema is 'like an innocuous and direct poison, a subcutaneous injection of morphine',[29] and this extreme, passive picture of the filmgoer (especially with the addition of almost sickly metaphors) has led many to theorise film as a dark force, drawing the poor unknowing and powerless filmgoer into its thinking.

Vivian Sobchack elucidates the event of filmgoing by seeing it as the activities of two bodies: the filmgoer's body and the film's body, which has its own perception of a world. As Merleau-Ponty writes, other bodies become 'the theatre of a certain process of elaboration ... a certain view of the world',[30] of which Sobchack comments: 'How better to pose the experience of visually engaging the nature of the film's visible visual behaviour.'[31] But unlike our perception of other people, the film's 'body' is almost as invisible to us as our own body (this is why our mind and the filmind become so easily mixed). As Sobchack puts it, the film's vision is 'lived though intentionally, introceptively, visually as "mine" ... the film's visual conduct is given to me as homologous to my own visual conduct in watching it'.[32] For Sobchack, the filmgoer perceives the film *within* their own lived body. The film's existence is lived as the filmgoer's body. And filmosophy would agree, though not put so much stress on the sense of body. Filmosophy sees a mix of *minds* rather than bodies – our bodies remain with us, merely forgotten, redundant. We are the film, the mixed active minds of film and filmgoer. It is not so much our thinking that we leave behind, but our 'being', our body. Until we glance at our watch, or we need to go to the toilet, film succeeds in cloaking our body – we simply pay no attention to our selves. (This is perhaps why theories of voyeurism have had such an impact on film studies.) In a sense the filmgoer's body dies, and the mind fully takes over. But, in another sense, are we saying that we forget our own thinking, in that the thinking that the film asks us to do is specifically 'different'? In a 1971 piece fittingly called 'The Extra-terrestrial', J. M. G. Le Clezio called cinema 'a science of visual impressions, forcing us to forget our own logic and retinal habits'.[33] Le Clezio beautifully indicates the way film moves us to construct new ways of thinking in order to accompany the film on its parathoughtful journey. It is in this sense that we *forget* our own being, our own habitual ways of thinking, and take part in the creation of a new being (the new third thought that is the encounter between film and filmgoer).

Filmosophical filmgoer

Part of the function of the filmosophical concepts of the filmind and film-thinking is to engender an active and creative attitude to film. This attitude develops out of the basic experience in the cinema, which is always markedly different to our daily sensations, with different expectations, and needs. Taking our seats we are expectant and thus attentive in the cinema – we are thinking with and against it, but we are thinking towards it, not passively positioned (in life we usually think *from* our experiences). If we go to the cinema for the sole reason of gaining some pleasurable experiences, then we have our 'pleasure thinking' at the ready, as it were, sifting out only those film-thoughts that supply this feeling, these pleasures of an impossible life.[34] Most important here are questions of how active the relationship between film and filmgoer is. In a very simple sense the filmgoer is active towards the film. The flat image is given peaks of importance as the filmgoer's attention shifts around the image, and differing parts of the image (faces, scenery, clues, guns) are brought 'forward' by the filmgoer. These variable peaks are part of the complex relationship between film and filmgoer. For Münsterberg film engenders 'a unique inner experience, which … brings our mind into a peculiar complex state'.[35] To say that film swamps our thinking is to misunderstand and underestimate the part played by the filmgoer's thinking (again, we are not discussing some hypothetical 'weak' filmgoer, nor some inattentive one).[36] Some (cultural) theorists have attempted to attend to the complete audience – when the filmgoer notices their popcorn, or their companion. But this seems less important (for our purposes) than attempting to understand just what is possible in the meeting of film and mind. At the other extreme, Münsterberg argues that the human mind still holds sway over any force the film might have – that is, our language and inherent theories and feelings and ideologies steer the film to the meaning we anticipate, expect or create – 'every shade of feeling and emotion which fills the spectator's mind can mould the scenes in the photoplay until they appear the embodiment of our feelings'.[37]

As with filmosophy, in Sobchack's embodied phenomenology the filmgoer's vision is a constitutive *activity*; the filmgoer projectively and prospectively engages with the film in an *act of becoming*.[38] This is thus a mutual sharing of the film-world, not biased subjection or passive identification. Sobchack recalls the words of Merleau-Ponty on the act of dialogue, where two minds are woven into a common ground or single fabric, 'a shared operation of which neither of us is the creator. We have here a dual being'.[39] The filmgoer engages in a virtual dialogue with the film – each thinks a certain way, and that collision results in a unique mix of thinkings. Sobchack writes illuminatingly on this mix:

> I am able to engage the visible in a dialogue that results from the marked similarities and re-marked differences between *what I see* and *what is seen by another* even as I see it … It is in this convergence and divergence of perception that the hermeneutic relation to cinematic technology arises in the spectator's experience.[40]

The filmgoer and film may have similar or dissimilar routes of thinking: we may converge with the thinkings of an action film (we want to see the explosion, and the film gives it to us), or diverge from the thinkings of a mystery thriller (we want to see who the killer is, but the film will not let us).

Whether converging or diverging, the filmgoer *feels* the film's thinking *directly*, *affectively* – they see and understand the objects of film *through* the film-thinking. Sobchack argues that the filmgoer can see what the film simply wants them to see, *or* can see the film intentions, see the film actively wanting us to see what it sees. But that seems to assert a separation of film-thinking and film-object. How can we see a character without seeing them through or via the film-thinking? It is only technicist rhetoric that creates a separation of object and style – a filmgoer holding a language of cameras and dollies could quite purposefully concentrate on the mechanics of the film. The filmgoer should not (be made to) experience technology (camera, zoom), but a dramatically intended film-world. Those who 'see' a 'camera' (moving, framing) are only seeing it via a technicist conceptualisation and rhetoric of film. Filmosophy is concerned to *organicise* and so remove the separation of film-object and film-thinking. Filmosophy argues that, with the concept of 'film-thinking' in their knowledge, the filmgoer can be simultaneously aware of both the object of the film's intention (the character) *and* the intention (framing, movement) itself. The filmosophical filmgoer immediately feels the character *through* their thinking and the film-thinking.

What I am developing here is an understanding of the encounter between film and filmgoer as a *mix of thinkings*. The film and the filmgoer combine their thinkings in a very special way – and theorising film as thinking helps us understand the powerful and special relationship that does exist. The filmgoer does not so much 'identify' with the film (or its characters) as 'join' it in the creation of a third thinking. Simply put, the encounter between film and filmgoer is so enjoyable and easy and powerful *because film is also thinking*. For Cavell (recalling Merleau-Ponty's words above), when reading a novel or simply experiencing life, our attention 'operates in the weave between them'.[41] We, as filmgoers, naturally weave our thinking into the films we experience. Not only do we naturally see different things, but our language and prior understanding may make us see some things above others. Münsterberg writes: 'Whatever is focused by our attention wins emphasis and irradiates meaning over the course of events.'[42] There becomes no such thing as one way vision: everything I look at looks at me.

At the level of cognitive processing, each of us has a unique subconscious and conscious strategy. We all look for certain things in movies, we all attend to and respond to different aspects of film. Theorising that multiplicity is almost impossible, other than pointing out that the variables are there. The filmgoing experience is one of constrained freedom – an endless push-pull mix of thinkings. Each filmgoer is invested in the film drama in their own particular (ideological, narcissistic, emotional) way. Their way of thinking attends to particular peaks of the image, particular elements of the narrative. But this undeniable aspect of all filmgoers *cannot be theorised*. We should thus be concerned with how filmgoers might *more fruitfully* interact with films, that is, to re-understand this engagement through a recognition of film's capabilities of thinking, and also *propose* (not just try to discover) a new way of encountering film.

Because we are all attentive in slightly differing ways, and because every film is thinking many possible aesthetic and kinetic and conceptual moments, the encounter between film and filmgoer produces a *unique* third thought, a unique mix. Film is constructed perfectly for our mind – we join our filmgoer-thinking with the film-thinking, and therefore include the film in our thoughts. *In* our mind. (This is why others have mistaken the filmgoing experience for a replacement of our thinking – relative immersion in a film does not mean that we are not still being selective and active in our experience.) It can sometimes feel like we are thinking the film ourselves. The experience of the film, our 'thinking' of the film (the attendings we make throughout the film), is the 'mix', the third thought, and our personal 'version' of the film. As Münsterberg wrote: 'The objective world is molded by the interests of the mind.'[43] Both filmgoer and film mould the film-world. Not least, the natural saccadic motion of the filmgoer's eyes makes for a kind of constant searching. The mixing of film and filmgoer is always an original journey – the filmgoer adds the filmind's film-thinking to their own, naturally or subconsciously reconfiguring it in the process. Even when we are 'losing ourselves' in the film, we are still thinking with and against the film. The relationship between film and filmgoer in filmosophy is thus an energy, a vital mix of thinkings. The filmgoer and the film affect each other, are correlated with one another. Our vision is not separate to our bodies, our being: we remake the film via our concepts, and the film remakes our vision. In the cinema we thus have a particularly filmic mode of attention – we begin to see 'filmically'.

Again, what is important is recognising how active the filmgoer can be, and what this activeness consists of.[44] We are always selecting and choosing – whether parts of an image to concentrate on, or parts of a narrative line. We select from those film-thoughts in any way we choose. The film appears to us, we are positioned in some respect to it, our thinking chooses a way of joining the film, the background to our being informs this choosing, and we (consciously and subconsciously) select parts of the film to attend to.[45] The filmgoer is never thoughtless – there is always content. A theory of thought is a theory of its content. Thinking is, conventionally, an activity: thinking is always 'about' something. So in the cinema we continue, but differently. As our mind meets the filmind so the collision produces a third thought (which is our thought of the film). But this is a third thought without there being a first and second. We could not identify or isolate the two thoughts of film and filmgoer, only experience (as a filmgoer) the third. (A film has no one concrete field of thinking – so one cannot say that the filmgoer necessarily only experiences a 'percentage' of the film's 'actual', or complete range of thoughts.)

The film plus the filmgoer's environment of experience, cultural inclinations, historical position and general needs and desires (time and background), all combine to create the meaning experienced. Yet it is hardly worth stating that there is no meaning in a film in itself ('all it can do is *block* a number of possible investments of meaning', as Roger Odin wrote[46]). Thus we have a conception of the filmgoer as active participant in the film, often instinctively selecting unique fields and swathes of film-thoughts. A ghostly participant, outside the film, yet integral (essential) to its thinking, the filmgoer can be deeply involved, and pragmatically evolves a meaning structure for the film (based on the concepts the filmgoer brings to the cinema, as we shall see below). For example, when we see a character on film, we do seem to feel we are just 'seeing' that person, *but we are seeing that person through another (kind of) mind*; we are seeing that person (with the help of) how the filmind wants us to see that person (soft, or looming, or close, and so on). We see via the filmind, but it is still up to us how much we accept the filmind's viewpoint. Our thinking *plus* film-thinking designs this coalesced, third thinking. It is an encounter, a joining, a dialogical connection. So the next question concerns what kind or sorts of experience and possible knowledge does the film/filmgoer encounter produce?

Affective film-thinking

Considering the route we have taken in noting the direct and unique connection between film and filmgoer, just what kind of thinking *is* going on? What is the sense we have of films? At this level of formal film-thinking (before dialogue and the references of objects), it seems that the base (formal) sound-image-thinking of film is an 'affective thinking' that communicates directly with a non-linguistic (perhaps subconscious) part of our minds. Stanley Kubrick once said that films

> present the opportunity to convey complex concepts and abstractions without the traditional reliance on words ... *2001*, like music, succeeds in short-circuiting the rigid surface cultural blocks that shackle our consciousness to narrowly limited areas of experience and is able to cut directly through to areas of emotional comprehension.[47]

Affects we might call emotions or feelings that are part of or attached to ideas or concepts. *We understand and receive meaning as we experience the film*. The film prompts feelings, and thus affective knowledge, in the filmgoer. By mixing our thinking with the film's thinking we can allow ourselves an amount of relaxation *exactly in order to truly grasp the affective meanings of the film*. As V. F. Perkins notes: 'We are not aware of "reading" the image. No act of interpretation, no effort of imagination or comprehension seems needed.'[48] The filmgoer 'feels' the formal thinking of film as a direct impression. For Jean Louis Schefer film is an eye without a memory – cinema can only produce the effects of memory. Schefer is actually saying that, without real thought, cinema can only imitate thinking, and that film communicates directly with a non-linguistic side of our minds:

> the illusion proper to the cinema is that this experience and this memory are solitary, hidden, secretly individual, since they make an immediate pact (story, pictures, affective colours) with a part of ourselves that lives without expression; a part given over to silence and to a relative aphasia, as if it were the ultimate secret of our lives – while perhaps it really constitutes our ultimate subjecthood. It seems that in this artificial solitude *a part of us is porous to the effects of meaning without ever being able to be born into signification through language.*[49]

Film bleeds ideas. The rupturing or violence of complex film-thinking creates spaces for ideas to appear. Thus some knowledge gained by the filmgoer can be conceptual. This kind of knowledge arrives by way of different types of moving sound-images – different complexes and movements of film-thinking – whether it is a shift from one image to another, or the description of a space by the film. These film-concepts are both new and direct; as Godard once said (in *La Chinoise*), 'we must replace vague thoughts with clear images'. The ending of *The Scent of Green Papaya* becomes a *thinking of* the relationship of the two lovers; it encompasses and feels their situation; and in a sense the image becomes a concept of their state, and thus possibly (can be *felt to be*) an idea of mutual love. The arrival of concepts is helped by the fact that film 'means' in a way that is much more human than, say, painting. In life we naturally frame a scene to suit our feeling of it – say, keeping one person in our view while talking to someone else. If we see this action in film we are more suited to experiencing the meaning of it than colour or form in painting. (In this sense film is a life thought-out – just a different artificial life and a new kind of thought.) For Artaud film is 'an inorganic language which moves the mind by osmosis and with no sort of transposition in words'.[50] The thinking that film does (with the filmgoer) has exactly this non-linguistic newness: in experiencing a film we are respondent to new, *different*, specially created values of pleasure and knowledge and entertainment. We are creating these fields of reception as we engage in the film. (Furthermore, it is important to recognise that images are part of our knowledge. As we shall see in the final chapter, a theory of thinking needs to take into account our continual aesthetic attention.)

In the face of film's thinking, we may recognise the relative 'impower' of the film-goer's thinking, not in terms of the relationship between film and filmgoer (the film does not totally swamp the mind of the filmgoer), but in terms of the power of film-thinking to create and show new ideas and concepts through the moving sound-image. Our impower lies in being unable to think images (or image-concepts) as clearly as film. Deleuze called this gap in our ability the unthought in thought, and Cavell found a similarly disabled filmgoer: the filmgoer's thinking seems invisible, and yet it is *joined* with the film (it is silent yet active: choosing and selecting from the film). This sense of invisibility is seen by Cavell as 'an expression of modern privacy or anonymity … as though the world's projection explains our forms of unknownness and of our inability to know'.[51] What Deleuze further argued was that a certain kind of cinema attempted to fill this gap in the filmgoer's thinking by effecting a 'shock to thought'. As noted earlier, there are two overlapping areas to Deleuze's thought-cinema: that film causes thought in the filmgoer; and that film is a kind of thought itself. (Deleuze arrives at this latter conception of thought-cinema *through* his account of images that produce thought in the feeler.) There are thus *two* shocks, from the image to conscious thought, then our image-thinking takes us back to the film images. Similarly, for Walter Benjamin, film can produce a 'shock effect', forcing the mind to cushion them with a 'heightened presence of mind'.[52] With the automatic movement of film, Deleuze writes, 'the artistic essence of the image is realised: *producing a shock to thought, communicating vibrations to the cortex, touching the nervous and cerebral system directly*'.[53] (This movement produces a kind of spiritual automaton in the filmgoer.) The essence of the image for Deleuze is thought-cinema, which for him is when movement becomes *automatic*, when time and movement exist for themselves, forcing the filmgoer to think *through* (against/with) this new construction of time and movement. Film here produces a 'nooshock': not only the forcing of thinking, but the forcing of a new kind of thinking. The noosign produces a nooshock and new thinking, and this shock to thinking is automatic.

Deleuze acknowledges Heidegger when he notes the difference between the possibility of thinking and the doing of thinking – in communicating the shock cinema gives us thinking (makes us think *and* shows thinking). Deleuze casts this relationship as direct and physiological, using the Artaudian/Eisensteinian terms 'shock' and 'sensation' to underline his view that thinking is an unavoidable result of film – an effect on the cortex. We *feel* the film much more than we see or hear it. *This is sensory thought; affective intelligence.* Deleuze sees Eisenstein's decomposition of the 'shock' in cinema as 'the very form of communication of movement in images … from the image to thought, from the percept to the concept'.[54] Montage creates or leads to a thinking of the Whole, via the effect of images on the cerebral cortex; we 'feel' the images, there is a total physiological sensation. Here Deleuze becomes prescriptive, arguing that the image (to be rightly termed 'thinking') must force us to think. For all this Deleuze still sees cinema as a primitive '*internal monologue*, a drunken monologue, working through figures, metonymies, synecdoches, metaphors, inversions, attractions...',[55] a cinema of resonance but not linguistic palpability or certainty of expression.

For Eisenstein film produces physiological sensations – as regards sound he writes, 'the term "I hear" is no longer strictly appropriate. Nor "I see" for the visual. For both we introduce a new formula: "I feel".'[56] Deleuze uses this formula, and sees a 'movement-image developing its vibrations in a moving sequence which *embeds itself within us*'.[57] Film, and its vibrations of thought, fuses with the filmgoer, and produces 'suprasensory relations ... this is the shock wave or the nervous vibration, which means we can no longer say "I see, I hear", but I FEEL'[58] *To be 'followed' by I THINK*: 'The cinematographic image must have a shock effect on thought, and force thought to think itself as much as thinking the whole. This is the very definition of the sublime.'[59] For Deleuze, when films start thinking, *we feel* a rupturing of thought (and a rupturing of our filmgoing experience), and this automatically results in a doing of thinking.

Following on from Deleuze then, the filmgoer can be said to be taking part in the creation of thought – which may be of an uninteresting sort with boring films, and powerful and prolonging with good ones. This is an intuitive relationship (even though later we may decide to add interpretation and writing). *These are thinkings we understand intuitively rather than metaphorically.* Currie says we 'interpret the visual images on screen by imagining that we actually see before us the fictional events they represent.'[60] Yet there is no need for an 'interpreting' via an 'imagining', it is possible to see and understand immediately. Take two people in a cinema, both with an understanding of how film can be thoughtful: one (perhaps sat at the back, with the screen's frame and other filmgoers in clear sight) sees an action of form and appreciates the thinking, and derives an interpretation; the other (perhaps near the front) is completely involved in the film, and *feels* a meaning for those moments when they appear – and only afterwards may remember the feeling and set about relating those moments through interpretation.

Meaning thus has a beginning (immediately in the experience), a middle (through reflection and interpretation during and after the film), and seemingly never an end. The film's moving sound-image thinking has the *possibility* of meaning – we hold the only capacity to give meaning to film, by experiencing it.[61] And the concept of the filmind does not presume a 'message': everything is intended but there is no message to be missed or misunderstood or completely, exhaustively understood.[62]

There are certainly 'conventions' in film (via other films), but they are never atoms of meaning as in language – they are conventions which affect meaning, rather than determine meaning. The affective meanings of film-thoughts are gained, pragmatically, through use; through the filmgoer's changing, adaptive, contextual response to them.

The specifically *formal* film-thought initially stimulates us to an affective meaning; the meaning is in the experience. This is not the same sort of 'meaning' that we achieve through interpretation, or that we might gain from identifiable (meaningful) gestures and actions and objects 'in' the film. This (formal-thinking) meaning is what we *feel* when watching the thing, and that immediate feeling is our useful (and hopefully interesting) truth of the film. When other writers note that 'meaning' is only one result of film-thinking, they are arguing along similar lines (but with differing semantics: sensation/sense/meaning, and so on) – that a profound and impressive impact is being made at a more immediate, affective level (and furthermore that not all films need be resolved into meanings – that they can be experiences beyond or before meaning).

The thoughtful, formal actions of film produce this immediate meaning – think of a film circling its hero: we get a sense, a feeling of his situation directly. But perhaps the most important thing to say about the kind of thinking film-thinking is is that it is indistinct, almost vague. An act of the image (say focusing) is not reducible to a succinct meaning, making the type of knowledge that film produces a 'rough' knowledge. The *affects* of film produce immediate, pure meaning – fluid, changing, ill-defined. These meanings we feel are tentative, gut-like ones, shaky in their location – the filmgoer may not know exactly where she 'received' a meaning from. Filmosophical (affective) 'meaning' is therefore that which arises directly from experiencing the film – we are given meaning. The thinking of film (its actions of form) is the primary source of these hazy meanings and distinct feelings. These are basic meanings which coalesce invisibly, inseparably, with the meanings we gain from actions and dialogue to become the whole thought of the moment. How (linguistically) ready we are to receive those meanings, and what we do with them in post-film writing, is the concern of the next chapter.

nine | film writing

You will see that this little clicking contraption with the revolving handle will make a revolution in our life – in the life of writers. It is a direct attack on the old methods of literary art. We shall have to adapt ourselves to the shadowy screen and to the cold machine. A new form of writing will be necessary.

– Leo Tolstoy (1908)[1]

Film studies has struggled to verbalise *how* an action of form seems to convey a feeling or a meaning. Films are praised for their 'tracking shots' or innovative framing, but seldom are these forms revealed in more fruitful ways. A fair amount of film theory impoverishes our experience of film by using a language (a descriptive terminology) that is removed and unsuitable to the very actions and movements of film form – *we should not be taught to see 'zooms' and 'tracking shots', but led to understand intensities and movements of feeling and thinking*. And even if style *is* granted meaning or 'intention' it is usually in a metaphorical or symptomatic way: the tracking shot 'symbolises' the link between two spaces, an strange framing 'reflects' the character's psychological state. In these kinds of analyses form and content are still resolutely separated[2] (even though the writer may think they are bringing them together) – the form acts on or responds to the content, *like two railway tracks that criss-cross each other every so often*. Form has still been seen as separate, usually brought in only when its actions *confirm* an interpretation of the film's story. This last point is important, as the route to interpretation should always be via the whole film, not biasing form or content. Of course a character is *separate* from a movement of the film, but the thinking of the film at that moment encompasses both. Using the concept of film-thinking the character and room and framing and movements become one (the thought of the filmind).

In this chapter I will thus be concerned with how the language and rhetoric of the concepts of the filmind and film-thinking might shape the filmgoer's routes of interpretation. Filmosophy here approaches the key question of the description and understanding of the formal make-up of film. What is important here, and what will be the subjects of the next few sections, are the relationship between thought and language, the current language and rhetoric of film studies, how form and meaning are bonded together by the concept of film-thinking, the language used to reveal and revel in film-thinking, how this new language changes our experience of film, the encouragement of a more open and personal style of interpretation, the encouragement of a performative writing style, and how these writings on film should positively affect the experience of film for others.

Language

My premise is low-level: that how we think, how we perceive, is dependent (to some extent) on the knowledge and experience we bring to the event of seeing and hearing, and that much of that knowledge and experience is stored in language. As Yvette Biró writes, 'we do not know what we see, but rather the opposite is true: we see what we know.'[3] We think with images *and* language. Our mental images are always changing and darting around, usually rough and hazy. At a certain age we learn the words for some images, and thought becomes partially linguistified. We start to 'interpret' things with our particular set of terms and concepts. We think using many different cognitive processes, and we use language to grab at some of them – either to communicate to others, or to resolve a thought for ourselves.[4]

We all think via language: we unconsciously use terms to handle, to mould experience and knowledge. Language attempts to translate thought – *concepts learnt and absorbed begin to direct our thinking*. How we see is dependent on how we understand what we see, which arrives through our linguistic capacity. It is not that we think entirely *in* language, but that a significant mark of our engagement with and understanding of what we experience is the sort of language we have. Eskimos 'see' more in snow because they have so many differing terms for it (while we only have slushy, crunchy, dirty, and one or two others). Our language of thought *reveals* itself in perceiving, in organising our visual and auditory fields. This is why we can say that the Eskimo really does 'see' more in snow, and not just that they can interpret snow in more varied ways (for even to do that they must be perceiving more, and not simply looking with more concentration).

A consequence of this is that we may only 'net' from an image what our language trawls in; we come to regard images through words (and translate importantly felt images into interpretations), but that is not to say that we automatically translate all images into language, that images are composed by language, reducible to language, or completely indebted to language for all their possible meanings. We just may not be able to recover and verbalise the *meaning we felt* – perhaps because our language (and whatever theoretics organising it) is pulling us to another kind of interpretation. Therefore my main argument is that the filmgoer's experience of film can be enhanced by more suitable and poetic reference terms for moving sound-image actions of form, and that these terms can come from understanding film as a new mode of thought. If the film circles the hero, and our language consists of technical and metaphorical terms, then our understanding of that scene will be steered by that language. An analogy can be made with how differing soundtracks can influence the meaning of images: *our descriptive language (of moving sound-images) is the musical mood of our audio-visual experience.*

The possession of words and categories affects our experience of film. The filmgoer almost matches their concepts to the film: an actor watching a film will hold concepts of drive and performance, and will latch onto those moments in the film; a railwayman's concepts will steer a different experience of *Europa*; an architect's concepts will pull certain affects from *Blade Runner*, etc. And we are not talking about interpretation yet, but the concepts that drive attention and knowledge and perception. Michael Baxandall has written beautifully on this area in regard to the history of Italian painting: 'Fifteenth-century medicine trained a physician to observe the relations of member to member of the human body as a means to diagnosis, and a doctor was alert and equipped to notice matters of proportion in painting too.'[5] Comprehension may not *require* previous experience or training, but it can be enhanced by a more suitable language and rhetoric (words and word arrangements). The encounter between film and filmgoer produces much meaning, but our capacity to receive those affective film-thinkings is somewhat dependent on whether we are 'ready' linguistically. If our minds do organise images to conform to the logic and meaning and capacity of its language, *then reconfiguring (renaming) forms of film with thoughtful poetics (the feelings of thinkings) will change the experience of film for the filmgoer.* This hopefully leads to a new organisation of the whole – a new mode of attention for the filmgoer.

So what is the current language of film studies?[6] How does it handle film style? The removed, metaphorical nature of some film writers' attempts to bring form and style into their interpretations will be discussed in a moment. But at source much writing is technicist – being grounded (and steered) by the language of filmmaking. It is as though we were to interpret books using the technical language of printing presses, ink resolutions and copy-editing symbols, instead of the affective power of story worlds. Some film theorists who get a taste of filmmaking revel in that language – talking of lenses and technical shots – to show off their knowledge (and almost infer that they could be making films too). An analogy can be made with film critics' use of actors' names instead of character names: for example, Donald Skoller persists in calling the characters in *Vertigo* Kim and Jimmy! In cultural theory and popcorn criticism this can be illuminating and fun, but most films deserve more than this. Technical terms – such as panning, tracking, zoom-in, close-up, off-camera, shot/reverse shot, long take, hand-held, medium shot, filter, deep focus, asynchronous sound – litter the texts of much writing. *This lumpen technological terminology obscures the possible poetic experience of film.* Speaking of books full of filmmaking terms Parker Tyler compares them to 'anatomy lectures over human corpses that explain how a living man, in general, "works", how this or that of his organs functions'.[7]

Film writing was technical in the beginning because quotation was impossible and writers so dearly wanted to get across what they were talking about, and no other way of description existed. But after a hundred years can we not move on? For example, even though it is low-impact rhetoric, and we all seem to accept its usage, where exactly is the 'camera' in films? The camera does this, responds to that, moves in on a character. I can see the film moving round a room, searching for clues, but no camera. I use this example because most film theorists would find this nit-picky and pedantic, and it is always nice to start with the borderline rather than the obvious. *Filmosophy aims for the complete re-understanding of film as possible poetic thinking* – not just the general elucidation of interesting and active 'film-thinking' in essayistic and abstract film, but the attempt to re-situate (and resuscitate) all film as affective thinking. Therefore, the first task is to philosophically reconceptualise its actions of form – not something done once and then used, but something pragmatically growing from the emergence of forms in world cinema (look at *Sonatine's* rethinking of the time-space of action and gun-play, with its many waitings and silences).

What are our terms for the horizontal-moving shot? The 'tracking shot'! Is that it? When V. F. Perkins finds movements *conveying* 'confusion' or 'exhilaration',[8] it is not that he is wrong in his assessments, only somewhat clunky in his relaying of those assessments. An action of form does not convey meaning, it inhabits thinking – there is no gap between action and meaning. The filmind can reconfigure it as a thought, as a feeling, and a dramatic way of understanding the characters it is attending to, or sounds that accompany it. Think of the movements of *Distant Voices, Still Lives* – to only call these 'tracking shots' is an insult to the power of the film: they are movements 'of' time, bringing us through the time of the characters, thinking a passage of life. Elsewhere these movements might be a thinking of connection, or of the centrality of a character in a transient world (when the film keeps a character central in a passing world).

Technicist descriptive terms for moving sound-image forms obstruct the possible. They ground (limit) the meaning of forms in their technical make-up – the technical term pushes a certain understanding of the meaning of that particular form. A 'zoom-in', called as such, gives a limited framework for understanding its use, and constructs a certain response from the filmgoer. As Deleuze said, in a conversation published in 1985, 'technique only makes sense in relation to ends which it presupposes but doesn't explain'.[9] The ends are the concepts of cinema – and technical terms are empty compared to suitable concepts of poetry and form. We see colour, we do not (need to) see filters; we see a glide from pavement to heavens, we do not (need to) see a crane shot; we just see the top half of a person, we do not see a midshot. With these three forms we might say the film is feeling a certain tone, a kind of flight, and an amount of respect, perhaps. Stanley Cavell recounts one of his first seminars on film wherein the students were asked to describe the films they had seen:

> words flowed about every thing from low-angle shots to filters to timings and numbers of set-ups to deep focus and fast cutting, etc., etc. But all this in turn lost its sense … the only technical matters we found ourselves invoking, so far as they were relevant to the *experience* of particular films, which was our only business, are in front of your eyes. You can see when a shot begins and ends and whether it's long, middle or close; you know whether a camera is moving back or forth or sideways … Then what is the reality behind the idea that there is always a technical something you don't know that would provide the key to the experience.[10]

Why do writers think that by telling us exactly how a 'shot' was done we will understand or experience the moment any better? The point is that even though most writers are not this technical they still overwhelmingly employ technical terminology – not terminology that matches what we 'see', but terminology that (uselessly) tells us how someone made what we see. Know-how provides no-why – rather, it can make the reader/filmgoer forget to ask *why* the film did such-and-such. The logistics of film should be left to the creators.

This heavy rhetoric attempts to steer the filmgoer to see things that are not even there: we do not (need to) see a medium shot, or deep focus – we just see (simply) a certain impression of a character, or we see clearly two characters who are some distance apart. Again, this lumpen technological terminology *obscures* the possible poetic experience of film. Daniel Dayan argues that the filmgoer needs to discover the 'frame' in order to realise that the film is controlling what we see and hear, but this too is just technical reflexivity. Even a writer as good as George Wilson falls back on terms such as 'dolly' and 'camera tracks',[11] but perhaps only because no other basic 'descriptive' terms exist. Again, Wilson can still elucidate a great interpretation using these terms, but they sting in the text like glimpses of the microphone boom straying into shot – breaking the spell, if only for a moment.

Filmosophical language

The filmosophical filmgoer engages the film with their personality, backed by concepts that tie form to thinking, to build an interpretation of the film that responds to the whole film, colour and dialogue, shifts and plots. Even though filmosophy confines itself to 'composition', this itself affects any larger interpretation, meaning that if you start with a filmosophical attention then your interpretation, your writing about the film, will progress in a certain kind of way. Filmosophy aims to fuel interpretations with a better understanding of how colour and movement and framing are integral to a film's meaning. The question here is not so much whether there can be final and complete interpretations, but what basis any interpretation uses for its work – the argument being that much interpretation either ignores sound-image forms, or else only teleologically brings in examples when they conform to the interpretation gained from the raw action or plot. As indicated earlier, much film writing not only uses technicist terminology but also stumbles through crude metaphors when it attempts to link form to meaning. One of the wrong turns taken was the prioritising of the real. Especially now that film is as malleable as animation we need to understand it differently – conceive of its possibilities, and create a suitable language to meet it even half-way. The art of realism is still there, but *within* the possibilities of film, as *one way of thinking*.

The concepts of the filmind and film-thinking naturally give birth to humanistic terms of intention (belief, empathy, etc.). These terms then 'organically' steer the filmgoer to see film forms as dramatic rather than technical. Form becomes just more content. *Film-thinking organicises the 'link' between form and content.* In making 'style' integral to content, filmosophy hopes to enhance and emancipate the experience of the filmgoer. Realising film as thinking we can now understand moments more rhetorically: the film (through its affective forms) might be said to be crying in empathy, sweating out loud, feeling pain for the character. (The concept of the filmind should provoke these kinds of interpretations.) Even the most normal, invisible form is thinking – if only with that intention in mind: to let us see the drama clearly and unobtrusively. Responding to regular films only in terms of narration we would be paying attention to events and themes; thinking about film in terms of an active, intending filmind, we would also be paying attention to shape and fluidity and light and sound: *the complete film*. The concept of film-thinking leads to writing that describes ('images', almost) a whole thoughtful event, infinitely malleable (as opposed to writing that alternates crudely between a misperceived 'form and content').

The concept of the filmind allows us to understand a film's formal actions as emanating from the *heart* of the film, bringing us closer to the film, thus making our experience grow and mature, via an interpretation that prolongs and dwells in the experience. *Where technicist writings open a back-door to the film, conceptual-ising the film as thinking opens the front-door*. Experiencing a film as thinking produces a more meditative, contemplative filmgoer – unprogrammed and unpositioned, imaginative and open. The more 'human' concept of *thinking* allows our whole self to attend to the film – we then might think *with* it, instead of via stuttering terminology and against it. Filmosophy encourages this (un)thought, intuitive, flexible, original experience – an *extension*, less patronising perhaps, of what Perkins calls 'naïve'[12] and Cavell 'native'.[13] Film-thinking levels the playing field for film style. Previously, if the narrative of a film was found to be privileged against the characters then the film might have been called, derisively, 'metalanguage dominant'. Now, with a greater sense of the thinking that film can do without 'shouting' we can see all sorts of subversive meanings without resort to calling them Brechtian devices. These writings on film, these examples of thought, are working practices that, through their attempt to *close the gap* between phenomena and terms, simply encourage people to *see more* in the moving sound-image. *The filmgoer is encouraged to see thinking (thoughtful intention) rather than technique*.

If, as Jean Epstein noted, 'the words are lacking, the words have not been found', and the words we do have 'slither like wet cakes of soap around what we try to say',[14] what form should a new language take? We do not need instruction in how to 'read' film, we only need a better language *of* those moving sound-images – we are already well suited to understanding film. Filmosophy is concerned with the film *as it appears* – its movements and attentions. And, for filmosophy, the rhetoric of its various forms can be sliced from the languages of thinking (questioning, comparing, belief, passion, reasoning, love, empathy, imagining). A descriptive term should not wound the film, should not cut the film's surface to reveal its technological workings, but should open-up the image to reveal its thinking, *its belief about the people and objects it has gained*. Such terms would represent an understanding of film that relates to us, to our knowledge of space and objects, rather than to any hidden structures or filmmaker mechanics. We have a natural engagement with film, so it seems strange that much film writing obsesses on non-natural aspects. To advance and inform this natural connection is the purpose of filmosophical terminology, a language of film-thinking that sits easily with the filmgoer's thought (rather than grabbing the wheel and steering it into a brick wall of technology). These new concepts should flood the filmgoer's thoughts, providing a mode of attention upon future films.

In writing about a film, a new or newly-applied word immediately creates a new understanding, a new way of attending to the film for the person who reads that writing. The words give birth to a new aspect to the film, and visiting the film with those concepts can change the film. As the film feeds itself though the gate of the projector, the filmgoer feeds the film through their language – sees what their language allows them to see – then takes that experience and further whittles the film down into language-ideas in post-film writing. So, that first experience, itself mediated by language, is again reduced into conscious, communicable language. *We reduce its thinking to our thinking, and how suitable our thinking is depends on our knowledge and language*. Deleuze understood this:

> Cinema is not a universal or primitive language system [*langue*], nor a language [*langage*]. It brings to light an intelligible content which is like a presupposition, a condition, a necessary correlate *through which language constructs its own 'objects' (signifying units and operations)*. But this correlate, though inseparable, is specific: it consists of movements and thought-processes (pre-linguistic images), and of points of view on these movements and processes (pre-signifying signs). It constitutes a whole 'psychomechanics', the spiritual automaton, the utterable of a language system which has its own logic. The language system takes utterances of language, with signifying units and operations from it, but the utterable itself, its images and signs, are of another nature.[15]

Ontologically, film contains no language, but the filmgoer constructs linguistic objects from the moving sound-image (the utterable itself). Language helps us live our lives by ordering and clarifying phenomena, and in doing so necessarily generalises. In experiencing everything through language we break down and structure what we see in concert with our linguistifying of the images. Seeing becomes almost a speaking in and through images.

Film happens – it is an event in time – and we experience the meaning of film via an unconscious language system that is so far not suited to the moving image – not prepared for the possible thoughtful poetics of film. As I have argued, our thinking mixes with the film's thinking, and the range and depth of our attentions is steered by our linguistic capacity – which mirrors the language we employ when writing or discussing the experience of the film. New forms of cinema, whether in *Fight Club* or *The Thin Red Line*, create spaces for new thoughtful rhetorics, of colours and silences, and subjective flights and relations. (With *The Thin Red Line* I remember drinking-in the thread of character thoughts – the filmind passing through the heads of its characters like a metaphysical bird.) New films demand new vocabularies in order to understand (and communicate) their thinkings; new words that create better, more creative knowledge. This attempt to say the ineffable may require a certain hyper-metaphoricity, or catachresis (the deliberate misapplication of a word or straining of a metaphor – compare with Epstein's singing of knowledge, 'lyrosophy'). But first of all must be found the words, *the words that relate film to feeling, to imagination, to love or justice*, rather than to imported theory or filmmaker mechanics. To bring a new pressure on, and release of, the single word (Roland Barthes' *Writing Degree Zero* beautifully brings this out with regard to modernist poetry). Fragments can come to the fore – singled-out text; lonely questions. With these words the performative rhetoric of filmosophical film writing starts to take shape.

Concepts of film-thinking serve the multi-form that is film – as Biró notes, 'thought contains simultaneously what in speech occurs consecutively, should we not pay more attention to this simultaneity and examine more closely *the language best suited to record this dynamic simultaneity?'*[16] Just as our thought is ill-served by language, so the current language of much film writing either separates forms too much, or simply collates them and uses them wherever they confirm a meaning gained from the film's story. The subject here is the words for the experience, not a complete structure for larger interpretations. The route to this new vocabulary is via translating film forms (and filmgoer feelings) into thoughtful poetics. That is, recognising the thoughtful attentions of film to be emotive and affective. Filmosophy embraces the film and attempts a poetic translation of the third thought (those joined 'thinkings' of film and filmgoer). The rudiments of this writing can be ordinary words in differing contexts (poetry); ordinary words in different unions (compounds); and original words (neologisms). For someone like Heidegger, language can merely be a communication of what we know, or it can be a 'projective saying',[17] an innovative naming of things and concepts, helping us communicate further. But doubting old jargon is an early step on the route to rediscovering film. A simple example of film-thinking occurs near the beginning of *The Matrix* – Neo is introduced to Morpheus to be told what the Matrix is, and the film *empathises* with Neo's lack of knowledge, keeping half the film (literally) in darkness (using Morpheus's coat, or a chair). The filmind *feels* Neo's position, his knowledge of only half the story, and the filmgoer feels a sense of lack and anticipation too, especially when Morpheus begins to answer his question and the filmind *feels this revelation* by revealing the whole image again.

The words for this kind of experience can only come from the encounter between film and filmgoer. This encounter is a movement of film to filmgoer and filmgoer towards film, and thus forces the filmgoer to adapt (somewhat, not totally) to the film

– to think on their toes (and many other kinds of texts produce this 'encounter', but never in this way). The post-film writing is a recording, a relaying of that encounter, that adaptation, that alliance. As Deleuze writes: 'What the philosopher brings back from the chaos are variations … reconnections through a zone of indistinction in a concept'.[18] The filmosopher enters the chaos, the multitude of meanings and images of film, and brings back variations – and to be able to grab the best variations they must hold the best concepts available. Filmosophy regards a film's direct meanings (its forms of thinking) as the well-spring of its larger possible meanings. *What we feel on initial encounter becomes the path of suitable interpretation.* A game of cat and mouse, we chase film with words, with (hopefully) poetry.[19] The force of great writing comes from a *fully involved* initial experience, and the recognition of the effect the film has had on us – the interrogation of that after-effect: the feelings we had in the cinema, and the change (if any) in our body and thought as a result. What, for example, is your immediate desire as you leave? Your truth of the film starts in the affective meaning of that third (mixed) thought, and is finalised in the recognition of any change in yourself after you have left the film.

The concept of film-thinking, and the humanistic rhetoric that accompanies it, makes it easier to reveal and write about the initial encounter with film (our immediate response). Perhaps filmosophy can help reassess those 'difficult great films' that film critics applaud but do not seem to like or enjoy – did you feel its greatness, or work it out afterwards? Some films may seem to be interesting and impressive, but they may not have engaged us – we may not have moved our thinking towards the film. Millions may not go to see a Godard film, but, as he himself says, 'if they do go, they'll give 80% of themselves to the film. If you go and see *Titanic*, you'll only give 10% of your personality. Good films get smaller audiences, but more of the viewer.'[20] Feeling a film, feeling along with its (thoughtful) feeling of its subjects, is almost to be envious of its thinkings; as Lyotard wrote: 'The feeling is the immediate welcoming of what is given.'[21] The filmgoer intuitively welcomes the affective meaning of the film.[22]

Filmosophical interpretation

After bonding form to thoughtful intention via the concept of film-thinking, filmosophy encourages an opinionated and personal form of film interpretation. These filmosophies attempt to express the feelings felt during the film; working towards a humane, but not naïve response to the film – a humanist thoughtful poetics – less spiritual than interpersonal, preferring the emotional to the technological (but still contingent on the filmgoer's personal history and social context,[23] and integral with other filmgoers' responses). To interpret is to advance on the meanings we *felt*, to new, more considered meanings. But these do not necessarily relate to any 'deep' or 'shallow' meanings, nor line-up with any subject and subtext. The interpretation must simply be *fed* by that experience. Pleasurable, kinetic adventure films are ripe for this kind of personal recounting, as they often deny overly plot-led interpretations. And also with bad films about serious subjects – if the film only provides information and not emotional engagement then a personal recounting will reveal this lack. Filmosophy does not defer meaning (like formalism), but provides an integration of form and (possibilities of) meaning – the writer, in relaying the affective meanings felt, should offer an 'opinion' of the film's meaning. Writing about a film is also a writing about our desires and interests, and each filmgoer offers their feeling of what the thinking meant to them – not to say the film is always thinking 'this', but thinking 'this' *with me*. Our filmosophical interpretation is only our opinion of what the filmind's thoughts mean at any particular point. The filmgoer produces their own truth of the film (eliding objectivity), and our 'opinion' becomes just our *natural* immediate interpretation of the film.

The *arrangement* of words in filmosophical writing is very important. In order to trace, to chase the ineffable, the text has to move, has to strain and reach. Performative devices help to reveal the writer's experience; think of Lawrence Sterne's blank page in *Tristram Shandy*, or the askew typography in Samuel Richardson's *Clarissa*, attempting to reveal a mental state through text. Look at the typographical strategies of magazines like *Raygun*. Look at Gaston Bachelard's loose writing, a flow that weaves discourses together, yet still with rigour and meaning. Look at Mark Danielewski's *House of Leaves*, wherein the text becomes hard to follow (curving round the page in on itself) as the protagonist enters a mystery that he is finding hard to follow. Filmosophy's performative translation of film-thinking should be poetic, fluid, theatrical, using metaphors that transform the reality of appearances. All this can be embellished with opinion, but opinions that are clearly signalled and couched in philosophical openness. Heidegger's poetic language, Kierkegaard's textual voices, Nietzsche's stylistic perspectivalism, Wittgenstein's ordinary language and Derrida's notion of philosophical writing, all lead us to see that film writing, to become filmosophical, needs to recognise its own rhetoric and embrace a performative nature if it is to get as near as possible to the very experience of the moving image.[24] Filmosophy attempts to organically unite 'form and content' in the filmgoer's thought, and the argument concerning film writing is parallel: the form of your writing is also its content. To write with a perception for the sound and look of the words is to allow the sentences and paragraphs to carry more than the literal, and to allow the ideas to be more forcefully released. A rhyming maxim does grow in the mind more than one without style. The 'text' of modern publishing has stagnated and needs some sort of artificial resuscitation – textual design, such as that in the Danielewski book, is few and far between.

For the words to grow in the reader they must remain loose in meaning, context-dependent and pragmatic (each film has differing thoughts). Film-thinking encourages humanistic terms, and added to indirect, performative discourse, the film will hopefully be re-lit and revealed. *But essentially, all is towards making information and knowledge more suitable to understanding – making experience more communicable.* Each film has so many thinkings, and demands more and more practical ways to disseminate the experience of these thinkings, and filmosophers must amplify their words to respond truthfully to a film that has moved them. The concepts and attentions of filmosophy are not intended to provide complete interpretations, but can be used as a first step, a route to larger interpretations. Filmosophical interpretations simply work towards making the experience of film fuller. In order to allow 'difficult' films to be seen afresh, and to expand on why certain films move us, and make us feel certain ways, the content of the description must *open* rather than close the film. These interpretations should *return* the reader to the film's actions, should defer to them in the writing, and make the reader want to revisit the film.[25] As attempts to relay the ineffable, these writings must always bow to the film's power. Thus, when writing about a film, the idea is to point back to the film to let its whole voice be heard[26] – to always defer to the film, pragmatically, indicating that the reader's encounter *will give its own* mix of thinkings. This also relates to the personal nature of filmosophical writing, on the one hand with regard to the recounting of a personal experience, and on the other setting out this experience as one among many.

Everything in a film may well be interpretable, but not every formal moment has meaning, and arbitrariness is always possible. But a film is always thinking, because no matter how arbitrary the filmmaker's intentions may be, the filmgoer still perceives a relation of film to subject, a style of presenting that leads us somewhere in our thinking (I felt I was seeing the character *like this*). It will always be impossible to theorise the meaning of particular films, but filmosophy is concerned with how film *creates* meaning through form (not what those meanings definitely are). This results in writing that does not smother a film, but allows space for film to breathe, to allow gaps and surprises. Interpretation, in the form of meaning-locating (and creation) is only a *possible* follow-up to the encounter with film – 'meaning' is not paramount, it is not the result of every encounter, but only a possible by-product. Filmosophical writing 'continues' the film by reveling in its thinkings and 'opening' the film for others. Never to fix meaning (as if you could), but to *reveal the ingredients* that made the meaning you might have felt (to reveal the colourings and sounds that made you understand the film in a certain way). These are writings that should not deconstruct or rip open a film's innards, but attempt to reflect the film in power and passion and feeling – listening to a film's thinking, and *pointing* to the power that it has. The attempt should be to continue the film in words, to prolong its experience for the reader through a resonating excursion of writing. Here the rhetoric of this writing becomes so important, in that it must communicate the feeling without closing the experience: it must resound and illuminate when the reader becomes a filmgoer to the film it refers to, the writing growing and thickening as it comes back into contact with the film it bows to.

Filmosophical interpretation – the opinion within the open writing – concentrates on the affective thinking of the film. Take an image of a hand. Filmosophy is obviously less concerned with any gestural or symbolic meaning of the hand in that situation, than how the hand is shown: from which angle, between what images, for how long, in what shade of dark or light or colour, etc. Thus opinion about that thinking revolves around whether the thinking matched the tone of the situation, or how inventive, or how subtle or flagrant the thinking was. Assessing or valuing a film may become a question of integrity: how suitable was the thinking within its forms, how much affective thinking was being created? Was the thinking soft or crude, meditative or calculative? Did it come through the film, or stop it dead in its tracks just in order to flash some wild, ironic thinking? For example, Aleksandr Sokurov's *The Second Circle* brings its thinking towards its ostensible subject, the film feeling death and sadness *through* image: a young man prepares his father's body for a funeral, and at points the film cannot focus beyond the close-up, revealing, feeling the tired mourning of the son. The same director's *Moloch*, about Hitler and Eva Braun, feels its subjects through a dead greyness, a sick coldness.

Beyond these writings, critical filmosophy would be a gradual and conversational process. Filmosophy merely announces the possibilities of film-thought and through collective comparison filmosophers announce their most interesting and coherent interpretations. Filmosophies can be supplemented with whatever interpretive strategies a writer wishes to bring to the film. The film writer can use filmosophical concepts of meaning creation and add a psychoanalytical reading, or relate the film to its context or environment, or propose how the film creates a space for ideological critiques (complete with analyses of actions, plots, sets, motives, and so on). The questions resolve again into whether certain films are interesting, good, beautiful, intelligent… Good and bad, admissible and inadmissible interpretations, are simply judged by any community of filmgoers. The (wider) truth of a film is just the one that we find most interesting or invigorating within this community.

But steering filmosophical writings is the thought of the resultant action on the reader. The concept of the filmind, with its feelings and thinkings, is there to leak a rhetoric that gives us more powerful poetic eyes. Writings are there to help the reader (the next filmgoer) see film as thinking not technique. The point of these filmosophies, the point of performative writing, is to *impact* on the reader, to make him or her feel the effect the film had on the writer. Each filmosophy adds to the reader's mode of attention, providing words through which they then experience future films. In writing about a film our descriptions of its thinkings must be *useful* for the reader – they must communicate the impact we felt, record our experience of the film so as to transform it for others – to renew the experience for those others, to *rejuvenate* the film for the reader. Interpreting film via filmosophy creates a new relationship between film and filmgoer for the reader.[27] The reader will then see the film *with* the original filmgoer's writing, and, if the reader *feels* that the film has changed the writer, then they will view that film in the tone of that writing. The filmosopher's writing communicates concepts that create a new mode of attention. The filmosopher's writing becomes an event, an encounter with film – something that changes the reader, and thus changes the film.

ten | **filmosophy**

We involve movies in us. They become further fragments of what happens to me,
further cards in the shuffle of my memory, with no telling what place in the future.
Like childhood memories whose treasure no one else appreciates, whose content
is nothing compared with their unspeakable importance for me.

– Stanley Cavell (1979)[1]

In the last century it might be said that philosophy became filmic and film became
philosophical – this chapter aims to look into this meeting of image and writing.
Filmosophy is the study of film as thinking, and thus extends into the study of 'philosophical' film-thinking, as well as the philosophy of the filmind and film-thinking.
Part of the argument of this book has been that in order to philosophise the thought
of film, one must first adequately, practically, work through the thinking of film – to
spell-out how film actually might be said to be 'thinking'. It is too easy to just use
'film-thinking' as a premise, and not really show or explain exactly *how* film is thinking. Practically working through examples of film-thought means that when we
come to the point of making assertions about the philosophical possibilities of film
we can understand the event of filmosophy in a much clearer way. Having traced
film-thinking through film forms, examples of film-philosophy (filmosophical films)
can be rooted in and expanded through these identifiable forms and actions. As
a setting to this imagistic philosophy we can look at the way that philosophy, as a
written enterprise, has been gradually attempting to escape its own literal confines,
and has steered itself towards the 'imaging' of its problems. So, in this chapter, my
argument is that we can trace a line from the reflexive, poetic writing of such philosophers as Nietzsche and Derrida, through the meditative thinking of Heidegger,
and the image of thought in Deleuze and others, to arrive at the postmetaphysical
thinking of film. That is, at the 'end' of philosophy lies film.

What I am suggesting here is that film offers *another future* for philosophy. Filmosophy is not better than philosophy, but another kind of philosophy – an intuitive,

affective philosophical event. At the end of philosophy, beyond (or rather *outside* of) philosophy's capability, filmosophy is simply one separate route for philosophy. There is much new work being done on the impact of Deleuze's thought-cinema for philosophy, and I need to emphasise again that this book is primarily concerned with spelling out the impact of film-thinking for film studies and filmgoers. Much commentary on Deleuze's *Cinema* does not seem to enhance or illuminate the *experience* of cinema as much as it could. Some are simply studying Deleuze's work on film *for* the conceptual and philosophical advancement of Deleuzian studies, rather than for the advancement of our filmgoing experience. This final chapter may be concerned with the more philosophical side of our story, but I still want to keep the fruits of this philosophical enquiry tied to *filmgoing*. For example, what are the practical ways in which we might use this philosophical side to film to make films that work through ideas and problems? And, how does this theorising about philosophical images help us understand contemporary cinema?

Thought and metaphor

A quick look first at different types of our thinking. Experience-thought, language-thought and conceptual-thought are not set in a hierarchy; they are just differing types of thought, our minds being a complex of free and tightening thought forces. Firstly our naïve child-thought becomes gradually categorised and linguistified, resulting in mature, abstract conceptual-thought. 'Conceptual-thought' is theoretical and comprehensive, and creates order from chaos. Philosophy is generally developed through the application of this human conceptual-thought. 'Language-thought' is the most useful and most used. Language enables (and steers) conceptual-thought, providing the vocabulary for thinking. Language helps us discover things, steering and controlling our perceptions. 'Intuitive experience-thought' is the basis of all human thought, but is not confined to a time 'before' conceptual thought, but works all the time, if mainly in an inhibited role. Perception is judgement and not merely sensation, and this primal-like raw thinking continues in and around conceptual and linguistic thought (just as Deleuze's movement-images occur around and between time-images). Importantly for our discussion, this intuitive thinking is image-based.

For Aristotle, Descartes and Locke mental images are picture-like in the way they represent objects in (from) the world. They copy or resemble what we normally see. But philosophers of the mind have queried the make-up of mental images. How can they be pictorial if we do not 'see' them? How can they be pictorial if they are so often (some would say always) indeterminate? Perhaps they are not pictorial, but we experience them in a similar way to seeing. We might say that mental imagery is the video recorder of our eye-cam, and almost as replayable – try simply picturing something that happened to you yesterday: how clear is that mental movie? But, significantly, there is a knowledge that resides in our mental images of things, a kind of resonance, or reverberation – the communication of the image which bypasses knowledge. Images also fuel the imagination (imaginary from *imaginaire*: no existence), and for Marcel L'Herbier, the experimental filmmaker and theorist, writing in 1919, the image, 'is no more than the epiphany of an imagination'.[2] Sometimes viewed as the source of all knowledge, and as essential for the intuitive production of truth, imagination is above all a poetic reconnection with the world (scans of the brain even reveal that remarkably similar parts are involved when seeing and when imagining[3]). And it is imagination's free play – and the ability to imagine *almost* anything – that provides a certain kind of conceptual advancement, a testing out of ideas through images. The route from imagination to poetry to knowledge is never direct, but usually powerful. We can thus see that images are *part* of our knowledge. We see in the same way, but entertain differing visions (perception being the extracting of meaning from an image). We are aesthetic beings (not just when contemplating art), and aesthetic experience is a *valid mode of knowledge*. And any theory of thinking needs to take into account this continual aesthetic attention of ours.

Thus, as we come to discuss the *writing* of philosophy, we can start to see that images might be able to play an important role. The route to this realisation can be seen in the straining of philosophical rhetoric to contain ideas, and the rejection of philosophy for 'thinking'. For Martin Heidegger 'thinking' is less about argumentation than poetry and meditation, while it was Wittgenstein who initiated the problem of the 'end of philosophy', and questioned whether it is an event that does in fact end philosophy or an event within philosophy that thus serves to continue it (filmosophy operates in the gap between these two possibilities). As philosophy nears this 'end', it is exactly this loosened thinking and metaphorical rhetoric that pragmatically stages posts of thought, each marking a different direction that can be taken.

Following on from the world of Arthur Schopenhauer, Friedrich Nietzsche collapsed reality and representation into *will*, and studied the relationship between concepts and reality (the combination that usually provides 'truth'): that there may be no leaf that matches the theoretical template, the concept, 'leaf'. Thus concepts work like metaphors, and change our experience of the world. Philosophical writing uses metaphors both in persuasion and concept creation, and analytical philosophers would say that continental philosophy is full of and thus weakened by its fancy metaphoricity, and itself favours 'directness' over indirectness, while hiding its own rhetorical leaps. Metaphorical language can be used overtly: self-consciously, and perhaps ironically; and covertly: unconsciously, but subtly there. The structure of metaphor is relevant to this discussion only in helping us to understand the philosophical use of metaphor. Metaphoricity exists where there is a lack of fit between two or more related terms, for example 'John is a tiger'. Metaphors cannot have one meaning, for that would be contradictory to their definition. We cannot then speak of any exact referent for a metaphorical expression, but perhaps only of the area it attends to – in this case the animal qualities of a man. A metaphor can mean this, or it can mean that, but it *does* mean. Metaphors work, in fact, to open up meanings; they are there to be *completed* by the reader. In their book, *Metaphors We Live By*, George Lakoff and Mark Johnson claim that most of our conceptual thinking is metaphorically structured, that concepts derive metaphorically from each other. Though they argue that these metaphorical conceptual systems are grounded in the literal, they find that, because we use metaphors to understand the world and ideas, truth, in being based on understanding, is therefore dependent on metaphor – thus metaphors can be both meaningful and true.

But *should* philosophy be attempting to address our hearts and emotions – to make us feel the argument? Is poetic language appropriate for setting out what is on one's mind, if a writer cannot control the meaning of poetical utterances? Should philosophy not strive for clear, transparent language that does not get in the way of the ideas that are being communicated, rather than being annoyingly indeterminate? *Why should we aim to be indirect, roundabout, imprecise, vague, ambiguous, and thus indefinite in our results?* Where we can begin is in asking just how figural descriptions are problematical within philosophical writing. Does their indeterminacy halt the flow of understanding, resulting in lost 'efficiency'? As Lakoff and Johnson have written, metaphor clearly indicates a myth of philosophical objectivism 'which fails to account for the way we understand our experience, our thoughts and our language'.[4] We can see how metaphors are used to *crystallise* abstract topics, and thus help us visualise the particular argument, because, after all, indirectly is how our understanding is normally changed. Metaphors clarify, they are less obstacles to thought than magnifying glasses. *Complex concepts and theories are usually only finally emancipated by metaphorical encapsulation.*

We might now ask whether rationality and metaphoricity *are* incompatible? Tropes can please the senses, but can they be relied on to instruct? How metaphor works in philosophical writing can be answered in a positive way. Metaphors enliven a work, making it vital and graphic. A good metaphor is a Pandora's box, overflowing with suggestive interpretations (hopefully like this one), that lead you elsewhere to a parallel case that the writer obviously feels will be informative. Some analogies may even turn out to be profitably re-usable (such as Locke's 'blank slate' for the mind before it has anything inscribed upon it). Richard Rorty has argued that metaphors should be viewed as 'a third source of beliefs' because, even though they may seem to be 'a voice from outside logical space', they are really 'a call to change one's language and one's life'.[5] The relation between philosophy and metaphor can thus be viewed as almost dialectical, in being able to play off each other to create tension, leading to *new* thought. Furthermore, if philosophy is about belief and convictions that are to be communicated then metaphors are important to philosophical writing in order to give force and life to that act of communication.[6] We could then extrapolate that for philosophical writing to work it must adequately persuade, and not just lie there, whispering to be taken up and practiced. As images and analogies, metaphors seem to create an immediate connection with the reader, and within philosophical writing they further work to invite appraisal, in pushing different lines of enquiry for us to actively realise and construct.

Nietzsche and Derrida

In a lecture from the 1870s called 'The Relation of the Rhetorical to Language' Nietzsche outlines some definitions of rhetoric, responding to the misconception of it as being *not natural*. While admitting that it 'appeals chiefly to the ear, in order to bribe it', Nietzsche points out that: 'There is obviously no unrhetorical "natural-ness" of language to which one could appeal; language itself is the result of pure-ly rhetorical arts [and] is based just as little as rhetoric is upon that which is true, upon the essence of things'.[7] Nietzsche argues that all words are tropes, that all lan-guage is figurative, and that the relationship between word and object is indirect and metaphorical. Therefore truth, for Nietzsche, is merely an illusion, or, 'a mobile army of metaphors, metonyms, anthropomorphism, in short, a sum of human rela-tions which were poetically and rhetorically heightened, transferred and adorned, and after long use seem solid, canonical and binding to a nation'.[8] Nietzsche is a philosopher within philosophy. He criticises other philosophers for preferring a 'handful of "certainty" to a whole cartful of beautiful possibilities', philosophers who 'lie down and die on a sure nothing rather than on an uncertain something'.[9] How Nietzsche conceives of philosophical enquiry can be ascertained from his interpre-tation and deconstruction of the traditional claims of philosophy – by showing that they rest on *purely rhetorical foundations*. Nietzsche argues that a full and essential knowledge of the world cannot be had because there is the screen of language inbe-tween, and thus that there can be no adequate expression of 'reality'; and even the demand for a common adequate mode of expression seems senseless. This disman-tling of metaphysical language secures the next step in Nietzsche's transvaluation of values.

In his essay 'On Truth and Lying in an Extra-moral Sense' from 1873 Nietzsche continues to view the relationship between word and object (and thus philosophy and its concepts) as indirect and metaphorical: 'The arrogance associated with knowledge and sensation lays a blinding fog over man's eyes and senses and deceives him about the value of existence by instilling in him a most flattering estimation of this faculty of knowledge.'[10] Something like 'truth' is not something out there to be *discovered* or found, 'but something that must be created ... as a *processus in infinitum*, an active determining – not a becoming-conscious of something that is in itself firm and determined'.[11] Nietzsche does not aim to indicate a way out of language, only that alongside the development of consciousness should go the parallel *transformation* of language. And though Nietzsche does not seem to allow for the presence of both the rational (which he calls a dignified mask) and the intuitive in one person, a linking in some way of linguistic rigour and interpretive pluralism can be the only possible way to come to terms, *understandably*, with Nietzsche's work.

The purpose of language in his eyes is not to pass on abstract truths but rather to communicate an individual's emotions and judgements. Nietzsche points out that we really do not know what we thought we knew because language (for him an act of abbreviation) 'gets in the way'. Richard Rorty finds this line of thought in tune with the view that philosophical language is not some pure reasoning, but is created by a history of thinkers. He finds that writers of this ilk

> permit us to feel the force of their metaphors in the days before these had been leveled down into literal truths, before these uses of words were changed into familiar meanings of words ... not to reweave our fabric of belief and desires but only to remind us of [philosophy's] historical contingency.[12]

Can we 'save' these schemes from their rhetorically infused conception? In the etymology of such abstract words as 'force' (from the Latin *fortis*, strong), or 'matter' (*materia*, timber), one will find the dredges of metaphorical mythology, leading us to realise that there may be no 'pure thought'. (It is perhaps the very metaphorical nature of language that makes metaphysics possible.) It seems that not in writing, nor even in thought, can we overcome the metaphorical origin of all philosophical inquiry, and that the ideas of philosophy can be viewed as a *history of metaphor*, where we come up against the limits of our knowledge.

For example, in Wittgenstein's *Philosophical Investigations* there are many voices: ironical, comical, stern, but always moved in together, shoving and pushing to get themselves to the front of our attention. Wittgenstein writes, as he himself has said in *Culture and Value*, as near to a kind of poetic form as possible, to make it clear that he is not teaching a 'method' to be taken up solidly.[13] Logico-literal language does not stretch far enough for Wittgenstein's purposes, which is to make us *think* in a different, wider way. Wittgenstein realises that there can be no direct link between philosophy and the audience's beliefs, and this recognition is shown in his attempt to *indicate* rather than state 'truth'. Philosophical writing can use metaphorical expression in a *new* way, can 'image' problems, thus furthering the expansiveness of meanings, requiring us to use *our* thinking to a far greater extent. Writing in the narrow sense is that of linear inscription on paper, but writing in Jacques Derrida's post-deconstructive sense is already *in* the conventions of social structure, is present *before* the appearance of inscription, meaning that speech already 'involves' writing. For Derrida, language is *becoming* writing, which has a completeness not found in 'language', in that it designates, 'not only the physical gestures of literal pictographic or ideographic inscription, but also the totality of what makes it possible'.[14] Writing is thus to be seen as a sort of 'inscribing'; not in any way a 'representation' but an origin.[15]

Derrida was sceptical about the values of 'truth', and argued that we should continue on the path begun by Nietzsche and put rhetorical and philological questions to the history of philosophy. In fact the history of metaphysics has made philosophical enquiry impossible: 'something of this presence of meaning, of this truth which nonetheless is the philosopher's great and only theme, is *lost* in writing', and hence, so as to stay within logocentric metaphysics, 'the philosopher writes against writing, writes in order to make good the loss of writing, and by this very gesture forgets and denies what *occurs* by his hand ... in order to erase and to forget that when he speaks the evil of the cipher is already there in germ'.[16] Here again Derrida asserts that the rhetorics of writing simply and inescapably 'occur'. Rorty sides with Derrida in many ways, yet feels he has, in fact, replaced philosophy's terms with his own, finding Derrida's use of terms such as 'trace' close to a constructive philosophy of language, to an onto-theology, in that it 'can be shown but not said, believed but not known, presupposed but not mentioned'.[17] While for Derrida all forms of philosophy and literature are effects of *écriture*, for Rorty they are kinds of *narrative*. This allows Rorty to hold the history of philosophy together, to *converse* with it using the same terms, and to 'de-thematise' those problems of philosophy which attempt 'to create unique, total, closed vocabularies'.[18]

Thus the rhetoric of philosophy moves closer to attempting to 'image' problems and thoughts through words.[19] For Richard Dienst theory is 'a highly mobile kind of cultural practice' understood as 'the invention of concepts, or more precisely, the invention of *theoretical images*'.[20] Writing needed to discover the image, such that in attempting to imitate the image the writing flowed with more movement. Just posing the question of how language might become more imagistic brings us to a whole new set of possibilities. Image becomes writing, 'in such a way as to reveal the origin of the idea and what has gone into its production', as Sigrid Weigel writes.[21] Walter Benjamin wrote of thinking-in-images (*Bilddenken*) – using images to think: for instance, that it is only as an image that the past can be apprehended. These images within thought, these thought-images (*Denkbilder*) in writing, attempt to reveal ideas more directly than before.

Heidegger

For Heidegger 'philosophy' is metaphysics or Western rationality. Thinking, rather, is not primarily concerned with definitions and arguments. If philosophy is teaching, then thinking is *learning* – a learning that elucidates structures of being. At various points Heidegger gives differing ultimate 'definitions' of thinking: that it is heart and memory, devotion and commemoration, thanking and paying heed, minding and divination. This is thinking that dwells closer to poetry and reflective feeling than reasoning or categorisation. But at its base, thinking casts a light onto things, transfigures things. Philosophy can call thinking to attend to things, but, for Heidegger, philosophers also need to attend to the *space* of thought itself. The task of thinking is thus the 'surrender of previous thinking to the determination of the matter for thinking',[22] in other words the recognition of current kinds of rational thinking, and the development of future kinds.

Humanity is capable of thinking, but rarely does. For Heidegger, current thinking is *thoughtless* – we are thinking less and less, mainly because the absorption of information and technology denies a place for thinking (thus my argument against technicist film terms). Thoughtlessness is an 'uncanny visitor': 'nowadays we take in everything in the quickest and cheapest way, only to forget it just as quickly, instantly … man today is in *flight from thinking*. This flight-from-thought is the ground of thoughtlessness.'[23] Thoughtlessness is also the failure to remember – memory is the gathering of thought, the reflection and meditation of thought. And we could say that the majority of popular film today has taken a similar flight from thinking, with a similar denial of its thoughtlessness, opining that their enquiry is full with possibilities, but is in fact weak in terms of reflection. Thoughtless film-thinking (not to be confused with film-thinking that brings out the unthought within thought) is slave to the drama perhaps, linking and moving only where the clear narrative demands.

Heidegger thus made the distinction between 'calculative' and 'meditative' thinking. Calculative thinking is a mode that merely *computes* possibilities economically; a thinking that 'never stops, never collects itself',[24] that takes in and then quickly forgets. This thinking is a normal, rational, somewhat scientific thinking that attempts to plan, research, organise and investigate. In filmosophical terms, calculative film-thinking would be crudely dialectical forms, or films that enact a single-track message delivery. It is filmmaking that bludgeons the filmgoer with its point-making, positioning them through tight expressionism, and film-thinkings that limit the amount of interpretations. But it is not by definition a negative kind of film-thinking – it can simply be more forthright in directing our attention to certain images and ideas, attempting to reason and argue through images and movements. The films of Oliver Stone and Paul Thomas Anderson might be examples here: think of *JFK*'s strategic image colourings, or *Magnolia*'s rushing movements and quickening shifts.

For Heidegger, part of the reason for the appearance of calculative modes of human thinking is technology. Technology is *closer* than reality, than beauty or nature or life, and we now often experience technology before reality (or reality via technology). This technology, this uncannyness, threatens the rootedness of man. Heidegger foresees a future in which, in every mode of his existence, man will be surrounded and suffocated by the forces of technology. We are thinking less and less because the absorption of information and technology denies a place for thinking. Now not only can this relate to the filmgoer's experience of the technology of film and media, but we can also see it in the use of technological imagery (special effects) in cinema. Films can often be overrun by special effects, leaving no room for thinking – they can be an easy and quick route to satisfaction.

So meditative thinking is needed to contemplate that which is close to us, that which is becoming bonded to us – this technology. Thus Heidegger's solution to the impact of technology is a mode of thinking that can calmly take it or leave it; a thinking that uses technology then lets it go. Meditative thinking lets in technology as much as it leaves it outside; Heidegger calls this a *'releasement towards things'*,[25] a calmness in the face of charging technology. And because technology hides its meaning from us, man also needs an *'openness to the mystery'*.[26] These two attitudes give man a vision of a new rootedness. Fluid film-thinking can be seen as such a usage, fluidly merging technology and life, adding one to the other rather than opposing them (think of the films of David Fincher, the Wachowski brothers, or even David Lynch and David Cronenberg). But meditative thinking does not just have a role in respect of technology, it is a thinking which 'contemplates the meaning which reigns in everything that is', and 'demands of us not to cling one-sidedly to a single idea'.[27] Meditative thinking is thus unassuming intuitive thinking that is a constant interplay of thought and argument, a slow and deep mode of attention that re-roots us. Just as Heidegger asserts as regards man, we might say that film's essential nature is meditative – it is only that crude filmmaking has revealed a calculative side, one which attempts to reduce film to story, to language, to technology. The concept of the filmind returns this meditative film-thinking to the heart of cinema, and allows us to contemplate the meaning that possibly reigns in every moment of film-thinking.

Heidegger's concept of meditative thinking recalls his earlier comments on re-flection: 'Reflection is the courage to make the truth of our own presuppositions and the realm of our own goals into the things that most deserve to be called into ques-tion.'[28] This looking around, circumspection, or pause can be found in the interpre-tive seeing of being (and so the interpretive film-thinking of the filmind). Meditative thinking becomes a poeticising of thought, an attempt to move thinking beyond language, towards a 'primordial poetry' – as all *poeticising* begins with thinking. For Heidegger, meditative, poetic thinking goes some way towards revealing the un-thought in thought: the unthought (as was first noted in the section on Deleuze in chapter four) is the not yet thought, the future of thought which brings the chaos of the 'outside' into rational thought. This reflective thinking considers a space, or clearing, where thoughts can be cared for and dwelt on, a space to ponder, allowing thinking to grow and ripen. Dialectical thinking, intuition, evidence – all are depen-dent on the availability of such a clearing, such a space for thought; a space for the (true) presencing of things to appear. The task of thinking (apprehending) is thus to attend to the clearing of Being (presence), and 'unconcealment' (truth) is 'the ele-ment in which Being and thinking and their belonging together exist'.[29] Meditative thinkers realise truth, unconceal truth, and so 'experience the untrembling heart of unconcealment'.[30] Where Heidegger leads us to is the realisation that formal film-thinking encounters truth without categories and language (these actually detract from the encounter). An inverse mirror of this relationship can be seen in the film-goer's experience of film via technicist rhetoric – categories and language reduce the film, marking it as a structural skeleton obscured by confusingly excessive flesh. When we start analytically examining the encounter too much, we have essentially transformed it and moved into the realm of the technical and the linguistic.

Heidegger saw truth as a kind of art – truth as the encounter with Being. In this sense film is not just about beauty and pleasure, it is not a thing we can only *give* value to – film can show us what 'things' are, can give us an image of things. Writing of Van Gogh's painting of a peasant's shoes, and how it gives us a sense of the func-tionality of shoes, Heidegger says: 'the equipmentality of equipment first genuinely arrives at its appearance through the work'.[31] The painting gives an image of equip-ment (the shoes transcending their matter) – the work reveals the nature of things. For Heidegger, art is invention, creation and projection which *illuminates* the ordi-nary, unconceals beings. Light, illumination, unconcealment. In Heideggerian terms then, films are bestowed with the gift of truth, which is addressed to the work's pre-servers, the filmgoers. The mix of film and filmgoer becomes a (somewhat Eisenstei-nian) leap forward. Film, in its meditative state, is thus the *happening* of truth. For the Heideggerian cinephile, film-thinking lets truth leap forth, and truth becomes a kind of film-thinking.

Yet thinking is not the summation of film, but its constituting means. A film can-not be without thinking; it has no distance from thinking. Film is a thinking. *Thinking is the ground of the world of film, and the ground of the life of filmosophy*. The filmind can thus be a calculating or meditating being, and many gradations inbetween. For Heidegger, art carries the subject off 'into uncommon, but often merely common, realms of the imagination, and gives the illusion of a world that is no world'.[32] Film can become this uncommon or unthought realm of the imagination, producing a world that is similar but significantly different to our own world. And it is medita-tive, sensible (sensitive) film-thinking – quiet, open, reflective film-thinking – that can reveal this unthought in thought. Meditative film-thinking enacts a fluidity of instinct that *dwells* on moments, actions, scenes, or other aspects of the film-world. The filmind and film-thinking unconceal the real world by re-thinking a film-world; film's being and thinking therefore exist in their togetherness. For Heidegger medi-tative human thought makes the far near and the familiar strange; film in its most meditative modes does the same, 'affectively'. The filmind thinks from and toward the *difference* that escapes attention because of its simplicity – that is, film can show the complexity of things through simple images. Beyond logic, meditative human thought is sensitive not just to the world, but to memory, and the fore-sensing of future possibilities. Meditative film-thinking is also active and open, and can relate any moment to a past or future moment by free-shifting through multiple spaces. We have reviewed the meditative film-thinkings of Michael Heneke, Béla Tarr and the Dardennes brothers, but the films of Abbas Kiarostami and Terrence Malick are also exemplary of this kind of film-thinking.

Thought-images

Thinking is also connected to 'seeing': perspective, interpretation, representation ('will to power' for Nietzsche). Film merges the two meanings of 'representation': it seems to be re-presenting something again (the real world), but can also be said to be creating something where there was nothing before (the film-world). We dwell in 'seeing', and an image is the presentation of 'seeing', a perspective or a generalisa-tion in which one may dwell. Meditative, poetic thinking thus produces images of thought. And there are many human thought-images: our present image (sent to the brain from our senses); memory and future (expected) images; mental (imaginative) images such as daydreaming; and ideational (graphical, map-like) images which balance our linguistic thinking. These make up our visual thinking, our visual knowledge. The significance of thought-images is their ability to coalesce ideas, merge concepts, unite the many. The unity of the multiple (assembled in the space of thinking) is given in thinking, in an image of thought – images that gather the various into a singular multiplicity.

For Deleuze there are always two kinds of knowledge: seeing and saying, light and language, the sensual and the intelligible. In the philosophy of Deleuze concepts are born as much from the *affects* and *percepts* that accompany images, as they are born from traditional knowledge. This third period, where he studied art and cinema, was just as much 'philosophy' as before – in a conversation published in 1988 he said: 'Percepts aren't perceptions, they're packets of sensations and relations that live on independently of whoever experiences them. Affects aren't feelings, they're becomings that spill over beyond whoever lives through them.'[33] These three powers – affect, percept and concept – are inseparable, and move from art to philosophy and back again. For Deleuze this throws up a new area of study: 'noology', the study of images of thought (the prolegomena to philosophy); 'The image of thought is what philosophy as it were presupposes; it precedes philosophy, not a nonphilosophical understanding this time but a prephilosophical understanding.'[34] The image of thought, having infinite movement (and an infinite collection of concepts), guides the creation of concepts: 'as it unfolds, branches out and mutates, [it] inspires a need to keep on creating new concepts, not through any external determinism but through a becoming that carries the problems themselves along with it.'[35] Descartes creates 'mind-body dualism' within a particular image of thought; Wittgenstein creates the concept of 'private language' within a particular image of thought. The image of thought is that original change in ideas, a creation of thought that fuses or coalesces into an image, a new aspect to thinking. The 'image of thought' comes before, as it were, actual rational argumentation.

But what relationship does this imagistic-thinking have to language? For Ricciotto Canudo, writing in 1923, cinema takes us 'back to the great, true, primordial, synthetic language, visual language, prior even to the confining literalness of sound. The moving image does not replace words, but rather becomes a new and powerful entity of its own.'[36] Filmosophy studies a thinking beyond and yet within language, just as in a similar way a filmgoer may be unable to describe a feeling after seeing something and have to drag their friends to see what they *mean*. And though Eisenstein ostensibly links film to *human* cognition and to language, he certainly understands film as having its own powerful emotional (formal) logic: 'The shot never becomes a letter but always remains an ambiguous hieroglyph.'[37] Eisenstein was seeking to show thought *beyond* language.[38] In *Looks and Frictions* Paul Willemen asserts that there is no escape from the verbal, that the communicative quality of film is derived necessarily from language, and that images contain and are structured by verbal signifiers. But, as argued in the previous chapter, though we may automatically translate parts of images into language (regard images through words), and importantly felt images into interpretations, that is not to say that images are composed by language, reducible to language, or completely indebted to language for all their possible meanings. Images may never escape language, and in films there is usually some sort of verbal presence in the visual, but leaving meaning only to language is not helpful, as affective meaning is there in abundance. Language can then be understood just one *route* for meaning.

Much analytical philosophy, rooted in rational linguistic construction, denies the possibility of conceptual advancement through images. Ian Jarvie, for example, criticises the idea that film can be a medium of 'discursive thought' from the reasoning that this idea entails a theory of film as language. Jarvie argues that for film to be a medium for this kind of thought 'some equivalent to negation' is needed, as well as 'some equivalent of the conditional or the subjunctive, without which positions cannot be entertained for the purposes of the argument only', adding for good measure that each of these requirements 'is doubtful of fulfilment'.[39] Apart from anything else, and as I hope to have shown, film's thinking should not be discussed as though it was in any way similar to linguistic thinking or discourse. Language too often supplants thought, and film (the thinking of the filmind) reveals this unthought within thought. As we have seen, for Heidegger, meditative, poetic thinking goes some way towards revealing the unthought in thought, but film immediately puts into relief our inability to think in such pure, visual ways, exposing the powerlessness of our thinking. As was noted at the end of chapter four, film is an event where thought is brought face to face with its own impossibility – the powerlessness of our thought in contrast with film-thought; the impossibility of our thinking film-thoughts – while at the same time film gives knowledge of the powers of thought that we do have. For a philosopher such as Spinoza the task of philosophy was just this: giving knowledge of *our* powers of thought, rather than providing knowledge of things.

Filmosophical concepts

So what kind of concepts are produced by film-thinking? How would philosophy term these concepts, this thinking? And what, later, is *filmosophical* thinking? Film-thinking is a movement of instinct that can glide effortlessly into (more active) intuition in more filmosophical films, but it is not intellectual thinking, as that presumes a feeding off the history of linguistic ideas. Most importantly this film-instinct, this action-thought, is a force of creation. *The film-thought rests in the filmgoer's mind – it soaks it with its mood, its attention, its movement.* Think again of that moment in *Casablanca* when the film almost touches Rick's hand, before revealing his face and recoiling, staggering back a little – initially thinking obsequiously or teasingly, then feeling surprise or perhaps respect. Think of the powerful 'forward' thinkings of *Magnolia* (where the film repeatedly pushes in on its characters and spaces), the film thinking (making us feel) both inquisitiveness and the hunger of the various characters to move forward with their lives – the film almost attempts to 'become' their search for a better future.

Primal, like a child's thought, messy and archaic almost, this emotional intelligence, is *general*, primitive, loose, indicative, in the realm of the sensorial, the empirical. This non-rational (Balázs) vision without perception (Perkins) that can picture emotions (Münsterberg) is evocative, fuzzy, intuitive and affective. Movement, for instance, can act like music, in that the movement itself may not relate to anything we may do in our lives, but it creates a feeling for the subjects or objects within the movement.[40] The *showing* of affective meaning in film also relates to a quality of 'allusion' – Yvette Biró finds that 'the true originality of allusion lies in the fact not only that it resuscitates memories, but also that the forces of emotion and will are not separated from it'.[41] Part of the power of film-thinking is its ability to *order* the sort of senses and experiences we find in memory and imagination. Biró also relates film to 'action' – both being a kind of pre-thought: 'the embodiment of invisible messages, intents, emotions and judgements'.[42]

What does film-thinking produce? What philosophical mode of thinking is film? What is the relation of film to reason, concept, logos, philosophy? For Emile Vuiller-moz, writing in 1918, cinema 'can effect audacious associations of ideas through the rapprochement of images', and recreates the world as if seen 'though a temperament'.[43] In 'Aesthetics, Obstacles, Integral *Cinégraphie*', written in 1926, Germaine Dulac traces the movement from filmed drama to the 'visual idea' and a 'cinema of suggestion'.[44] In a general sense film-thinking enacts a kind of non-rational, figural non-communication ('communication without communication', as Lyotard would put it), a pointing not saying. Film form conveys without solidly, linguistically communicating. As V. F. Perkins perceptively writes:

> films are unlikely to replace speech or writing as the medium for examining and conveying ideas. Moral, political, philosophical and other concepts can attain in words an (at least apparent) clarity and precision which no other medium can rival.

The movie's claim to significance lies in its embodiment of tensions, complexities and ambiguities. It has a built-in tendency to favour the communication of vision and experience as against programme.[45]

It is exactly these 'tensions, complexities and ambiguities' that mark film-thinking as a new kind of thought, and point to the possibility that a better understanding of certain philosophical areas comes from using images to 'non-communicate' (or, recalling Heidegger and Derrida's assert/deny stylistic, film heralds communication, and thus perhaps idea, concept, philosophy.) This thinking of the skin of reality builds evocation upon basic movements and durations.[46]

In 'Reflections on the Seventh Art', written in 1923, Canudo saw a future where 'films will reach us with the supreme clarity of ideas and visual emotions', being 'the synthesis of all the arts and the profound impulse underlying them ... a lucid and vast expression of our internal life'.[47] Antonin Artaud saw film-thought as playful rather than rational, whereby film attempts to reveal 'the actual functioning of thought ... in the absence of any control exercised by reason ... the disinterested play of thought'.[48] Yet Artaud's link with any possible, actual, prelinguistic human thought must remain sidelined – that ur-thinking is non-existent, while film-thinking plays out in front of us at each cinema house. Interrogating what film-thinking does is more important than empirical verification, and 'playfulness' is as good as any way to describe the 'ideas' that film thinks, and thus the collision and interplay of these ideas. Film-ideas are perhaps even more useful than analytic concepts – the emotional concepts of film (perhaps those concerning subjectivity, memory, and so on) seem to be more tuned to our living and being. In giving us aesthetic ideas film is creating a different kind of thinking in our minds, provoking us towards a less restrictive or literal mode of thought.

In his book, *Filming and Judgment*, Wilhelm S. Wurzer refers to filming as both a kind of cinematic thinking and a post-rational mode of *human* thinking (we film the world, we coat the world with a layer of our thinking). Filming (both cinematic and human) is post-rational perception/thinking -- aligned with imaginative and aesthetic free-play. Filming is a free and open way of apprehending something; a shining-though of non-essential being (*phainestai*); a letting go; a kind of thinking beyond simple representation; a disjunctive kind of judgement (*gelassenheit*). But in the end Wurzer is perhaps less interesting for his discussion of actual films (where he relies mainly on interpretations of story), than for his rethinking of what films might be doing (acting out judgements).

For Béla Balázs film can convey 'associations of ideas more completely than the verbal arts, because words are loaded with too many conceptual elements, while a picture is a purely non-rational image'.[49] That 'any' picture is 'non-rational' seems fine, but film-thinking greatly extends this arena, posing a question to rationality itself: *what can rationality prove that film cannot show a direct belief in?* Biró understands this, asserting that sensory thinking is not simply a diluted form of rational thinking; but, of course, on the other side of the coin, reason has its own hidden images, its own metaphoricity – the relation of reason to figure (Nietzsche) – as was mentioned earlier. But film-thinking reveals truly fluid content, and as such disrupts dialectics, lying beyond truth, and residing in open judgement, creating a specifically filmic kind of truth. Consider here Dziga Vertov's newsreel-documentaries, which were named *Cine-Pravda* (Cinema Truth), and which inspired the French *cinéma vérité* filmmakers.

For a writer such as Sigrid Weigel the image is 'dialectic at a standstill'[50] – inhabiting the gap between positions, *forcing* an understanding beyond dialectics. For Alan Spiegel film technique 'relates to a way of thinking and feeling – about time, space, being and relation – relates, in short, to a body of ideas about the world that has become part of the mental life of an entire epoch in our culture'.[51] Thus, beyond the attempts of figurative philosophical writing, film spies a land, a vista of uninhibited creation. And what this thinking creates is … beyond specific interpretation; is unsayable. But we can, tentatively, point at something like *archetypes*; Biró writes: 'This thinking stays alive only because in its images and mode of associations are dormant those "archetypal patterns" which contain basic answers and reactions of human consciousness.'[52] Again linking with primitive mental images, film-thinking *actively pursues* what we may or may not have been born with. This movement of non-rational thinking leads us to Jean-Luc Godard's pronouncement that films present loose ideas over right or just or true ideas. In considering Godard's theories of cinema, Deleuze says:

> the just ideas are always those that conform to accepted meanings or established precepts, they're always ideas that confirm something … While 'just ideas' is a becoming-present, a stammering of ideas, and can only be expressed in the form of questions that tend to confound any answers.[53]

Film-thinking reveres and contemplates the belief of its images – it holds, or stutters in the presence of what it images. In creating affective meaning this sensory thinking ('magical' in a way) bypasses logic and forms pure *image-ideas* (and associational shifts of ideas). Münsterberg concludes similarly (again, more anthropomorphically): film 'has the mobility of our ideas which are not controlled by the physical necessity of outer events but by the psychological laws for the association of ideas'.[54]

But, beyond (non-)ideas, can film-thinking be said to create anything in the way of 'concepts'? A concept is understood as an abstract idea that corresponds to some (distinct) entity, or to its essential features – and it would seem that film fulfils this definition, perhaps even more suitably than linguistic concepts. How can that be? In a 1929 essay titled 'Perspectives' Eisenstein considers, via Berkeley, the bruising of knowledge by the word-concept, and so begins to investigate the possibility of a 'pure idea'. He looks at 'form', and notes that in a Russian dictionary of foreign words form is *obraz*, 'image', which itself is a combination of the concepts of 'cut' and 'disclosure'. An image's content at once links to and isolates itself from its surroundings, and content is an organisation principle, and therefore the content of a work is this thoughtful organisation. Eisenstein then restages 'cognition', not as abstract passive contemplation, but as an act that has immediate effects. Thinking is productive construction, and the new art of film 'must restore to science its sensuality. To the intellectual process its fire and passion. It must plunge the abstract process of thought into the cauldron of practical activity.'[55] Eisenstein's answer is, as we have seen, 'intellectual cinema', bringing together logic and image in extreme cognition and sensuality 'that has mastered the entire arsenal of affective optical, acoustical and biomechanical stimulants'.[56] Concepts are traditionally part of reason and language, yet the term derives from the Latin *conceptum*: something conceived – from the *imagination*. Spiegel speaks of D. W. Griffith and Joseph Conrad and their striving for 'a union of image and concept, of visual fact and value'.[57] And it is the value of the fact, the leaning of the idea, the motive of the concept that has always been hidden in traditional concepts. Film unifies movement and idea, creating a purer concept, an action-concept.

The final movement of Deleuze's mental image is the extending of film's thought into the conceptual. Deleuze admires the films and programmes directed by Godard because they are loosened images: more image than representation. This in turn relates, as we have mentioned, to how the films present *loose ideas* over right and just and true ideas. Godard's films equalise language and image, confronting one with the other, undermining one through the (usually montaged) presence of the other. That an *idea* can be expressed through image or word or model is, for Deleuze, a kind of 'indiscernability' – or equivalence. On the relation between image and concept Deleuze is worth quoting at length. In an interview for *Hors-cadre* in 1986 he spoke of the intertwining of image and concept:

> The relation between cinema and philosophy is that between image and concept. But there's a relation to the image within the concept itself, and a relation to the concept within the image: cinema, for example, has always been trying to con-

struct an image of thought, of the mechanisms of thought. And this doesn't make it abstract, quite the reverse.[58]

Then on the final page of *Cinema* he writes:

A theory of cinema is not 'about' cinema, but about the concepts that cinema gives rise to and which are themselves related to other concepts corresponding to other practices … It is at the level of the interference of many practices that things happen, beings, images, concepts, all kinds of events. The theory of cinema does not bear on the cinema, but on the concepts of the cinema, which are no less practical, effective or existent than the cinema itself.[59]

And the final words of *Cinema* succinctly proposes the unique nature of film's concept creation:

Cinema's concepts are not given in cinema. And yet they are cinema's concepts, not theories about cinema. So there is always a time when we must no longer ask ourselves, 'What is cinema?' but 'What is philosophy?' Cinema itself is a new practice of images and signs, whose theory philosophy must produce as conceptual practice. For no technical determination, whether applied (psychoanalysis, linguistics) or reflexive, is sufficient to constitute the concepts of cinema itself.[60]

Deleuze's philosophy embraces a constructive pragmatism that develops in the shadow of film: 'Philosophy works with the concepts which cinema itself gives rise to.'[61] Philosophy's playdoh, the ideas and concepts that it manipulates, are there in animated form at the cinema – and Deleuze asks us to use cinema's concepts when advancing philosophy. Film-thinking asks us to realise that knowledge is better fuelled in this age by the use of the nonconcept; that linguistic concepts can possibly disfigure thought, and that film can be the help-line out of this dead-end. Film, as its own thought, its own energy, creates intuitive image-concepts (of time, of desire, of justice) – nonconceptual affects, fractured perspectives, that meet directly with our own minds.

Film, as nonphilosophy (not pre-philosophical, as Deleuze would argue), becomes the 'Eros' to philosophy's 'logos'. Film disrupts principles of reason and judgement, and so becomes a *truth* with its own will. The filmgoer feels the generalisations that film-thinking produces, feels the truth of and in the movement/action of film-thought. Thus film is a new metaphysic, a postmetaphysic, in that it can provide a direct thinking of such abstract concepts as being, knowing, substance, cause, identity, time, space. In its almost automatic consideration of things transcending reality, physics or nature, film cannot help but become metaphysical. In the opening images of *L'Humanité* the film-thought considers the space of detachment, the beauty of landscape, and the relation of man and earth – the film understands its objects and persons and relates them via its film-will. *L'Humanité believes* through images and sound, providing, leaking, film-concepts of purity and forgiveness.

Beyond our thinking film has its own speed and movement and attention of thinking. In the cinema our knowledge is detoured through images, even though it may have been expecting gains from more traditional linguistic routes – might we call this the imagistic brain bypass? Our knowledge may well be emancipated and energised by film in ways we never expect. The film-concept (the nonconcept, within a nonphilosophy: filmosophy) may provide a better understanding of certain philosophical areas. Can we now begin to philosophise with film rather than concepts? For Derrida there is thought in film that 'exceeds philosophical discourse and questions philosophy', which does not necessarily mean that a filmmaker 'has the means of questioning philosophy, but what she or he creates, becomes the bearer of something that cannot be mastered by philosophy'.[62] Derrida is closer to the shock to thought thesis of film-thinking, as he adds: 'The idea is to indicate in a polemical fashion that thinking is going on in the experience of the work, that is to say, that thought is incorporated in it – there is a provocation to think on the part of the work, and this provocation to think is irreducible.'[63] But it is also the capacity of cinema to provoke a feeling of understanding to a wide variety of cultures that accompanies its postmetaphysical suitability – Gerard Fort Buckle saw this in 1926: 'The film's greatest asset of all is its ability to appeal to men of all tongues, to convey the thoughts expressed by its creators without any loss or contortion consequent on translation to another tongue.'[64]

Filmosophical being

So what kind of being or mind is the filmind? It has assisted us in understanding the dramatic intention of film form, but what are its philosophical ramifications? Münsterberg sees a mind that leaves reality behind: 'this greater distance from the physical world brings it nearer to the mental world'.[65] Some tie film too closely with the mental and cling to the analogy – for Parker Tyler film embodies the way the mind works: 'The closest we can come to the world's *naked presence* through a medium…'[66] But the filmind is distant from both reality and the brain, being neither ontological nor anthropomorphic: it neither shows us how things 'really are', nor what or how we 'really think'. It is its own mind, a prelinguistic, affective world-mind, ready to think anything it wishes. Most importantly, its ability to conceive of anything in a flash means it is beyond our thought, beyond the capabilities of our minds.[67] Ideas of it resembling some previous or nascent form of human thought are less useful though; nor should we refer to is as some 'ultraconsciousness', or consciousness perfected – we have to create new terms for its thought (echoing the reason for coining 'filmind' itself). Just as early writers asked if film was art, and we gradually realised, with Perkins, that we should study film as film, so the filmind needs to be studied on its own playing field, with its own new rules for its own (other) kind of thinking. Walter Benjamin saw that the film camera 'introduces us to unconscious optics',[68] and the metaphors used to explain film-thinking are useful and sometimes powerful – the filmind as the grandfather and grandchild of consciousness.

As part of our description of this filmosophical being we must include its post-metaphysical nature. For Stanley Cavell, film presents us with the metaphysical, what is normally beyond our reach, because it satisfies 'the wish for the magical reproduction of the world by enabling us to view it unseen. What we wish to see in this way is *the world itself* – that is to say, everything.'[69] But film presents not our world unmediated, but its own world (especially with digitalisation, film no longer automatically reproduces an even recognisable world). Remarkably, film is an extension of seeing, of hearing, of thinking, and thus an extension of knowledge, *while existing at the skin of things*. This filmind that alters colours, or closes in on faces, or glides over fields of corn, or shifts from a burning match to a blazing Arabian sun, operates at the surface of things. Film is thus an event with no memory, context or history. Film displaces our world, and shows us another world. George Wilson suggests that the 'vision' of film is 'a metaphysically more accurate moving "picture" of the world'.[70] But in enacting this overcoming of physics, film becomes a new, 'other', *post*-metaphysics, with its own *new* principles of ground, telos and essence. With Lars von Trier's *Europa* we are treated to an experience of images that would normally be beyond our human perceptual capabilities: we experience the wide simultaneously with the close, the frozen with the active, and colour against monochrome.

Metaphysics hides being (hides human thought), and with this in mind we can see that there are no 'first-person' or 'third-person' films, just first-minded film. Film operates beyond the categories of objective and subjective thought, and in fact slides them together (into the 'filmind').[71] In *Fiction and the Camera Eye* Spiegel writes:

> The images produced by the motion picture camera *will only allow us to experience the object through a series of perspectives*; that the ontology of the image itself will never allow for an apprehension of the object as a whole. In this sense no other art is less equipped to present a godlike and omniscient view of human experience

than the cinema, and no other art form, therefore, represents a more accurate embodiment of a modernist and relativist metaphysics than cinematographic form.[72]

The filmind appeals to our own naïve physics: the spatial thinking we practiced as children. Film thus operates as if our cognitive, linguistic thought had never come. Our spatial reasoning – the primal thought of a pre-rational being – is called upon as the filmind reminds us of the *beginning* of our thought.

So how would philosophy term this filmosophical being, the filmind? How does our knowledge of the mind and consciousness help us understand the filmind? And vice versa. Being always conscious (always filming), it has no 'subconscious', and relates more to pre-reflective consciousness – *Befindlichkeit* (state-of-mind). Nor does film reveal an inner consciousness, but is perhaps its own nestled nonconsciousness, and even has more in common with ideas of collective consciousness, and less in common with the idealist Hegelian notion of the perfectibility of consciousness. These notes, more than anything, reveal the distance between film and human consciousness – as film is always between and betwixt our current references. Merleau-Ponty wrote that, 'if philosophy is in harmony with the cinema, if thought and technical effort are heading in the same direction, it is because the philosopher and the moviemaker share *a certain way of being, a certain view of the world* which belongs to a generation'.[73] At a basic level film shows us how we in fact produce our own 'realties'. Philosophy can learn from the intuitive thinking of film, and post-war European philosophy might now be seen as trying to become more filmic in its investigations – the fluidity of pragmatism and poetic writing leading this direction.

Film, beyond dialectics, without ever producing finality, presents a freeing of intention and the operation of open judgement – for instance, film can make us realise that time is not given, but created. Neither the re-presentation of reality nor the re-presentation of thought (vision, imagination, memory, dream) is strictly possible. The filmind is rather their mediation and conflagration (and thus perhaps the recognition that mind and reality are one). But it is how film orders and reasons through its images and sounds that reveals it as a kind of 'postmetaphysical thinking'. *A thinking that enacts reasoning without the language of metaphysics.* Cinematic filming becomes the model for a new kind of nonphilosophical investigation: a postmetaphysical postphenomenology. But film-thinking can be as kinetic and playful as it can be reasoning and questioning, and the future of this kind of study would extend into recognising and relating differing kinds of film-thinking, and thus differing levels of imagistic belief.

conclusion

We cannot make our eyes better than they have been made, but the movie camera we can perfect forever.

– Dziga Vertov (1923)[1]

We must be better connoisseurs of the film if we are not to be as much at the mercy of perhaps the greatest intellectual and spiritual influence of our age as to some blind and irresistible elemental force.

– Béla Balázs (1945)[2]

In the invention of cinema man found a short-cut to the control and conquest of re-ality (initially making it grey and soundless, as Maxim Gorky noted). In the invention of computer-generated images man created a whole new reality (as Jodie Foster noticed). Now original worlds can be created, or recordings of recognisable realities can be altered – even the expression on a baby's face.[3] In this conclusion I would like to briefly discuss the relationship between the new possibilities of cinema and the concept of film-thinking. To ask how filmosophy intersects with contemporary film practice, but also to discuss the impact of moving images on the filmgoer, and ask how film can change our perception of everyday life.

Germaine Dulac, berating the past arts for their attempted hold on cinema, ar-gued that what we should be doing, 'is to search, in what it offers us, for the expan-sion of our sensitive being in an *unexplored form'*.[4] The new possibilities of cinema can be seen in the following forms: digital animation (for example *Final Fantasy*); the new fluid image, mixing digital and recorded images (for example *Fight Club*); the evolving experimentation with traditional film form (for example *Julien Donkey-Boy*); the new gallery art film (for example *Disappearance at Sea*); and the subtle think-ing of poetic realism (for example *Secrets and Lies*). This technicist line is simply an excuse to look at some new forms – as has been emphasised over the course of this book; the interest lies not in the particular technical method, nor in exactly how a particular film mixes recorded and digital for example, *but in what kind of film-thinking these forms usher in*. Thus, in describing these films, the explication of effects and digital moments should be avoided – writing should simply refer to the thinking: the feelings and questions and motives of the forms. For example, for the writer of filmosophical reviews, *The Matrix* is on one plane of film-reality: there are no 'recorded' and 'digitally animated' parts, just one level of film-world.

Firstly, completely animated digital 'cinema', which is perhaps less interesting than fluid film-thinking (the recognisable altered) because its 'new world' is still very different to our own – here the filmgoer has an aesthetic connection over and above any natural connection. Traditional animation went digital with *Toy Story*, and has now taken the next step with *Final Fantasy: The Spirits Within*. This is digital animation that aims to have its 'actors' and settings look as real as possible. *Final Fantasy* apparently took 200 digital artists four years to make; a whole year was needed just to perfect the 60,000 hairs on the head of the heroine, Dr Aki Ross, the first photo-realistic 'synthespian' to lead a movie. Being completely animated means these films can do anything, be anywhere: such as the underneath angle of Aki standing on a liquid pool. To aid the realism, sometimes the image will be shaky and responsive, cheating the filmgoer into thinking there is a 'camera', and therefore a 'recorded' world. This attempt at photo-real graphics prefigures the next stage: animated films that really do look indistinguishable from recorded events. Cinema will then truly become its own new world – able to show anything, be anything, go anywhere, think anything – and animators will be the new gods of this world.

But the *mix* of traditional recorded cinema with digital effects announces a new kind of fluid film-thinking. As was discussed in chapter five, this new, malleable, animatable, fluid image enables filmmakers to alter the recorded reality of their fictions, and even to add completely animated 'real' scenes. With the image now entirely mappable by computer, any section of a recorded image can be changed or eliminated. In the new digital image everything is manipulable, everything is re-thinkable. Yet the ability of 'regular' cinema to inflect its images with digitally-created effects has been around for a while. An early usage was the invisible joining of sequence scenes – the film could travel up streets and through window panes and into houses with the ease of a truly free film-imagination.[5] This subtle use of digital effects to aid the aesthetics and narrative of the film is one of the most interesting aspects of the new fluid cinema. This is not so much a question of creating 'completely' new worlds, but of refreshing our image of (our way of *seeing*) the real world.[6] This mix (of photography and digital imagination) is the more interesting new world, the one that we can connect with, yet shows us new ways of seeing things, new thoughts of events and moments. *Contact* plays with this new fluid image, as does *Fight Club, A. I.: Artificial*

Intelligence and *The Matrix*. But filmosophy's interest is not in the technology, nor in delineating the amount of 'animation' in a film. Again, the interest is in recognising the new film-thinking that this revolution of the image creates. Cinema can now truly think anything. What could cinema think next? What should the cinema think next? With the appearance of these new images (photography plus computer-generated imagery) contemporary cinema is going through a change, a change almost as big in impact as its invention. *Contemporary technology has given us animatable film-worlds*. Vertov saw this coming. He knew that cinema was forever perfectible, that it could show us new things, that it would leave our eyes behind while simultaneously teasing them with what they could not (normally) see – thus showing the impower of perception/thought. This is why *Man with a Movie Camera* contains speeding images (from trains or airplanes), x-rays, time-lapse photography, and so on.

Fight Club is this new fluid cinema, this pure thought.[7] The new fluid cinema demands of us a great re-thinking of the cinematic image. *This new cinema extends and stretches and essentially confirms the transsubjective nature of cinema*. For a start, fluid film-thinking helps multiply the possible viewpoints available in cinema as it helps the film be anywhere: inside a trash bin in *Fight Club*, behind a bullet in *The Matrix* or travelling through a car's engine in *The Fast and the Furious*. But this new film perspective is not limited to digitally-altered cinema: *Dancer in the Dark* shows Selma from multiple angles, through multiple, repeating shifts.[8] The film searches for a way of seeing her, searches for a truth about her, with different angles of film-thinking. This becomes an almost never-ending attempt to *realise her three-dimensionally*. The film attempts to inhabit her world through multiple description, multiple framings, but Selma, as a character, as a person to be understood, seems to defy the film's questioning and descriptive thinkings.

Deleuze found that cinema resembled a higher, spiritual life: 'the domain of cold decision, of absolute determination (entêtement), of a choice of existence'.[9] Film's thinking, as we sit down in the cinema house, is set and immovable and thus untouchable, unchangeable – it is an unwavering intention. But what recent technologies show, and what the concept of film-thinking attempts to capture and serve, is cinema's ability to think anything – 'gigantic visions of mankind crushed by the Juggernaut of war and then blessed by the angel of peace may arise before our eyes with all their spiritual meaning', as Münsterberg noted.[10] This powerful filmind, which reveals itself in any form, is now able to re-think its characters and spaces, to mould and change its recognisable reality with pure intention.

But the fluid image does not automatically bring with it *interesting* thinking. Cinema is still finding its possibilities of thinking in original forms. In 1921 Epstein saw film poems of the future: '150 metres and 100 images like beads on a thread that

would approximate the thinking process.'[11] In 1982 Biró pronounced that 'the promise of film's intellectual potential is yet to be fulfilled.'[12] And since the 1990s a new
movement of 'gallery film' has appeared. A lot is simply recorded 'performance art',
and does not experiment with the images themselves, and much is ignorant of the
history of avant-garde, experimental, structuralist, materialist filmmaking (Stan Bra-
khage, Bruce Nauman, and so on). But some is rethinking cinema. The (intellectual,
attentive) context of the gallery persuades the filmgoer to complete the film, to use
their memory and thinking to fill in the blanks.[13] This is emphasised by the sometimes elliptical, fragmentary nature of the gallery film – films that use the 'punctums'
of traditional filmmaking, those moments in films we always remember: meetings,
departures, fights, births, deaths, dances, collapsing buildings…

The sculptors and filmmakers Jane and Louise Wilson create films that physically
describe space, tracing it with movements in screenings that collapse traveling shots
into the corners of exhibition rooms like kaleidoscopes. Their films (of disused facto-
ries and run-down spaces) 'become' the spaces they present, and feel the elements
that *reveal* an institution (like their1999 exploration of the Houses of Parliament).
Douglas Gordon's *24 Hour Psycho* slows Hitchcock's film down to take a whole day
to show, *revealing* the expressionism of the film; showing the *workings* of that style,
that thinking. Tacita Dean explores light and time in film – *Sound Mirrors* explores a
setting using time, time for the image (sea, groyne, horizon) to soak our mind, time
for the image to give all it has got. *Fernsehturm* offers a wide thin image (an historically 'cinematic' image) of a revolving restaurant, which travels into the sun and away
again, allowing silhouettes and colours to change and melt (colours which recall *So-
laris*; movement which recalls *2001: A Space Odyssey*). *Disappearance at Sea* 'becomes'
the bulb of a lighthouse: mesmeric and mechanical. The film offers a filmic anatomy
of a lighthouse, through a beam that glances off rocks: both the film and the light
beam stare into darkness, but can only glimpse the sea. The metaphysical is hinted at
(after the beam touches the film we are left with a ghost glare of light) while viewing
the beauty of the physical (a sunset).

Contemporary cinema has also provided some new thinking. *Gangster No.1* feels
the schizophrenia of the central character, *shattering the image itself* (where the classic metaphor is usually an actual broken mirror). *Magnolia* starts as it means to go
on: with an inquisitive thinking, pushing into its characters, rushing up to them, introducing them as parts of a whole. *Bringing Out the Dead* feels the boredom of the
ambulance crew, for whom time flits by with no action except … the passing of time,
revealing images of speeded-up movement through the streets. *The Limey* shifts
with loosened memory, feeling associations and glimpses, thinking a transcendent
position beyond past and present (a transcendent position that the father is look-

ing for, to discover what happened to his daughter). A similarly radical, yet different rethinking or re-inhabiting of memory can be found in *Memento*.

Julien Donkey-Boy is a radical and poetic film, with disturbed images and a haphazard narrative. As a way into it, the film might be said to be thinking its *own world* (Julien's world), searching for new ways to 'image' stories. In feeling Julien's schizophrenia, the film thinks an image of accentuated colours, juddering movements, hazy defocusings and multiplied refractions. Stuttering slowed film (of an ice skater, a road at night) reveals the images (blurs, fractures, colours) *between* images – those images lost in movement, and only found in pauses (and video pausing). We receive a discontinuity (jump cuts), and so come to feel Julien's fractured world-view. Even the joyous continuity of church cannot seep into the (visually) shattered home life. Sounds, especially poetic opera sounds, are cut short, broken, denied just as they are beginning to be felt (there is no room for love; love is always denied).

The film creates new images in its search for new ways to *show story*. At the beginning, the film alights on a face, then some bracken, then the background, then the face again, in an auto-attention, a jumping focusing of attention, glancing at this, seeing that for a second or less. This sensitised, destabilised image is a thinking of Julian's state, and comes moments before he kills a young boy. After which, the film locks itself to Julien, feeling his centrality to a shaking world. The film also expressively reveals and thinks the father's power and position, overlaying an image of his head while Julien ties his father's shoes. When the father hoses Julien's brother Chris, the film's heightened attention seems to catch each drop in the spray of water, and later, the closeness of the confession is thought *through* image, the film almost merging with the confessional booth. The film's elliptical shifts reveal the forced, lengthy repetition of the brother's exercises on the stairs. And, with the film's final dramatic conclusion, the film ends by showing Julien against the shocked whiteness of his bed sheets. *Julien Donkey-Boy* is a poetic story of images; an imaging of Julien's world – of surfaces, forms, ruptures (the film has a belief about Julien's world). The film attempts the interesting image, the beautiful image, the future image (alive with its surface, crackling with pixel-grains or ribbed with televisual lines), but importantly, this is an image-poetics *that relates to, and thinks about, the characters and situations*.

Some new cinema is also attempting to create an empathetic and humane kind of film-thinking (as we saw in the case of the Dardennes at the end of chapter seven). At its base, in the simple yet thoughtful capturing of recognisable life, film becomes a mirror to our own life. Significant is the easy relationship we have with film: it suits our thinking, and we comprehend it fairly quickly. It looks familiar (though different). As Richard Abel relates, for a writer such as Louis Delluc, cinema is 'a *photogenic* or *revelatory* medium of absorption and defamiliarisation'[14] – film can show us ordinary things in a new way, can make us look again at what we thought we understood, can make us see ordinary things anew. Film-thinking transforms the recognisable (in a small or large way), and this immediate transfiguration by film provokes the idea that our thinking can transform our world. For Walter Benjamin the photographic image, particularly slowed images, 'can bring out those aspects of the original that are unattainable to the naked eye ... can capture images which escape natural vision'.[15] Not just inhuman angles and close-ups, but (more interestingly) the subtle alteration of the normal, the revelation of everydayness. Benjamin saw that film offered an immediate significance, in comparison to something like painting, presenting 'an aspect of reality which is free of all equipment'.[16] A film such as *Secrets and Lies*, which shows little indication of the equipment of film (no special effects here), might therefore be said to 'mean' more closely, more suitably. Vertov's cine-eye almost implies that we might also begin to see reality with our own cinema-eye. Perhaps *L'Humanité*, with its deep and long 'looks' (a film that stares) at human action, might provoke meditative thinking about our experiences, might feed our own investigative looks.[17] The filmgoer might not just begin to understand their environment cinematically, but may begin to look for different 'information' in the world.

Much of the reason behind the restaging of the rhetoric of filmic description (shifts and flights and questionings) is to help along this transfiguring result. We then engage with film more fruitfully and suitably, and hopefully take away a better, closer understanding. The gift of our perceptual abilities deserves at least a non-technical language. These filmosophical terms may even *independently* work on our perception to relight our encounter with the world. Philosophically, film affects our way of understanding life, because it affects our ways of perceiving our lives. For Yvette Biró film is the miraculous of everyday things – film 'has tried to acquire everything that surrounds us: the bleak and the unadorned, the never-noticed superfluous, the ephemeral and the unworthy of observation ... [it] has taught us to be fascinated by everyday things'.[18] We *should* enjoy the visual experience for its own sake, but to appreciate film is to emancipate everyday understanding – *how* we understand film pools our understanding of life and being.

The re-thinking of the everyday through thoughtful image and sound is apparent in much cinema. *The Last September* thinks through a shrouded, shadow-edged image, encroaching on the characters, feeling the (inescapable) political violence creeping into their lives. *Ratcatcher* begins with the slowed twisting of a boy in a lace curtain, before being slapped back into reality by the boy's mother – the film undercutting the poetic with the realist. But then, once the boy has gone, the film rests on the untwisting curtain, reasserting the poetic (a stronger poetic, that needs the realistic to truly impact). In *Eyes Wide Shut*, when Alice recounts her story of imagined infidelity, the film questions Bill (head on), but only gives us Alice from the side. The film makes us feel that the significance and repercussions of the confession lies with Bill. The film *feels* the impact the story has for Bill. *At the Height of Summer* thinks passion indirectly (and perhaps more truthfully) – giving us warm olive skin against cool night blue, or the fading imprints of hot feet on the rust red wall above a bed. *The Low Down* scans bodies and touches, edges and glimpses, reactive to human movement – the film searching for knowledge about its two lovers. Other film moments resound: the time-spaces of *Limbo*, the grey decision-spaces of *The Insider*, the absorbing, ever-darkening thinking of *The House of Mirth*.

Secrets and Lies and Last Resort are two films that use and re-think our natural engagement with the 'real' to beautiful effect. *Secrets and Lies* reveals a simple, tender, respectful thinking. The film sits when the characters sit; the shifts link characters organically, linking their words about each other to images of each other; and the film allows characters moments of quiet reflection. We think we are simply seeing through the image, perceiving the characters directly, but the film is always *thinking with our perception*. After Cynthia hears from her new daughter, the film stands back, showing her from head to toe, giving her space, but also realising (thinking) the impact on her. When Cynthia and Hortense finally talk in the cafe, the film shows an understanding of their situation – allowing the image to soak us by not interrupting with shifts. *Last Resort* concerns a Russian woman and her son who arrive in the UK and are 'held' a small English seaside town while their application for asylum is processed. Their life is (thought) rough, through an image that is alive with grain. The film also knows when to shake and worry – and is most unsettled when she, our heroine, is unsettled. The film physically, thoughtfully, reacts to its characters' emotions (which resembles the close, empathetic thinking of *Rosetta*), and only seems to move when the woman does. The film concentrates on faces and immediate locale, and at only one or two important points shifts scale: when the woman is driven from the airport to the seaside town to be 'held', and when she and her son and her new friend 'escape'. Each time the imposing vista is introduced by the film, is allowed by the film to reduce the characters. The film also feels an openness for sound, allowing voices and interruptions to mount and fill (like the image). Sometimes the film image searches close to eyes, as if it were trying to catch an 'inside' to the characters – creating a humane and meditative film-thinking.

The most beautiful thinking arrives with naturally-filled images, fractured and busy without obscuring emotion or character: faces doubled in half-reflections through glass, eyes framed with fire or sea, bodies masked by fruit machines or bright lights. This loads the image with 'information' and makes us work to direct our attention (and feeds possible second viewings). The ending becomes a celluloid-Turner, with sea and blur and bodies and image-grain gliding and melting into a melancholic grey-blue. *Last Resort* (a film that opens and closes with its main characters facing us, but moving backwards) is open thinking, tender feeling, human-political image-thought – here surfaces are as important as depths, and (when the woman is seated on a bench under a streetlight on a harsh cold night) the tales of immigrants are perhaps given a single, beautiful thought-image: a small warm face that glows in the corner of a cold blue frame.

Filmosophy looks to all these forms – digital animation, fluid film-thinking, experimental forms, art films and empathetic realism – as film-thinkings that are ideally suited to *change* our perception of the world. Through movie fictions and television news we receive a construction of the world that in turn feeds and shapes our own interaction with it, and in order to cope with these media we need a knowledge of their form. The concept of film-thinking bonds form and content together, organically, meaningfully. Watching a film we may then see them as 'wholes' of thinking: the characters with the framing, the scene with the movement. The aim is to advance a new critical *mode of attention*, to see films as thinking is to credit them with power and creative intention. Filmosophy is guided by the aim of increasing this mode of attention as regards all moving images – whether cinema, television or even video games.[19] Moreover, filmosophy seeks to provide an ur-method that can grow as film progresses, can keep up with whatever film invents tomorrow. Once you understand the filmind you will not be flummoxed by its new moves, you might even anticipate the next one.

But the explosion of image-culture in the past two or three decades is simply an evolution (rather than a disease needing a cure). Our culture is not as oriented towards the written word as before. We have entered a new era of vision. We need to investigate these new image-worlds, these new worlds of representation. It has been coming: since the advance and handy miniaturisation of personal cameras we have been quietly replacing human memory with photographic media. And further advances in optical instruments begin to erode our faith in our own human perception. Questions grow: How does the multitude of images affect us? Have we lost sight of ourselves? Seeing film as 'another mind' also gives us clues to why cinema and television exert such a hold over society, and why governments feel the need to keep its power in check. Children need a suitable language to 'use' while experiencing images, to heighten their mode of attention. That the endless zooming-in of daytime soaps might be understood as a kind of false engagement; that the brightly coloured quiz and talk shows are forcing our eyes open in order to provide an immediate cheery feeling. For Deleuze television 'presentifies everything',[20] perhaps making us feel it to be a medium without past or future, that does not require us to remember it because of its denial of time – television only asks us to follow it for the time we have it switched on, so we forget it when it is off. But television does have a longer effect, and filmosophical terms might help us understand and control that effect.

George Wilson offers a note on life outside (and after) the cinema: 'the phenomena we witness often appear to us as puzzling, indeterminate, ambiguous and without a guiding structure', and thus one of the ideas within this arena of philosophy 'is to extend our perceptual powers in ways that cut through some of the limitations and unveil the perspectives that they hide'.[21] As Wilson recognises,

> it is still another possibility of film to invite its viewers to suspend and reappraise some of their automatic assumptions about how and where significance can be discerned in the workings of the world … and demonstrate the fragility of the categories that visual intelligence unhesitatingly imposes upon the views before our eyes.[22]

Film (especially empathetic film-thinking) can redraw those categories, can provide new categories – and conceiving film through an intending filmind can open these categories.

For early writers such as Epstein and Delluc cinema was an instrument of *revelation*, while for Canudo these 'light engravings … can prolong man's existence beyond the limits of space, time and death'.[23] But film must be careful not to become a 'translation' of philosophy; film that begins as an idea often ends up as just that, an illustrated idea (with no aesthetic growth, no ripples of meaning). Rather it must see, must seek, its own natural philosophicalness – that of revealing a new thinking, a new point of view about the world. For Wilson we need to interrogate this filmic 'point of view' in order to understand 'these reconstructed forms of being witness to the world'.[24] This book has emphasised the words of writers who witnessed the invention of cinema because their words now resound with the current re-invention of cinema forms. Filmosophy is a product of our current age of plastic malleable cinema. It is also a product of our age of knowledge about cinema conventions: an unlearning, a more 'suitable', more cinematic reconceptualisation. Seeing film as 'thinking' ties content, form and filmgoer together, such that the filmgoer perceives an organic whole of the film thinking about its characters and events through dramatic forms, rather than layers of story and style. Filmosophy thus offers a practice, a skill to *do* something; a strategy for being philosophical about film and seeing the philosophical in film. The filmosopher is the person of tomorrow and the days after tomorrow. The filmosopher engages in a thinking of and for the future (where film 'tells' us new things). In filmosophy film is the beginning *and the future* of our thought. We thought that we needed to calculate our beliefs about the world, but the end of philosophy, with its metaphorical pictures of that belief, might lead us to realise that we can understand the world in like manner – that we can 'film' our beliefs.

notes

introduction

1   Maxim Gorky (1996) 'Nizhegorodski Listok', in C. Harding and S. Popple (eds) *In the Kingdom of Shadows: A Companion to Early Cinema*. London: Cygnus Arts Press, p. 5

2   Yhcam (1988 [1912]) 'Cinematography', in Richard Abel (ed.) *French Film Theory and Criticism: A History/Anthology, 1907–1939, Volume I: 1907–1929*. Princeton, NJ: Princeton University Press, p. 69. Yhcam was pseudonym, and the writer's real identity is still not established.

3   Emile Vuillermoz (1988c [1918b]) 'Before the Screen: Hermes and Silence', in Abel, *French Film Theory and Criticism, Volume 1*, p. 158.

4   Vsevolod I. Pudovkin (1960) *Film Technique and Film Acting*. New York: Grove, p. 86.

5   Walter Benjamin (1999) 'The Work of Art in the Age of Mechanical Reproduction', trans. Harry Zohn, in *Illuminations*. London: Pimlico, p. 230.

6   Stanley Cavell (1979) *The World Viewed: Reflections on the Ontology of Film*, enlarged edition. Cambridge, MA: Harvard University Press, p. 105.

7   Stanley Cavell (1983) 'The Thought of Movies', in Cynthia A. Freeland and Thomas E. Wartenberg (eds) (1995) *Philosophy and Film*. New York: Routledge, p. 21

8   Cavell, *The World Viewed*, p. 226.

9   Ibid., p. 23.

10   Ibid., p. 129. For a writer such as Susanne K. Langer film is 'an eternal and ubiquitous present', creating an ever-changing 'future' or 'destiny' within 'an endless Now'; (1953) *Feeling and Form: A Theory of Art Developed from Philosophy in a New Key*. London: Routledge, p. 415.

11   V. F. Perkins (1972) *Film as Film*. Harmondsworth, Middlesex: Penguin, p. 69.

12   Ibid., p. 67.

13   Cavell, *The World Viewed*, p. 72.

14   The film philosopher Homer Simpson incisively commented on this as he began to tell a story in *The Simpsons*: 'Listen closely, as my words will conjure up pictures as clear as any television program'.

15   Hugo Münsterberg (1916) *The Photoplay: A Psychological Study*. New York: D. Appleton, p. 102. Münsterberg was a German-American psychologist and philosopher, who died the same year that *The Photoplay* was published.

16   André Bazin (1971) *What is Cinema?, Volume 1*, selected and trans. Hugh Gray, preface by Jean Renoir. Berkeley: University of California Press, p. 14.

17   Benjamin, 'The Work of Art in the Age of Mechanical Reproduction', p. 230.

18   Gilles Deleuze (1998 [1989]) 'The Brain is the Screen: Interview with Gilles Deleuze on *The Time-Image*', trans. Melissa McMahon, in Réda Bensmaïa and Jalal Toufic (eds) (1998) *Gilles Deleuze: A Reason to Believe in this World*, special issue of *Discourse: Journal for Theoretical Studies in Media and Culture*, vol. 20, no. 3, p. 48.

19   Gilles Deleuze (1985 [1983]) *Cinema 1: The Movement-Image*, trans. Hugh Tomlinson and Barbara Habberjam. Minneapolis: University of Minnesota Press, p. 201.

20   Deleuze, 'The Brain is the Screen', p. 49.

21   Gilles Deleuze (1995d [1986]) 'Doubts About the Imaginary', trans. Martin Joughin, in *Negotiations: 1972–1990*. New York: Columbia University Press, p. 64.

22   Ricciotto Canudo (1988 [1911]) 'The Birth of a Sixth Art', trans. Ben Gibson, Don Ranvaud, Sergio Sokota and Deborah Young, in Abel, *French Film Theory and Criticism, Volume 1*, p. 296–7.

chapter one

1   Emile Vuillermoz (1988a [1917]) 'Before the Screen: *Les Frères corses*', in Abel, *French Film Theory and Criticism, Volume 1*, p. 133.

2   Gilles Deleuze (1995c [1985]) 'On *The Time-Image*', trans. Martin Joughin, in *Negotiations: 1972–1990*. New York: Columbia University Press. p. 57.

3   Gerard Fort Buckle (1926) *The Mind and the Film: A Treatise on the Psychological Factors in the Film*. London: George Routledge and Sons, p. 19.

4   Bazin, *What is Cinema? Volume 1*, p. 62.

5   Interestingly, Small apparently found a lack of reception for film's handling of conceptual matter, and concluded that 'film theory's appreciation for this subject rests with Eisenstein's thwarted ambitions'; Edward S. Small (1980) 'Cinevideo and Mental Images', *Journal of the University Film Association*, vol. 32, nos. 1–2, p. 5.

6   Surrealist filmmakers see mental processes as mechanistic and align film with dreams and free imagination – a naïve untutored eye (although it is not clear where the divide lies between these two types of thought). Ramona Fotiade calls this type of film 'conscious hallucination', bridging reality and imagination; Ramona Fotiade (1995) 'The Untamed Eye: Surrealism and Film Theory', *Screen*, vol. 36, no. 4.

7   Parker Tyler (1972) *The Shadow of an Airplane Climbs the Empire State Building: A World Theory of Film*. Garden City, NY: Doubleday, pp. 72–3. Tyler was a poet and writer who was one of the first to study the representation of homosexuality in film.

8   Ibid., p. 229. Tyler also pastes on a value claim: that a subjective film is a good film because the creator has achieved total identity with his or her vision.

9   R. E. Jones (1941) *The Dramatic Imagination: Reflections and Speculations on the Art of the Theatre*. New York: Duell, Sloan and Pearce., pp. 17–18; quoted in Langer, *Feeling and Form*, p. 415.

10   Perkins, *Film as Film*, p.133. And inverting the analogy, it is possible to speak of the mind as being like a film – a cine-brain. For filmmaker Alain Robbe-Grillet, writing in 1965, the images of film are imaginings, and our imaginings 'are something like an interior film continually projected in our own minds … the total cinema of our mind admits both in alternation and to the same degree the present fragments of reality proposed by sight and hearing, and past fragments, or future fragments, or fragments that are completely phantasmagorical'; Alain Robbe-Grillet (1965) *Snapshots, or Towards a New Novel*, trans. Barbara Wright. London: Calder and Boyars, pp. 11–12.

11   Germaine Dulac (1988a [1924]) 'The Expressive Techniques of the Cinema', trans. Stuart Liebman, in Abel, *French Film Theory and Criticism, Volume 1*, p. 310.

12   See Abel, *French Film Theory and Criticism, Volume 1*, p. 333. The film *Time Regained* attempts to perform these associations, though mainly through the profilmic theatrical movements of settings and props.

13   Henri Bergson, quoted in Abel, *French Film Theory and Criticism, Volume 1*, p. 22.

14   Paul Douglass (1992) 'Deleuze's Bergson: Bergson Redux', in Frederick Burwick and Paul Douglass (eds) *The Crisis in Modernism*. Cambridge: Cambridge University Press, p. 381.

15   Emile Vuillermoz (1988b [1918a]) 'Before the Screen: La Dixième symphonie', in Abel, *French Film Theory and Criticism, Volume 1*, p. 170.

16   Ricciotto Canudo (1988b [1923]) 'Reflections on the Seventh Art', in Abel, *French Film Theory and Criticism, Volume 1*, p. 301. Although he points out the mistakes of filmmakers' representations of memory: 'In one's memories one does not see oneself', p. 298.

17   Paul Ramain (1988 [1925]) 'The Influence of Dream on the Cinema', in Abel, *French Film Theory and Criticism, Volume 1*, p. 363.

18   Jean Goudal (1988 [1925]) 'Surrealism and Cinema', in Abel, *French Film Theory and Criticism, Volume 1*, p. 357.

19   Gilles Deleuze (1989 [1985]) *Cinema 2: The Time-Image*, trans. Hugh Tomlinson and Robert Galeta. London: Athlone Press, pp. 159 and 165. He does, however, allow a dream-image (pre-time-image), calling it the 'onirosign', p. 273.

20   Cavell, *The World Viewed*, p. 67.

21   Cf. Bachelard on the difference between imaginary and image.

22   Yhcam, 'Cinematography', p. 75.

23   Christian Metz (1973) 'Current Problems of Film Theory', *Screen*, vol. 14, nos 1–2, p. 46.

24   Antonin Artaud (1972) *Collected Works: Volume Three*, trans. Alastair Hamilton. London: Calder and Boyars, p. 38.

25   Deleuze also moved through ideas of the subjective character-linked camera (most significantly as regards the moving camera of F. W. Murnau – the camera equally separating and linking itself to the characters) on his way to his own singular conception of thought-cinema. Reading Robbe-Grillet he realises that even objective-looking films must be subjective in the end: 'the most objectivist determinants do not prevent their realising a

"total subjectivity'"; Deleuze, *Cinema 2*, p. 7. The camera neither inhabits nor watches the character, but almost becomes the character – the inside of the image is the ultra-subjectivity of the character – a 'being-with' as John Marks has pointed out; (1996) *Gilles Deleuze: Vitalism and Multiplicity*. London: Pluto Press, p. 155.

26 Bruce Kawin (1978) *Mindscreen: Bergman, Godard, and the First-Person Film*. Princeton, NJ: Princeton University Press, p. 10; or as Avrom Fleishman puts it, 'film images coded as the mental images of a character'; (1992) *Narrated Films: Storytelling Situations in Cinema History*. Baltimore: Johns Hopkins University Press, p. 232, n. 2.

27 Kawin, *Mindscreen*, p. 10.

28 Ibid., p. 192.

29 George M. Wilson (1986) *Narration in Light: Studies in Cinematic Point of View*. Baltimore: Johns Hopkins University Press, p. 130.

30 Münsterberg, *The Photoplay*, p. 150.

31 Ibid., p. 184.

32 Ibid., p. 220.

33 Ibid., p. 97.

34 Mark R. Wicclair (1978) 'Film Theory and Hugo Münsterberg's *The Film: A Psychological Study*', *Journal of Aesthetic Education*, vol. 12, no. 3. p. 43; my emphasis.

35 Noël Carroll (1988) 'Film/Mind Analogies: The Case of Hugo Münsterberg', *Journal of Aesthetics and Art Criticism*, vol. 46, no. 4, p. 489.

36 Dudley Andrew (1976) *The Major Film Theories: An Introduction*. Oxford: Oxford University Press, p. 26.

37 Virginia Woolf (1996 [1926]) 'On Cinema', in Michael O'Pray (ed.) *The British Avant-Garde Film, 1926–1995: An Anthology of Writings*. Luton: University of Luton Press/John Libbey Media, p. 35; my emphasis.

38 Richard Allen and Murray Smith (eds) (1997) *Film Theory and Philosophy*. Oxford: Clarendon Press, p. 19; my emphasis. Although they go on to state that the idea of cinema as a model of consciousness (and the idea that modernist art is a weapon to transform consciousness) posits a relationship between consciousness and the world that is much too literal.

39 Richard Abel (ed.) (1988b) *French Film Theory and Criticism: A History/Anthology, 1907–1939, Volume 2: 1929–1939*. Princeton, NJ: Princeton University Press., p. 15.

40 Perkins, *Film as Film*, p. 155.

41 Roger Gilbert-Lecomte (1991) 'The Alchemy of the Eye: Cinema as a Form of Mind', trans. Phil Powrie, *Quarterly Review of Film and Video*, vol. 12, no. 4, p. 19.

42 Ibid., p. 22.

43 Ibid., p. 21. Gilbert-Lecomte is also one of the only writers who makes the point that certain forms of the mind cannot be directly reduced to film.

44 Ibid., p. 21.

45 Ibid.' pp. 21 and 22.

46 Béla Balázs (1952) *Theory of the Film: Character and Growth of a New Art*, trans. Edith Bone. London: Dennis Dobson, p. 145.

47   Ibid., p. 178 and 179.

48   Ibid., p. 179.

49   Stanley Kubrick (2001) *Interviews*, ed. Gene D. Phillips. Jackson, MI: University of Missis-
      sippi Press, pp. 89–90.

50   Yvette Biró (1982) *Profane Mythology: The Savage Mind of the Cinema*, trans. Imre Gold-
      stein. Bloomington, IN: Indiana University Press, p. 39.

51   Woolf, 'On Cinema', p. 35.

chapter two

1   Ludwig's 'absolute master of time and space', quoted in André Gaudreault (1987) 'Narra-
      tion and Monstration in the Cinema', *Journal of Film and Video*, vol. 39, no. 1, p. 32. Gaud-
      reault himself quotes this from an essay by William Kayser, titled 'Qui raconte le roman?',
      but gives no further reference. It is most likely taken from Ludwig's 1871 book *Shake-
      speare-Studien*.

2   Tyler, *The Shadow of an Airplane Climbs the Empire State Building*, p. 68.

3   Ibid., p. 220.

4   William Rothman (1988) *The 'I' of the Camera*. Cambridge: Cambridge University Press,
      p. xv.

5   Herwitz (1995) 'Screening *The 'I' of the Camera*', *Film and Philosophy*, vol. 2, p. 21.

6   Rothman, *The 'I' of the Camera*, p. xi.

7   Ibid., pp. 126–7.

8   Herwitz, 'Screening *The 'I' of the Camera*', p. 24.

9   Ibid., p. 28.

10   Rothman, *The 'I' of the Camera*, p. 172.

11   Tyler, *The Shadow of an Airplane Climbs the Empire State Building*, p. 104.

12   Susan Sontag (1970) *Styles of Radical Will*. New York: Delta Books, p. 170; quoted in Wilson,
      Narration in Light, p. 128.

13   Kawin, *Mindscreen*, p. 3.

14   Ibid., p. 192.

15   Wilson, *Narration in Light*, p. 129.

16   Kawin cites Allen Ginsberg's *Coming Apart* as 'a visual representation of what [Ginsberg's]
      mind decides to notice: in short, both mindscreen and discourse'; *Mindscreen*, p. 75.

17   Ibid., p. 12.

18   Rudolf Arnheim (1974) *Art and Visual Perception*. Berkeley: University of California, p. 328;
      quoted in George W. Linden (1970) *Reflections on the Screen*. Belmont, CA: Wadsworth,
      p. 225.

19   Linden, *Reflections on the Screen*, pp. 225 and 226.

20   Daniel Dayan (1974) 'The Tutor-Code in Classical Cinema', *Film Quarterly*, vol. 28, no. 1, p. 30.

21   Kawin, *Mindscreen*, p. 188.

22   Wilson, *Narration in Light*, p. 130.

23   Kawin, *Mindscreen*, p. 192.

24   Ian Jarvie (1987) *Philosophy of the Film*. New York: Routledge, p. 85.
25   Kawin, *Mindscreen*, p. 53.
26   Ibid., p. 54.
27   Emile Benveniste (1971) *Problems in General Linguistics*. Miami: University of Miami Press, p. 208.
28   David Bordwell (1985) *Narration in the Fiction Film*. Madison: University of Wisconsin Press, pp. 61–2.
29   Ibid., p. 62.
30   See ibid., p. 210. Compare with the strange club scene in *Twin Peaks: Fire Walk With Me*, where we have to strain to hear the dialogue.
31   Ibid., p. 225.
32   Strange because surely, as Cavell puts it, 'a narrator cannot cede his position to his protagonist'; *The World Viewed*, p. 129.
33   Gregory Currie (1995) *Image and Mind: Film, Philosophy and Cognitive Science*. Cambridge: Cambridge University Press, p. 245.
34   Seymour Chatman (1978) *Story and Discourse: Narrative Structure in Fiction and Film*. Ithaca, NY: Cornell University Press, p. 148.
35   Edward Branigan (1992) *Narrative Comprehension and Film*. New York: Routledge, p. 85.
36   Gaudreault, 'Narration and Monstration in the Cinema', p. 34.
37   Robert Burgoyne (1990) 'The Cinematic Narrator: The Logic and Pragmatics of Impersonal Narration', *Journal of Film and Video*, vol. 42, no. 1, p. 7.
38   Ibid., p. 14.
39   Wilson, *Narration in Light*, p. 50.
40   Ibid., pp. 133 and 86.
41   Ibid., p. 127.
42   Ibid., p. 133.
43   Ibid., pp. 136 & 137.
44   George M. Wilson (1997) '*Le Grand Imagier* Steps Out: The Primitive Basis of Film Narration', *Philosophical Topics*, vol. 25, no. 1, pp. 312 and 301.
45   Jerrold Levinson (1996) 'Film Music and Narrative Agency', in David Bordwell and Noël Carroll (eds) *Post-Theory: Reconstructing Film Studies*. Madison: University of Wisconsin Press, p. 252.
46   Wilson, '*Le Grand Imagier* Steps Out', p. 315.

chapter three

1   Maurice Merleau-Ponty (1964a) 'The Film and the New Psychology', in *Sense and Non-Sense*, trans. Hubert L. Dreyfus and Patricia Allen Dreyfus. Evanston, IL: Northwestern University Press, p. 59.
2   Maurice Merleau-Ponty (1964b) 'Eye and Mind', trans. Carl Dallery, in *The Primacy of Perception*, ed. James Edie. Evanston, IL: Northwestern University Press, p. 166; my emphasis.
3   Ibid. p. 166.

4   Merleau-Ponty, 'The Film and the New Psychology', p. 59.

5   Vivian Sobchack, (1992) *The Address of the Eye : A Phenomenology of Film Experience*. Princeton, NJ: Princeton University Press, p. 168.

6   Sobchack, *The Address of the Eye*, p. 216.

7   Ibid., p. 216.

8   Ibid., p. 24.

9   Ibid., p. 216.

10   Ibid.

11   Merleau-Ponty, 'The Film and the New Psychology', p. 59. For more on the 'body', the flesh, and perception, see Maurice Merleau-Ponty (1968) *The Visible and the Invisible*, trans. Alphonso Lingus. Evanston, IL: Northwestern University Press., pp. 139ff.

12   George Lakoff and Mark Johnson (1980) *Metaphors We Live By*. Chicago: University of Chicago Press, p. 19.

13   Sobchack, *The Address of the Eye*, pp. 205 and 209.

14   Vivian Sobchack (1990) 'The Active Eye: A Phenomenology of Cinematic Vision', *Quarterly Review of Film and Video*, vol. 12, no. 3, p. 35.

15   Merleau-Ponty, 'The Film and the New Psychology', p. 58.

16   Sobchack, *The Address of the Eye*, p. 204.

17   Ibid., p. 217.

18   Ibid., p. 285.

19   Ibid., p. 217.

20   Merleau-Ponty, 'The Film and the New Psychology', p. 59.

21   Sobchack, 'The Active Eye', p. 35.

22   Ibid., p. 25. Merleau-Ponty might well have called the zoom 'consciousness in the act of learning'; (1981) *The Phenomenology of Perception*, trans. Colin Smith. London: Routledge and Kegan Paul, p. 28.

23   A combination of bodily and optical movement is used in vertigo-inducing or world-altering moments (technically, the film moves forward, while the image zooms back outwards, and vice versa). The downward version is used most famously in *Vertigo*, where it is meant to appropriate the human feeling of queasiness or fear. Yet it should be obvious that humans cannot zoom out or in like a camera, and the human experience of vertigo does not exactly 'look' like it looks in cinema. But strangely that does not stop many writers from asserting that film replicates human perception.

24   Sobchack, *The Address of the Eye*, pp. 136 and 143.

25   Sobchack, 'The Active Eye', p. 22.

26   Wilson, *Narration in Light*, pp. 86–7.

27   Sobchack, *The Address of the Eye*, pp. 131, 243 and 183.

chapter four

1   Deleuze, *Cinema 2*, p. 9.

2   Germaine Dulac (1978 [1925]) 'The Essence of Cinema: The Visual Idea', trans. Robert Lam-

berton, in P. Adams Sitney (ed.) *The Avant-Garde Film: A Reader of Theory and Criticism*. New York University Press, p. 46.

3   Tyler, *The Shadow of an Airplane Climbs the Empire State Building*, p. 48.

4   Buckle, *The Mind and the Film*, p. xiii. Even though Williams continued by talking of film as a language that 'may make literature'.

5   Through what Deleuze calls 'properly perceptive montage'; *Cinema 1*, p. 70.

6   Balázs, *Theory of the Film*, p. 165.

7   Linden, *Reflections on the Screen*, p. 232.

8   Balázs, *Theory of the Film*, pp. 89 and 90.

9   Paul Sharits (1978) 'Cinema as Cognition', *Afterimage*, no. 7, Summer, p. 109.

10   Münsterberg, *The Photoplay*, p. 127.

11   Ibid., p. 129.

12   Ibid., p. 130.

13   Jean Epstein (1981) '*Bonjour cinéma* and Other Writings', trans. Tom Milne, *Afterimage*, 10, Autumn, p. 19.

14   Jean Epstein (1977) 'Magnification and Other Writings', trans. Stuart Liebman, *October*, 3, Spring, p. 15.

15   Abel, *French Film Theory and Criticism, Volume 2*, pp. 14–15.

16   A term that was initially developed in the writings of Louis Delluc; see Abel, *French Film Theory and Criticism, Volume 1*, p. 110. In fact Epstein was so taken with the sublime of cinema that he renamed it 'the photography of illusions of the heart'; (1978) 'For a New Avant Garde', trans. Stuart Liebman, in P. Adams Sitney (ed.) *The Avant-Garde Film: A Reader of Theory and Criticism*. New York: New York University Press, p. 28.

17   In his commentary on Epstein, Richard Abel writes that these images 'would be linked together, not through sequentiality, but through simultaneity, so that their suggestive, connotative or metaphorical significance would be foregrounded'; Abel, *French Film Theory and Criticism, Volume 1*, p. 213.

18   Ibid., p. 205.

19   Artaud, *Collected Works: Volume Three*, p. 19.

20   Ibid., p. 59.

21   Ibid., pp. 66 & 66-67.

22   Ibid., p. 67.

23   Ibid., p. 20.

24   Ibid., pp. 20-21.

25   See Marie Seton (1978) *Sergei M. Eisenstein: A Biography*. London: Dennis Dobson, p. 148.

26   Sergei M. Eisenstein (1988d [1932]) 'Help Yourself!', in *Selected Works, Volume 1: Writings, 1922–34*, ed. Richard Taylor. London: British Film Institute, p. 234. For Deleuze, Eisenstein made cinema 'the internal monologue of the brain-world'; *Cinema 2*, p. 211.

27   Sergei M. Eisenstein (1988d [1933]) 'Pantagruel Will Be Born', in *Selected Works, Volume 1: Writings, 1922–34*, ed. Richard Taylor. London: British Film Institute, p. 247.

28   Eisenstein, 'Help Yourself!', p. 236.

29   Sergei M. Eisenstein (1988a [1929]) 'The Dramaturgy of Film Form', in *Selected Works, Vol-*

ume 1: Writings, 1922–34, ed. Richard Taylor. London: British Film Institute, p. 164.

30   Sergei M. Eisenstein (1988b [1929a]) 'The Fourth Dimension in Cinema', in *Selected Works, Volume 1: Writings, 1922–34*, ed. Richard Taylor. London: British Film Institute; my emphasis.

31   According to Jacques Aumont, this 'second period' Eisenstein, after the revolutionary shock of montage, is a somewhat idealistic Eisenstein, pursuing a chimerical total and synthetic art. Eisenstein believed in Marx's working of Hegel: Thesis vs Antithesis = Synthesis. See Jacques Aumont (1987) *Montage Eisenstein*, trans. Lee Hildreth, Constance Penley and Andrew Ross. London: British Film Institute, p. 67. Deleuze also noted this link to Hegel – for him Eisenstein was a 'cinematographic Hegel'; *Cinema 2*, p. 210.

32   For David Bordwell this organic period is shaped by a particular theory of mind: a behaviourist or associationist epistemology, contrasting with the dialectical epistemology of his earlier period. According to Bordwell's thesis that is – it is arguable whether early Eisenstein can be reduced to just being 'dialectical'. See David Bordwell (1993) *The Cinema of Eisenstein*. Cambridge, MA: Harvard University Press.

33   Sergei M. Eisenstein (1994b [1939]) 'Montage 1938', in *Selected Works, Volume 2: Towards a Theory of Montage*, edited by Richard Taylor and Michael Glenny. London: British Film Institute p. 326.

34   Or as Susanne Langer calls it, 'the matrix, the commanding form'; *Feeling and Form*, p. 414.

35   Eisenstein, 'Montage 1938', p. 308.

36   For Deleuze, Eisenstein 'gives the dialectic a properly cinematographic meaning', reaching 'an essentially dialectical conception of the organism'; *Cinema 1*, p. 37.

37   See ibid.: 'the parts are produced by each other in their set and the set is reproduced in the parts, so that this reciprocal causality refers back to the whole as cause of the set and of its parts, according to an internal finality'.

38   This does not simply mean there is an organic unity of opposites, 'but the pathetic passage of the opposite into its contrary', as Deleuze notes; *Cinema 1*, p. 35.

39   Sergei M. Eisenstein (1987 [1964]) *Nonindifferent Nature: Film and the Structure of Things*, trans. Herbert Marshall. Cambridge: Cambridge University Press, p. 35.

40   Ibid., p. 14.

41   Which recalls the words of Virginia Woolf in 1926: 'If so much of our thinking and feeling is connected with seeing, some residue of visual emotion which is of no use to either painter or to poet may still await the cinema'; 'On Cinema', pp. 35–6.

42   Eisenstein, *Nonindifferent Nature*, p. 35.

43   Remember, for Eisenstein 'ex stasis (out of a state) means literally the same thing as "being beside oneself" or "going out of a normal state" does'; *Nonindifferent Nature*, p. 27.

44   Ibid.

45   For Dudley Andrew, filmgoers 'are led away from logic to re-experience our primary mode of understanding'; *Major Film Theories*, p. 74; while Jacques Aumont posits that ecstasy could be the result of an organic fusion between the principles of human thought and the structure of montage, 'between the "process of symbolisation" and the efficacy inherent in montage'; *Montage Eisenstein*, p. 196, though he questions the purpose of indefinitely

losing oneself through ecstasy; see ibid., p. 65.

46 Eisenstein, *Nonindifferent Nature*, p. 12.

47 Eisenstein, 'Montage 1938', pp. 304 and 305.

48 The filmgoer is 'called on to use his imagination, to create his own experience of the story', as Langer puts it; *Feeling and Form*, p. 414.

49 Eisenstein, 'Montage 1938', p. 309. This final image is what Deleuze would term an image of thought – a collision of ideas that fuses or coalesces into an image.

50 Sergei M. Eisenstein (1994a [1937]) 'Unity in the Image', in *Selected Works, Volume 2: Towards a Theory of Montage*, edited by Richard Taylor and Michael Glenny. London: British Film Institute, p. 268.

51 Eisenstein, *Nonindifferent Nature*, p. 4.

52 Ibid., pp. 8–9.

53 Ibid., p. 11.

54 Yvette Biró considers Eisenstein's plan to film Karl Marx's *Das Kapital*, and finds him 'looking for a mode of depiction that, instead of developing gradually, would reveal the whole of what is to be communicated by means of sensory recognition, of sudden exposure. He wants to produce abstraction out of crude images and simple events. But every picture-event is of a dual nature. One the one hand, it is extremely 'primitive', locking meaning into a single action; on the other, the suggestive and lucid arrangement of the picture-events conveys meaning to us – almost with brutal force – as a wide, unbroken whole'; *Profane Mythology*, p. 25; my emphasis.

55 Deleuze adds: 'Psychoanalysis has subjected these famous images of the creamer and what follows to such puerile treatment that it has become hard to rediscover their simple beauty'; *Cinema 1*, p. 181.

56 What Bordwell terms 'felt concepts'; *The Cinema of Eisenstein*, p. 178.

57 Geoffrey Nowell-Smith (1994) Geoffrey, 'Eisenstein on Montage', in Eisenstein, *Selected Works, Volume 2: Towards a Theory of Montage*, edited by Richard Taylor and Michael Glenny. London: British Film Institute, p. xvi. And as Aumont notes: 'Eisenstein was only interested in metaphor and metonymy as figures of thought – as fundamental figures of the very processes of thought'; *Montage Eisenstein*, p. 195.

58 From the 'percept to the concept' as Deleuze puts it; *Cinema 2*, p. 157.

59 Ibid., p. 23.

60 For D. N. Rodowick the movement-image is 'defined by an organic will to truth, or a fundamental philosophical belief in the representability of the whole'; (1997) *Gilles Deleuze's Time-Machine*. Durham, NC: Duke University Press, p. 185.

61 Deleuze, *Cinema 2*, pp. 187–8.

62 Artaud, *Collected Works: Volume Three*, p. 59.

63 Deleuze, *Cinema 1*, p. 198.

64 As Richard Dienst noted in 1994, it is not any traditional ideas of representation or indexicality that matter to Deleuze, 'but the mapping of energies and actions that might be released with any given set of images'; (1994) *Still Life in Real Time: Theory After Television*. Durham, NC: Duke University Press, p. 147; my emphasis.

65 Deleuze, *Cinema 2*, p. 23.

66 Ibid.; second ellipsis Deleuze's own.

67 For instance, Godard's films are 'trying to "see borders", that is, to show the imperceptible'; Gilles Deleuze (1995a [1976]) 'Three Questions on *Six Times Two*', trans. Martin Joughin, in *Negotiations: 1972–1990*. New York: Columbia University Press, p. 45.

68 Gilles Deleuze (1995b [1983]) 'On *The Movement-Image*', trans. Martin Joughin, in *Negotiations: 1972–1990*. New York: Columbia University Press, p. 54.

69 Ibid., p. 52.

70 Deleuze, *Cinema 2*, p. 165

71 Ibid., p. 161.

72 Deleuze, *Cinema 1*, p. 215

73 Deleuze, *Cinema 2*, p. 159; Deleuze's own ellipsis.

74 Deleuze, *Cinema 1*, p. 206. In other words, the mental image effects a rupturing of Deleuze's previous classifications (action-image, perception-image, etc.) from the first volume of *Cinema*.

75 Deleuze, *Cinema 2*, pp. 12 and 19.

76 Ibid., p. 201. As John Marks has written: 'As a form of thought, cinema offers us the possibility of discovering the "inner becomings of things": a world of constant modulation'; (1996) *Gilles Deleuze: Vitalism and Multiplicity*. London: Pluto Press, p. 144.

77 Ibid., p. 263.

78 Ibid.

79 Ibid., p. 262.

80 Ibid., p. 263.

81 Deleuze quotes Marie-Christine Questerbert on *The Central Region*: 'This is a film as concept where the eye has reached the point of no seeing', *Cinema 2*, p. 331, n. 11.

82 Deleuze, *Cinema 2*, p. 267.

83 Artaud, *Collected Works: Volume Three*, p. 61; my emphasis.

84 Ibid., p. 63.

85 Antonin Artaud (1988 [1933]) 'The Premature Old Age of the Cinema', in *French Film Theory and Criticism: A History/Anthology, 1907–1939, Volume 2: 1929–1939*. Princeton, NJ: Princeton University Press, p. 122; my emphasis.

86 Ibid., p. 123.

87 Artaud, *Collected Works: Volume Three*, p. 78; my emphasis.

88 Deleuze, *Cinema 2*, p. 161.

89 'Thought has no other reason to function than its own birth, always the repetition of its own birth, secret and profound'; ibid., p. 165. Perhaps film here is an indication of thought before linguistic consciousness – Deleuze cites Bazin on Welles' *Macbeth*: the indiscernible boundaries of earth and water, sky and land, good and evil, constituted a 'prehistory of consciousness'; ibid., p. 169.

90 Ibid., p. 178.

91 Like Nietzsche, tearing belief from every faith in order to give it back to rigorous thought. See ibid., p. 176.

92 Ibid., p. 172.

93 Rodowick, *Gilles Deleuze's Time Machine*, p. 185. For Deleuze, authorship is the keystone of his theory of cinematic thought, leaving most readers with the impression that the director thinks the film. But the whole impetus behind the idea of the time-image is that film is thinking for itself; not just to show sequential actions, but to be time.

94 Deleuze, *Cinema 2*, p. xi.

95 Ibid., p. xii.

96 For example, through neorealism's innovation, 'we no longer have much faith in being able to act upon situations or react to situations, but it doesn't make us at all passive, it allows us to catch or reveal something intolerable, unbearable, even in the most everyday things'; Deleuze, 'On *The Movement-Image*', p. 51.

97 Deleuze, *Cinema 2*, p. 179.

98 Ibid., p. 180.

99 Ibid., p. 167.

100 Ibid., p. 278.

101 Ibid., p. 168.

102 Ibid., pp. 168 and 169.

103 Ibid., p. 160.

104 Ibid., p. 167; 'man today is in flight from thinking. This flight-from-thought is the ground of thoughtlessness'; (1966) *Discourse on Thinking*, trans. John M. Anderson and E. Hans Freund. New York: Harper and Row, p. 45.

105 Ibid., p. 201.

chapter five

1 Bill Viola (1995) *Reasons for Knocking at an Empty House, Writings 1973–1994*, ed. Robert Violette. London: Thames and Hudson, p. 148.

2 Deleuze: 'the object of cinema is not to reconstitute a presence of bodies, in perception and action, but to carry out a primordial genesis of bodies', *Cinema 2*, p. 201.

3 As Gregory Currie's realises in the very last line of *Image and Mind*: 'Film shows the need for a category of unreliable but narratorless narratives'; *Image and Mind*, p. 282.

4 Samuel Beckett (1993) *Murphy*. London: Calder, p. 63.

5 Merleau-Ponty, 'The Film and the New Psychology', p. 51.

6 Ibid., p. 52.

7 Bazin, *What is Cinema?, Volume 1*, p. 13.

8 Yet Sobchack does note that the film's visual 'body', 'represents to us its own presence to and partial constitution of object movement', signalling that she does eventually see the film's body 'as' both the film and its objects (if only partially); 'The Active Eye', p. 31.

9 Gilles Deleuze (1998 [1989]) 'The Brain is the Screen: Interview with Gilles Deleuze on *The Time-Image*', trans. Melissa McMahon, in Réda Bensmaïa and Jalal Toufic (eds) *Gilles Deleuze: A Reason to Believe in this World*, special issue of *Discourse: Journal for Theoretical Studies in Media and Culture*, vol. 20 no. 3, p. 49.

10   Merleau-Ponty, *The Phenomenology of Perception*, p. 29.

11   Sobchack, *The Address of the Eye*, p. 247.

12   Ibid., p. 132.

13   Woolf, 'On Cinema', p. 36.

14   Sobchack, *The Address of the Eye*, p. 256.

15   Cavell, *The World Viewed*, p. 138.

16   Münsterberg, *The Photoplay*, p. 104.

17   See Slavoj Zizek (2001) *The Fright of Real Tears: Krzysztof Kieslowski Between Theory and Post-Theory*. London: British Film Institute, pp. 33–4.

18   Ibid., pp. 71–2.

19   As Robert Burgoyne would say, 'the character-narrator has to earn his authentication authority'; 'The Cinematic Narrator', p. 11.

20   It should also be mentioned that the filmind includes the possibility of completely thinking its characters – such as Jar Jar Binks from *Star Wars: Episode 1 – The Phantom Menace* – and the future of film may lie in such a pure animatable film-reality.

21   See Paul Messaris (1994) *Visual 'Literacy': Image, Mind and Reality*. Boulder, CO: Westview Press, pp. 29–31.

22   Shlomith Rimmon-Kenan (1983) *Narrative Fiction: Contemporary Poetics*. New York: Taylor and Francis, p. 88; quoted in Burgoyne, 'The Cinematic Narrator', p. 11.

23   Gilbert-Lecomte, 'The Alchemy of the Eye', p. 22.

24   Sobchack, *The Address of the Eye*, p. 302.

25   Tyler, *The Shadow of an Airplane Climbs the Empire State Building*, p. 49.

26   Sobchack, *The Address of the Eye*, p. 245. Compare this film's slave-to-the-body-ness with *The Son*'s metaphysical action-being style – see the end of chapter seven.

27   Carroll, 'Film/Mind Analogies', p. 489.

28   Ibid., p. 491.

29   Epstein, *'Bonjour Cinéma and Other Writings'*, p. 19.

30   See Wicclair, 'Film Theory and Hugo Münsterberg's *The Film*', p. 43: 'the analogue between filmic devices and mental processes should be construed functionally rather than phenomenologically'.

31   Kawin, *Mindscreen*, p. 192; my emphasis.

32   Artaud, *Collected Works: Volume Three*, p. 59.

33   Although it is important to note that in this realm of the relation-image Deleuze also allows such things as Groucho's absurd reasoning – 'either this man is dead, or my watch has stopped' – and symbols, those bearers of various relations (such as keys in Hitchcock), to deliver a mental image.

34   Deleuze, *Cinema 2*, p. 168.

35   Bergson, quoted in Abel, *French Film Theory and Criticism, Volume 1*, p. 22.

36   Balázs, *Theory of the Film*, p. 145.

37   See Deleuze, *Cinema 2*, p. 172.

38   Stanley Cavell (1995) 'Time after Time', *London Review of Books*, vol. 17, no. 1, p. 8. Although Cavell is mainly referring to the concepts that film drama gives rise to in philosophical

readings of plot and character and gesture (even if they are moments chosen by the film).

39 Balázs, *Theory of the Film*, p. 179.

40 Sobchack, *The Address of the Eye*, p. 171.

41 Merleau-Ponty, 'The Film and the New Psychology', p. 57.

42 Eisenstein, 'Unity in the Image', p. 268.

chapter six

1   Deleuze, 'On *The Time-Image*', p. 58.

2   David Bordwell (2003) 'Who Blinked First?', in Lennard Højbjerg and Peter Schepelern (eds) *Film Style and Story: A Tribute to Torben Grodal*. Copenhagen: Museum Tusculanum Press, p. 54.

3   Bordwell, *Narration in the Fiction Film*, p. 287.

4   David Bordwell (1989) *Making Meaning: Inference and Rhetoric in the Interpretation of Cinema*. Cambridge, MA: Harvard University Press, p. 266.

5   David Bordwell (1997) *On the History of Film Style*. Cambridge, MA: Harvard University Press, p. 157.

6   Bordwell, *Narration in the Fiction Film*, p. 281.

7   Ibid., p. 209.

8   Richard Allen (2001) 'Cognitive Film Theory', in Richard Allen and Malcolm Turvey (eds) *Wittgenstein, Theory and the Arts*. London and New York: Routledge, p. 208

9   Robert Stam (2000) *Film Theory: An Introduction*. Oxford: Blackwell, p. 236.

10 Currie, *Image and Mind*, p. 2.

11 Thomas Elsaesser and Warren Buckland (2002) *Studying Contemporary American Film: A Guide to Movie Analysis*. London: Arnold, p. 169.

12 Bordwell, *Narration in the Fiction Film*, p. 287.

13 Stam, *Film Theory*, p. 241.

14 In the new cinema of attraction (*Charlie's Angels, The Matrix Reloaded*, I would even include *The Royal Tennenbaums*) continually changing spectacle seems more important than rational narrative progression.

15 Bordwell, *Narration in the Fiction Film*, p. 281.

16 Ibid., p. 282.

17 Ibid., p. 288.

18 Ibid., p. 285.

19 Ibid., pp. 281 and 210.

20 Ibid., p. 209.

21 Ibid., p. 212.

chapter seven

1   Yhcam, 'Cinematography', p. 72.

2   Sergei M. Eisenstein (1988c [1929b] 'Perspectives', in *Selected Works, Volume 1: Writings,*

1922–34, ed. Richard Taylor. London: British Film Institute', p. 159.

3   Germaine Dulac was perhaps the first real formalist of film; he considered shooting angles, close-ups, superimposition, dissolves, fades, soft focus, distortions – effects that 'bring a whole visual philosophy to cinema', because the shot, 'simultaneously defines the place, an action, and a thought'; 'The Expressive Techniques of the Camera', pp. 312 and 309.

4   And I am using the term 'image' to cover all depictions, and thus not always to denote being 'of' something (people, objects), as with representation – I will not be talking about an image of grey haze in the sense that there is a grey haze out there that the film captures. This distinction is even more important in the midst of current technology, as the film image can now be just about anything.

5   As Deleuze argues: 'the new spiritual automatism and the new psychological automata depend on an aesthetic before depending on technology'; *Cinema 2*, p. 267.

6   Roy Huss (1986) *The Mindscapes of Art: Dimensions of the Psyche in Fiction, Drama, and Film* (Rutherford, NJ: Fairleigh Dickinson University Press, p. 185.

7   Münsterberg, *The Photoplay*, p. 209.

8   Buckle, *The Mind and the Film*, pp. 88–9 and 82. The director Ingmar Bergman, writing about his film *Cries and Whispers*, saw a direct link between colour and identity: 'Ever since my childhood I have pictured the inside of the soul as a moist membrane in shades of red'; (1995) *Images: My Life in Film*. London: Faber and Faber, p. 55.

9   Edward Branigan (1976) 'The Articulation of Color in a Filmic System: *Deux ou trois choses que je sais d'elle*', *Wide Angle*, vol. 1, no. 3, pp. 20 and 21.

10   Deleuze, *Cinema 1*, p. 52; Sergei M. Eisenstein (1970 [1948]) 'Color Film', in *Notes of a Film Director*. New York: Dover, p. 128.

11   For further notes on colour see Daniel Frampton (1996) 'Filmosophy: Colour', in Colin MacCabe and Duncan Petrie (eds) *New Scholarship from BFI Research*. London: British Film Institute.

12   Roger Gilbert-Lecomte understood this back in 1933: 'The acoustic possibilities of the cinema will be clear when the role of sound is specifically investigated in its subordination to the succession of images: a great luminous cry, the modulations of water as it lies in pools'; 'The Alchemy of the Eye', p. 22.

13   Perkins, *Film as Film*, p. 94–5.

14   A painter such as Gerhardt Richter understands this, crafting defocused images in oil – painting a space inbetween artist and subject.

15   Epstein (1975) *Ecrits sur le cinéma, Volume II*. Paris: Seghers, p. 67; quoted in Deleuze, *Cinema 1*, p. 223, n. 12.

16   Buckle recognised this way back in 1926: 'In the turning of the camera, lies the greatest means of allowing introspection and retrospection to come into play when so desired'; *The Mind and the Film*, p. 56.

17   Cavell, *The World Viewed*, p. 243, n. 55. While for Canudo, film's capacity to study plant growth with speeded-motion 'is an affirmation of its stupendous capacity to renew the representation of life itself, fixing the instant-by-instant movement of beings and things'; 'Reflections on the Seventh Art', p. 296; my emphasis.

18   Gilbert-Lecomte saw that film's mobility in time 'can reproduce that of the mind in rela-
     tion to the mobility of life, and these variations in speed, hitherto unknown to the senses,
     allow consciousness to discover new rhythms . . . the movements of dreams; a man flying;
     the flight of angels; the motion of ghosts'; 'The Alchemy of the Eye', p. 22.

19   Buckle, *The Mind and the Film*, pp. 27–8.

20   Cavell, *The World Viewed*, p. 232, n. 13.

21   Wilson, *Narration in Light*, p. 87

22   I recall the filmmaker Paul Schrader referring to the 'psychology' of his camera, as in *Light
     Sleeper* when the hero enters a bar and the film leaves his viewpoint to rise and tour the
     large mural on the wall, before returning to him at the other side of the bar.

23   Cavell, *The World Viewed*, p. 129.

24   Jean Epstein (1977) 'Magnification and Other Writings', trans. Stuart Liebman, *October*, 3,
     Spring, p. 236. As Béla Balázs wrote: 'The close-up not only isolates objects in space, but
     seems to lift them out of space entirely and transfer them to a conceptual space in which
     different laws obtain'; *Theory of the Film*, 147.

25   Münsterberg, *The Photoplay*, p. 37.

26   Dulac, 'The Expressive Techniques of the Camera', p. 310.

27   As Bazin notes about *Germany Year Zero*: 'The preoccupation of Rossellini when dealing
     with the face of a child … is the exact opposite of that of Kuleshov with the close-up of
     Mozhukhin'; *What is Cinema?, Volume 1*, p. 37.

28   What was to be a real biography before Murnau's estate blocked publication.

29   Jim Shepard (1999) *Nosferatu in Love*. London: Faber and Faber, p. 73.

30   Bazin, *What is Cinema?, Volume 1*, p. 69.

31   Biró, *Profane Mythology*, p. 53; my emphasis.

32   Ibid., p. 53.

33   Seymour Chatman (1990) *Coming to Terms: The Rhetoric of Narrative in Fiction and Film*.
     Ithaca, NY: Cornell University Press, p. 52.

34   Apart from anything else, steadicams and the new digital mobility of filmmaking means
     'tracks' do not always need to be used. Sobchack is aware of the dangers of technicist lan-
     guage: 'the film's own bodily movement gets called "camera movement", which overlooks
     the film's own existence as the subject of its vision [that] expresses all of the movement
     visible on the screen of its consciousness'; 'The Active Eye', p. 30.

35   David A. Cook notes that *Cabiria*'s moving shots, 'permitted the camera to roam around
     freely among the vast sets, moving in to isolate the characters in close-up and moving out
     again to re-frame the shifting action'; (1990) *A History of Narrative Film*, second edition.
     New York and London: W. W. Norton, p. 59.

36   See Cavell, *The World Viewed*, p. 144.

37   Buckle, *The Mind and the Film*, p. 33.

38   Gilbert-Lecomte, 'The Alchemy of the Eye', p. 22.

39   Tyler, *The Shadow of an Airplane Climbs the Empire State Building*, p. 63.

40   Perkins, *Film as Film*, p. 98.

41   See Karel Reisz and Gavin Millar (1968) *The Technique of Film Editing*. London: Focal Press,

p. 215.

42   Bazin, *What is Cinema?, Volume 1*, p. 38. Perkins concurs, arguing that 'the more a film benefits from rapid change of image, the less it can draw on the equally expressive possibilities of change within the image'; *Film as Film*, p. 115.

43   Deleuze, *Cinema 2*, p. 158.

44   Giorgio Agamben (1996) 'Repetition and Stoppage', trans. Brian Holmes, in *Documenta X: Documents 2*. Kassel: Cantz Verlag, p. 69.

45   See Colin MacCabe (1985) *Theoretical Essays: Film, Linguistics, Literature*. Manchester: Manchester University Press, p. 44.

46   Alan Spiegel (1976) *Fiction and the Camera Eye: Visual Consciousness in Film and the Modern Novel*. Charlottesville, VI: University Press of Virginia, p. 166.

47   Münsterberg, *The Photoplay*, p. 120. Another way of understanding this freedom was noted by Tyler: 'This is … cosmic space identifying itself in every millimetre of the reel as consistent and the same, whatever images it may carry as features of the action'; *The Shadow of an Airplane Climbs the Empire State Building*, p. 230.

48   Münsterberg, *The Photoplay*, pp. 96-97.

49   Cavell, *The World Viewed*, p. 137.

50   Münsterberg, *The Photoplay*, pp. 95 and 96.

51   Deleuze, *Cinema 2*, p. xi.

52   Ibid., p. xii.

53   Dienst, *Still Life in Real Time*, p. 155.

54   Münsterberg, *The Photoplay*, p. 181.

chapter eight

1   Goudal, 'Surrealism and Cinema', p. 22.

2   Kubrick, *Interviews*, p. 106.

3   Jean Louis Schefer, (1995) *The Enigmatic Body: Essays on the Arts*, ed. and trans. Paul Smith. Cambridge: Cambridge University Press, p. 112

4   Questions about the person or persons who experience film have always been slightly steered by the choice of name for those individuals. What do we call the meaning-producing film-cognitiser? Spectators seem to dumbly sit in awe; readers coldly deconstruct; viewers are obviously deaf; while experiencers (?) sound like they are on drugs. 'Filmgoer' is fairly neutral, perhaps somewhat archaic and certainly cinema-centric. Later I will outline the make-up of a 'filmosopher'.

5   Perkins, *Film as Film*, p. 134.

6   To clarify these terms: our consciousness is everything we are aware of at any particular moment; the subconscious is the part of the mind of which we are not fully aware, but which influences our actions and feelings; both, I would argue, are part of human 'thinking'. Psychoanalysts prefer the terms unconscious and preconscious, which refer more to repressed and/or recallable/unrepressed memories and emotions – i.e. from which we can only recall thoughts that have not been repressed. In some definitions the 'uncon-

scious' is completely inaccessible to the conscious mind, but still affects behaviour and emotions. The term is also used for when we are unaware of doing something, and, more confusingly, for when we have passed out.

7   Messaris, *Visual 'Literacy'*, p. 91. Gregory Currie also argues that film images 'are naturally generative in virtue of their similarity to real things … it is likeness that plays the role for cinematic images that conventionality plays for language'; (1993) 'The Long Goodbye: The Imaginary Language of Film', *British Journal of Aesthetics*, vol. 33, no. 3, p. 215.

8   Wilson, *Narration in Light*, pp. 86–7.

9   Liebman, quoted in Melinda Barlow (1990) 'The Peculiar Light of Thought: Jean Epstein and the Sublime', *University of Hartford Studies in Literature*, vol. 22, nos. 2–3, p. 10.

10   Münsterberg, *The Photoplay*, pp. 51–2, my emphasis. Münsterberg thus holds film to be a window on the world and a type of mental image; a window (a lot of the time), but always with a different cognitive state.

11   See, for example, Kendal Walton (1978) 'Fearing Fictions', *Journal of Philosophy*, vol. 75, no. 1, pp. 5–27.

12   Noël Carroll (1990) *The Philosophy of Horror; or, Paradoxes of the Heart*. New York: Routledge, pp. 74–5.

13   Ibid., pp. 80 and 81.

14   See Karen Bardsley (2002) 'Is It All in Our Imagination? Questioning the Use of the Concept of the Imagination in Cognitive Film Theory', in Kevin L. Stoehr (ed.) *Film and Knowledge: Essays on the Integration of Images and Ideas*. Jefferson, NC/London: McFarland.

15   Allen, 'Cognitive Film Theory', p. 194.

16   Cf. Allen's 'projecting illusion' thesis; (1995) *Projecting Illusion: Film Spectatorship and the Impression of Reality*. New York: Cambridge University Press.

17   Bazin, *What is Cinema?, Volume 1*, p. 14. This directness to the photographic image was later taken up – less proto-scientifically and more poetically – by Roland Barthes in *Camera Lucida*.

18   Martin Heidegger (1971) 'The Origin of the Work of Art', in *Poetry, Language, Thought*, trans. Albert Hofstadter. New York: Harper and Row, p. 66.

19   See Allen, 'Cognitive Film Theory', pp. 179–80.

20   Münsterberg, *The Photoplay*, p. 211.

21   Merleau-Ponty, 'The Film and the New Psychology', pp. 57 and 58.

22   Artaud, *Collected Works: Volume Three*, p. 60. Even Artaud's physician, Dr René Allendy, wrote about film, finding in it a unique blend of the subjective and objective, where the unconscious takes the form of symbolism, which can 'arouse intense feelings in us without our having the least intellectual notion of its meaning' quoted in Abel, *French Film Theory and Criticism, Volume 1*, p. 337.

23   Messaris, *Visual 'Literacy'*, p. 17.

24   Ibid., pp. 39–40.

25   Balázs, *Theory of the Film*, p. 17.

26   Buckle, *The Mind and the Film*, pp. 47, 17, and 14; retrospection being 'the act of considering things from a different angle of view', p. 14.

27   Cavell, *The World Viewed*, pp. 157, my emphasis, and 244, n. 60.

28   Quoted in Deleuze, *Cinema 2*, p. 166; originally from Georges Duhamel (1930) *Scènes de la vie future*. Paris: Mercure de France, p. 52. According to Richard Abel, in *Scènes de la vie future* Duhamel 'ridiculed anyone foolish enough to work in the cinema'; *French Film Theory and Criticism, Volume 2*, p. 63, n. 1.

29   Artaud, *Collected Works: Volume Three*, p. 60.

30   Merleau-Ponty, *The Phenomenology of Perception*, p. 353.

31   Sobchack, *The Address of the Eye*, p. 140.

32   Ibid., p. 138.

33   J. M. G. Le Clezio (1971) 'The Extra-terrestrial', *L'Arc*, no. 45, p. 28; quoted in Deleuze, *Cinema 2*, pp. 18–19.

34   For Jung the cinema 'makes it possible to experience without danger all the excitement, passion and desirousness which must be repressed in a humanitarian ordering of life'; quoted in Roger Manvel (1950) *Film*. Harmondsworth, Middlesex: Penguin, p. 8.

35   Münsterberg, *The Photoplay*, pp. 56–7.

36   What part of our mind remains outside or uninvolved with the film?– what Perkins called the 'residue of detachment', *Film as Film*, p. 140. Is it the consciousness of noticing the cinema exit signs or more subtly the unending referencing that our minds do with the thoughts up on the screen?

37   Münsterberg, *The Photoplay*, p. 173.

38   See Sobchack, 'The Active Eye', p. 21. A 'co-operative visual exploration of the visible world', as she notes in *The Address of the Eye*, p. 141.

39   Merleau-Ponty, *The Phenomenology of Perception*, p. 354; quoted in ibid.

40   Ibid., p. 194.

41   Cavell, *The World Viewed*, p. 157. As Samuel Guttenplan helpfully puts it: 'sensations produced in us by objects blend with our ways of thinking of and understanding those objects'; (1994) *A Companion to the Philosophy of Mind*. Oxford: Basil Blackwell, p. 463.

42   Münsterberg, *The Photoplay*, p. 74.

43   Sobchack, *The Address of the Eye*, p. 106.

44   In his 1937 book *Art and Prudence* the writer Mortimer Adler argued that film does not remove the rational and the active in the filmgoer, who is still capable of making prudent decisions on the information given.

45   In *Matter and Memory* Bergson argued that we select what interests us from the range of matter before us, and our memory then acts on this selected matter, bringing up knowledge that helps us understand the chosen matter; our thoughts, in perceiving, move from the virtual (memory) to the actual (action).

46   Roger Odin (1995) 'For a Semio-Pragmatics of Film', in Warren Buckland (ed.) *The Film Spectator: From Sign to Mind*. Amsterdam: Amsterdam University Press, p. 214.

47   Kubrick, *Interviews*, p. 90; my emphasis.

48   Perkins, *Film as Film*, p. 138.

49   Schefer, *Enigmatic Body*, p. 112; my emphasis.

50   Artaud, *Collected Works: Volume Three*, p. 21.

51 Cavell, *The World Viewed*, pp. 40-41.

52 Benjamin, 'The Work of Art in the Age of Mechanical Reproduction', p. 232.

53 Deleuze, *Cinema 2*, p. 156.

54 Ibid., p. 157.

55 Ibid., p. 169; Deleuze's ellipsis.

56 Eisenstein, 'The Fourth Dimension in Cinema', p. 186.

57 Deleuze, *Cinema 2*, p. 157; my emphasis.

58 Ibid., p. 158. Compare to Eisenstein's fourth dimension of cinematic duration, which registers things impossible for natural perception: 'Cinema begins where the collision between different cinematic measures of movement and vibration begins'; 'The Fourth Dimension in Cinema', p. 192.

59 Deleuze, *Cinema 2*, p. 158.

60 Gregory Currie (1992) 'McTaggart at the Movies', *Philosophy*, vol. 67, no. 3, p. 347.

61 For Merleau-Ponty, 'the meaning of a film is incorporated into its rhythm just as the meaning of a gesture may immediately be read in that gesture: the film does not mean anything but itself'; 'The Film and the New Psychology', p. 57.

62 As Bordwell writes, 'films produce effects, of which meanings are certain types'; (1996) 'Convention, Construction, and Cinematic Vision', in David Bordwell and Noël Carroll (eds) *Post-Theory: Reconstructing Film Studies*. Madison: University of Wisconsin Press, p. 93.

chapter nine

1 Quoted in Spiegel, *Fiction and the Camera Eye*, p. 162.

2 One should note here that simply using the terms 'form' and 'content' does not negate or problematise the argument for their inseparability.

3 Biró, *Profane Mythology*, p. 40.

4 If we say that thought is thus previous to language, the next question, beyond the scope and need of this chapter, is whether thought can then exist without language? Are our mental images forever scored with language?

5 Michael Baxandall (2000) 'Painting and Experience in Fifteenth Century Italy', in Keith Whitlock (ed.) *The Renaissance in Europe: A Reader*. New Haven, CT and London: Yale University Press, p. 131.

6 And I am not going to even start on the interpretive strategies of much film writing – especially those analyses that may as well have been about the book-of-the-film they ignore so much going on in the image.

7 Tyler, *The Shadow of an Airplane Climbs the Empire State Building*, p. 88.

8 Perkins, *Film as Film*, p. 87.

9 Deleuze, 'On *The Time-Image*', p. 58.

10 Cavell, *The World Viewed*, pp. xxi–xxii.

11 Wilson, *Narration in Light*, pp. 48 and 49.

12 Perkins, *Film as Film*, p. 157: 'To recapture the naïve response of the film-fan is the first step towards intelligent appreciation of most pictures. The ideal spectator is often a close

relation of Sterne's ideal reader who "would be pleased he knows not why and cares not wherefore"'

13   Cavell, *The World Viewed*, p. 202: 'Criticism, as part of the philosophy of art, must aspire to philosophy. Its goal is the native view; the desophisticated.'

14   Epstein, '*Bonjour Cinéma* and Other Writings', pp. 13 and 26.

15   Deleuze, *Cinema 2*, p. 262; my emphasis.

16   Biró, *Profane Mythology*, p. 24; my emphasis.

17   Heidegger, 'The Origin of the Work of Art', p. 74.

18   Gilles Deleuze and Félix Guattari (1984) *What is Philosophy?*, trans. Graham Burchell and Hugh Tomlinson. London and New York: Verso, p. 202.

19   Cavell calls it the 'immediate and tremendous burden on one's capacity for critical description of cinematic events'; *The World Viewed*, p. x.

20   Quoted in Jonathan Romney (2000) 'An Audience with Uncle Jean-Luc', *Guardian* Friday Review, 11 February, p. 2.

21   Jean-François Lyotard (1991) 'Something Like: "Communication … without Communication"', in *The Inhuman: Reflections on Time*. Oxford: Polity Press, p. 111.

22   For a very personal experience of a film look at Nick Cave's words on Sokurov's *Mother and Son*, 'I Cried and Cried, from Start to Finish'.

23   We might say that the first 'film' we see is the one of our life. The second, now, is television. Only then do we see our third, the cinema film. The thinking there is initially, partially understood, only to be refined and flowered in collision with other cinema films. Thus the thinking of a film is understood by us in relation to all other films (audiovisual experience) and their types of thinking – this is the sense in which we might better understand Cavell's statement that 'a movie comes from other movies'; *The World Viewed*, p. 7.

24   Philosophy, no matter how ostensibly analytic and dry, is always inherently literary, and writers such as Nietzsche and Derrida have shown how philosophy can use this literary nature to trace the archaeology of philosophical ideas – more on this in the next chapter.

25   Perkins understood this, and his version of a useful theory of film is one that 'will have to redirect attention to the movie as it is seen, by shifting the emphasis back from creation to perception'; *Film as Film*, p. 27.

26   Cavell sees in this kind of 'humane criticism … the power of the missing companion'; *The World Viewed*, p. 13.

27   This matches Richard Rorty's idea that descriptions 'are evaluated according to their efficacy as instruments for purposes'; (1992) 'The Pragmatist's Progress', in Stefan Collini (ed.) *Interpretation and Overinterpretation*. Cambridge: Cambridge University Press, p. 92.

chapter ten

1   Cavell, *The World Viewed*, p. 154.

2   L'Herbier, in 1919, quoted in Abel, *French Film Theory and Criticism, Volume 1*, p. 108.

3   In fact the line between imagining and seeing is not so clear – as we use imagination

when we see, to bolster a view with memory, or to fill in an object we only glanced at. We are certainly very active viewers, anticipating and mixing with memory and imagination.

4　Lakoff and Johnson, *Metaphors We Live By*, p. 210.

5　Richard Rorty (1991) *Essays on Heidegger and Others: Philosophical Papers, Volume 2*. Cambridge: Cambridge University Press, pp. 12–13.

6　As Cavell has argued, Wittgenstein's writing 'wishes to prevent understanding which is unaccompanied by inner change'; (1962) 'The Availability of Wittgenstein's Later Philosophy', *Philosophical Review*, vol. 71, no. 1, p. 93.

7　Friedrich Nietzsche (1989) *On Rhetoric and Language*, ed. and trans. Sander L. Gilman, Carole Blair and David J. Parent. Oxford: Oxford University Press, p. 21.

8　Ibid., p. 250. Although what Nietzsche does not attend to is the question of the results of overt and covert uses of metaphorical language crossing paths.

9　Friedrich Nietzsche (1972) *Beyond Good and Evil*, trans. R. J. Hollingdale. Harmondsworth, Middlesex: Penguin, §10.

10　Nietzsche, *On Rhetoric and Language*, p. 246.

11　Friedrich Nietzsche (1968) *The Will to Power*, trans. Walter Kaufman and R. J. Hollingdale, ed. Walter Kaufman. New York: Vintage Books, §552d.

12　Rorty, *Essays on Heidegger and Others*, p. 16.

13　See Ludvig Wittgenstein(1980) *Culture and Value*, trans. Peter Winch, ed. G. H. von Wright and H. Nyman. Chicago: University of Chicago Press, §24.

14　Jacques Derrida (1976) *Of Grammatology*. Baltimore: Johns Hopkins University Press, p. 9.

15　Derrida would probably say there is no language of cinema, only the writing, the inscribing of cinematography (which recalls the *cinécriture* of Agnes Varda).

16　Jacques Derrida (1982) *Margins of Philosophy*, trans. Alan Bass. Brighton: Harvester Press, p. 291; my emphasis.

17　Richard Rorty (1982) *Consequences of Pragmatism*. Brighton: Harvester Press, p. 102.

18　Richard Rorty (1984) 'Deconstruction and Circumvention', *Critical Inquiry*, 11, September, p. 19.

19　Recalling the words of Emile Vuillermoz, writing in 1920, who argued that film is 'a supple and expressive language ... a form of ideographic writing'; 'Before the Screen: Aesthetic', p. 227.

20　Dienst, *Still Life in Real Time*, p. x.

21　Sigrid Weigel (1996) *Body- and Image-Space: Re-Reading Walter Benjamin*. London: Routledge, p. 52.

22　Martin Heidegger (1993) 'The End of Philosophy and the Task of Thinking', trans. Joan Stambaugh, in *Basic Writings*. London: Routledge, p. 449.

23　Heidegger, *Discourse on Thinking*, p. 45.

24　Ibid., p. 46.

25　Ibid., p. 54.

26　Ibid., p. 55.

27　Ibid., pp. 46 and 53.

28   Martin Heidegger (1977) 'The Time of the World-Picture', in *The Question Concerning Tech-nology and Other Essays*, trans. William Lovitt. New York: Harper and Row, p. 116.

29   Heidegger, 'The End of Philosophy and the Task of Thinking', pp. 445–6.

30   Ibid., p. 444.

31   Heidegger, 'The Origin of the Work of Art', p. 36.

32   Heidegger, *Discourse on Thinking*, p. 48.

33   Gilles Deleuze (1995e [1988]) 'On Philosophy', trans. Martin Joughin, in *Negotiations: 1972–1990*. New York: Columbia University Press, p. 137.

34   Ibid., p. 148.

35   Ibid., p. 149.

36   Canudo, 'Reflections on the Seventh Art, p. 296.

37   Eisenstein, 'The Fourth Dimension in Cinema', p. 182. On the hieroglyph see also Vaschel Lindsay's *The Art of the Moving Picture*, published in the same year as Münsterberg's *The Photoplay* (1916).

38   Another possible relationship of language to filmmaking arises: is there something in the grammar of French that led the *nouvelle vague* to experiment in such a way – or was it rather something in the French style of thinking that prompted their design?

39   Jarvie, *Philosophy of the Film*, p. 356, n. 8.

40   As Münsterberg writes: 'None of our actions in practical life is related to tones from musi-cal instruments, and yet the tones of a symphony may arouse in us the deepest emotions … energies which awaken our own impulses, our own tensions and relaxations'; *The Pho-toplay*, p. 166.

41   Biró, *Profane Mythology*, p. 14. Biró bases her ideas around myth, which for her consist of emotional meanings much like film; see, pp. 74–5.

42   Ibid., p. 27. The filmmaker and writer Raúl Ruiz also refers to an image-idea as being 'an idea-act'; (1995) *Poetics of Cinema 1: Miscellanies*, trans. Brian Holmes. Paris: Dis Voir, p. 71.

43   Vuillermoz, 'Before the Screen: Hermes and Silence', p. 158.

44   Germaine Dulac (1988b [1926]) 'Aesthetics, Obstacles, Integral *Cinégraphie*', trans. Stuart Liebman, in Richard Abel (ed.) *French Film Theory and Criticism: A History/Anthology, 1907–1939, Volume I: 1907–1929*. Princeton, NJ: Princeton University Press, p. 393.

45   Perkins, *Film as Film*, p. 155.

46   As D. N. Rodowick asks, is 'the flow of images as an internal monologue equivalent to the movement of prelinguistic thought?'; *Gilles Deleuze's Time Machine*, p. 189.

47   Canudo, 'Reflections on the Seventh Art, p. 293.

48   Quoted in Phil Powrie (1991) 'Film-Form-Mind: The Hegelian Follies of Roger Gilbert-Lecomte', *Quarterly Review of Film and Video*, vol. 12, no. 4, p. 27; my emphasis.

49   Balázs, *Theory of the Film*, p. 180.

50   Weigel, *Body- and Image-Space*, p. 52.

51   Spiegel, *Fiction and the Camera Eye*, p. xii.

52   Biró, *Profane Mythology*, p. 15.

53   Deleuze, 'Three Questions on Six Times Two', pp. 38–9.

54 Münsterberg, *The Photoplay*, p. 97.
55 Eisenstein, 'Pespectives', p. 158.
56 Ibid., p. 158.
57 Spiegel, *Fiction and the Camera Eye*, p. xii.
58 Deleuze, 'Doubts About the Imaginary', pp. 64–5.
59 Deleuze, *Cinema 2*, p. 280.
60 Ibid..
61 Ibid., p. xv.
62 Jacques Derrida (1993) 'The Spatial Arts: An Interview', in Peter Brunette and David Wills (eds) *Deconstruction and the Spatial Arts: Art, Media, Architecture*. Cambridge: Cambridge University Press, p. 24.
63 Ibid., p. 25.
64 Buckle, *The Mind and the Film*, p. 102.
65 Münsterberg, *The Photoplay*, p. 175.
66 Tyler, *The Shadow of an Airplane Climbs the Empire State Building*, pp. 72–3, my emphasis. Quoted earlier.
67 Münsterberg realises this: 'the photoplay is doing all this more richly than any chance imagination would succeed in doing'; *The Photoplay*, p. 172.
68 Benjamin, 'The Work of Art in the Age of Mechanical Reproduction', p. 230. 'Can the optical field ... have an unconscious?' asks Rosalind E. Krauss (1993) *The Optical Unconscious*. Cambridge, MA: MIT Press, p. 179.
69 Cavell, *The World Viewed*, pp. 101–2; my emphasis.
70 Wilson, *Narration in Light*, p. 98. For Heidegger, technology arises out of the tradition of metaphysics and signals the closure of metaphysics. Technology is a mode of revealing and thus an extension of metaphysics – and it is our blind use of technology that is overwhelming us.
71 Similarly Karl Popper talked of a third world of the objective content of thought – beyond the first world of things, and the second world of private thought.
72 Spiegel, *Fiction and the Camera Eye*, p. 32; my emphasis.
73 Merleau-Ponty, 'The Film and the New Psychology', p.59; my emphasis.

conclusion

1 Dziga Vertov (1967) 'Kinoks-Revolution', in Harry M. Geduld (ed.) *Film Makers on Film Making*. Harmondsworth, Middlesex: Penguin, p. 93.
2 Balázs, *Theory of the Film*, p. 17
3 The example of *Contact* reminds me of another curious instance: in a television advert for the UK supermarket chain Tesco, a baby being carried by its mother has its face digitally altered in order to give it more adult expressions – making it look surprised, or questioning. The effect is quite disconcerting.
4 Dulac, 'The Essence of Cinema: The Visual Idea', p. 39; my emphasis.

5   Remember Münsterberg's words: 'The massive outer world has lost its weight, it has been
     freed from space, time and causality, and it has been clothed in the forms of our own con-
     sciousness. The mind has triumphed over matter and the pictures roll on with the ease of
     musical tones;' *The Photoplay*, p. 220; quoted earlier.

6   The final words of Neo in *The Matrix* (addressing the 'artificial intelligence') become a com-
     mentary on the possibilities of the new thinking cinema: 'I'm going to show these people
     what you don't want them to see. I'm going to show them a world, without you. A world
     without rules and controls, without borders or boundaries. A world where anything is
     possible.'

7   *Fight Club* is also the site of a new reflexive thinking as well, one that has more in common
     with avant-garde cinema – projection signals are pointed out, and the sprockets of the
     celluloid rattle into the picture at one point, the film thinking the violent powerful intent
     of its hero(es) through the image.

8   A style of thinking that recalls the opening of Ruiz's *Three Lives and Only One Death*,
     wherein the film scans and surveys its protagonist, thinking him from above and below
     and everywhichway (trying to 'get an angle on him' as it were).

9   Deleuze, 'The Brain is the Screen', p. 48.

10   Münsterberg, *The Photoplay*, p. 102.

11   Quoted in Abel, *French Film Theory and Criticism, Volume 1*, p. 213.

12   Bíró, *Profane Mythology*, p. 11.

13   What if a film such as Tarr's *Damnation* had been released through a gallery? – think of the
     new context, and thus the new reactions (although, think of people walking in and out,
     glancing at it, discussing it as it plays). Sokurov's painterly *Mother and Son* would certainly
     have suited a gallery context.

14   Abel, *French Film Theory and Criticism, Volume 1*, p. 115.

15   Benjamin, 'The Work of Art in the Age of Mechanical Reproduction', p. 324.

16   Ibid., p. 332.

17   Which reminds me of a thought: what I always want to beware of, and yet am so aware
     and cannot escape, is the trace of looking at a favourite image – a looking that exhausts
     that image over time. So much so that we subsume and devour and soak-up that image,
     until we see nothing in it except our memory of it (like a dying relationship).

18   Bíró, *Profane Mythology*, p. 57.

19   How are games 'thinking'? What happens to our sense of subjectivity and involvement on
     playing them? A game such as *Silent Hill* (almost Lynchian in its weirdness) is famous for
     being immeasurably more creepy and absorbing than your regular horror film (including
     the recent film of the game itself).

20   Deleuze, 'The Brain is the Screen', p. 54.

21   Wilson, *Narration in Light*, p. 90.

22   Ibid., p. 95.

23   Canudo, 'Reflections on the Seventh Art', p. 302.

24   Wilson, *Narration in Light*, p. 207.

bibliography

Abel, Richard (ed.) (1988a) *French Film Theory and Criticism: A History/Anthology, 1907–1939, Volume I: 1907–1929*. Princeton, NJ: Princeton University Press.

____ (ed.) (1988b) *French Film Theory and Criticism: A History/Anthology, 1907–1939, Volume 2: 1929–1939*. Princeton, NJ: Princeton University Press.

Adler, Mortimer J. (1937) *Art and Prudence*. New York: Longmans.

Agamben Giorgio (1996) 'Repetition and Stoppage', trans. Brian Holmes, in *Documenta X: Documents 2*. Kassel: Cantz Verlag.

Allen, Richard (2001) 'Cognitive Film Theory', in Richard Allen and Malcolm Turvey (eds) *Wittgenstein, Theory and the Arts*. London and New York: Routledge.

____ (1995) *Projecting Illusion: Film Spectatorship and the Impression of Reality*. New York: Cambridge University Press.

Allen, Richard and Murray Smith (eds) (1997) *Film Theory and Philosophy*. Oxford: Clarendon Press.

Andrew, Dudley (1976) *The Major Film Theories: An Introduction*. Oxford: Oxford University Press.

Arnheim, Rudolf (1974) *Art and Visual Perception*. Berkeley, CA: University of California.

Artaud, Antonin (1972) *Collected Works: Volume Three*, trans. Alastair Hamilton. London: Calder and Boyars.

____ (1976) *Selected Writings*, ed. Susan Sontag, trans. Helen Weaver. New York: Farrar, Strauss and Giroux.

____ (1988 [1933]) 'The Premature Old Age of the Cinema', in *French Film Theory and Criticism: A History/Anthology, 1907–1939, Volume 2: 1929–1939*. Princeton, NJ: Princeton University Press.

Astruc, Alexandre (1968 [1948]) 'The Birth of the New Avant-Garde: La Caméra-stylo', in Peter Graham (ed.) *The New Wave*. Garden City, NY: Doubleday.

Aumont, Jacques (1987) *Montage Eisenstein*, trans. Lee Hildreth, Constance Penley and Andrew Ross. London: British Film Institute.

____ (1989) 'The Point of View', trans. A. Denner, *Quarterly Review of Film and Video*, vol. 11, no. 2.

Balázs, Béla (1952) *Theory of the Film: Character and Growth of a New Art*, trans. Edith Bone. London: Dennis Dobson.

Bardsley, Karen (2002) 'Is It All in Our Imagination? Questioning the Use of the Concept of the Imagination in Cognitive Film Theory', in Kevin L. Stoehr (ed.) *Film and Knowledge: Essays on the Integration of Images and Ideas*. Jefferson, NC/London: McFarland.

Barlow, Melinda (1990) 'The Peculiar Light of Thought: Jean Epstein and the Sublime', *University of Hartford Studies in Literature*, vol. 22, nos. 2–3.

Barthes, Roland (1967) *Writing Degree Zero*, trans. Annette Lavers and Colin Smith. London: Jonathan Cape.

____ *Camera Lucida* (1980), trans. Richard Howard. London: Flamingo.

Baxandall, Michael (2000) 'Painting and Experience in Fifteenth Century Italy', in Keith Whitlock (ed.) *The Renaissance in Europe: A Reader*. New Haven, CT and London: Yale University Press.

Bazin, André (1971) *What is Cinema?, Volume 1*, selected and trans. Hugh Gray, preface by Jean Renoir. Berkeley: University of California Press.

Beckett, Samuel (1993) *Murphy*. London: Calder.

Benjamin, Walter (1999) 'The Work of Art in the Age of Mechanical Reproduction', trans. Harry Zohn, in *Illuminations*. London: Pimlico.

Benveniste, Emile (1971) *Problems in General Linguistics*. Miami: University of Miami Press.

Bergman, Ingmar (1995) *Images: My Life in Film*. London: Faber and Faber.

Bergson, Henri and Michel Georges-Michel (1914) 'Henri Bergson nous parle du cinéma', *Le Journal*, 20 February.

Biró, Yvette (1982) *Profane Mythology: The Savage Mind of the Cinema*, trans. Imre Goldstein. Bloomington: Indiana University Press.

Bischoff, Michael, 'The End of Philosophy and the Rise of Films', <http://www.freenet.msp.mn.us/people/bischoff/thesis.html>; accessed 20 September 1999.

Bordwell, David (1985) *Narration in the Fiction Film*. Madison: University of Wisconsin Press.

____ (1989) *Making Meaning: Inference and Rhetoric in the Interpretation of Cinema*. Cambridge, MA: Harvard University Press.

____ (1993) *The Cinema of Eisenstein*. Cambridge, MA: Harvard University Press.

____ (1996) 'Convention, Construction, and Cinematic Vision', in David Bordwell and Noël Carroll (eds) *Post-Theory: Reconstructing Film Studies*. Madison: University of Wisconsin Press.

____ (1997) *On the History of Film Style*. Cambridge: Harvard University Press.

____ (2003) 'Who Blinked First?', in Lennard Højbjerg and Peter Schepelern (eds) *Film Style and Story: A Tribute to Torben Grodal*. Copenhagen, Denmark: Museum Tusculanum Press.

Branigan, Edward (1976) 'The Articulation of Color in a Filmic System: *Deux ou trois choses que je sais d'elle*', *Wide Angle*, vol. 1, no. 3.

____ (1992) *Narrative Comprehension and Film*. New York: Routledge.

Buckle, Gerard Fort (1926) *The Mind and the Film: A Treatise on the Psychological Factors in the Film*. London: George Routledge and Sons.

Burgoyne, Robert (1990) 'The Cinematic Narrator: The Logic and Pragmatics of Impersonal Narration', *Journal of Film and Video*, vol. 42, no. 1.

Canudo, Ricciotto (1988a [1911]) 'The Birth of a Sixth Art', trans. Ben Gibson, Don Ranvaud, Sergio Sokota and Deborah Young, in Richard Abel (ed.) *French Film Theory and Criticism: A His-
tory/Anthology, 1907–1939, Volume I: 1907–1929*. Princeton, NJ: Princeton University Press.

____ 'Reflections on the Seventh Art' (1988b [1923]), in Richard Abel (ed.) *French Film Theory
and Criticism: A History/Anthology, 1907–1939, Volume I: 1907–1929*. Princeton, NJ: Princeton
University Press.

Carroll, Noël (1988) 'Film/Mind Analogies: The Case of Hugo Münsterberg', *Journal of Aesthetics
and Art Criticism*, vol. 46, no. 4.

____ (1990) *The Philosophy of Horror; or, Paradoxes of the Heart*. New York: Routledge.

Casebier, Allan, *Film and Phenomenology: Toward a Realist Theory of Cinematic Representation*
(Cambridge: Cambridge University Press, 1991).

Cave, Nick, 'I Cried and Cried, from Start to Finish', <http://www.iae.nl/users/maes/cave/disc/
sunday.html>; accessed 23 June 2000.

Cavell, Stanley (1962) 'The Availability of Wittgenstein's Later Philosophy', *Philosophical Review*,
vol. 71, no. 1.

____ (1979) *The World Viewed: Reflections on the Ontology of Film*, enlarged edition. Cambridge,
MA: Harvard University Press.

____ (1995a) 'Time after Time', *London Review of Books*, vol. 17, no. 1.

____ (1995b [1983]) 'The Thought of Movies', in Cynthia A. Freeland and Thomas E. Wartenberg
(eds) *Philosophy and Film*. New York: Routledge.

____ (1997) *Contesting Tears: The Hollywood Melodrama of the Unknown Woman*. Chicago: University of Chicago Press.

Chatman, Seymour (1978) *Story and Discourse: Narrative Structure in Fiction and Film*. Ithaca, NY:
Cornell University Press.

____ (1990) *Coming to Terms: The Rhetoric of Narrative in Fiction and Film*. Ithaca, NY: Cornell
University Press.

Christie, Ian (1994) *The Last Machine*. London: British Film Institute.

Cook, David A. (1990) *A History of Narrative Film*, second edition. New York and London: W. W.
Norton.

Cormier, Harvey, '*2001*: Modern Art, and Modern Philosophy', in Cynthia A. Freeland and Thomas E. Wartenberg (eds) (1995) *Philosophy and Film*. New York: Routledge.

Currie, Gregory (1992) 'McTaggart at the Movies', *Philosophy*, vol. 67, no. 3.

____ (1993) 'The Long Goodbye: The Imaginary Language of Film', *British Journal of Aesthetics*,
vol. 33, no. 3.

____ (1995) *Image and Mind: Film, Philosophy and Cognitive Science*. Cambridge: Cambridge
University Press.

Danielewski, Mark (2000) *House of Leaves*. New York: Doubleday.

Danto, Arthur C. (1992) *Beyond the Brillo Box: The Visual Arts in a Post-Historical Perspective*. New
York: Noonday Press.

____ (1993) 'A Future for Aesthetics', *Journal of Aesthetics and Art Criticism*, vol. 51, no. 2.

Davidson, Donald (1984) *Inquiries into Truth and Interpretation*. Oxford: Clarendon Press.

Dayan, Daniel (1974) 'The Tutor-Code in Classical Cinema', *Film Quarterly*, vol. 28, no. 1.

Deleuze, Gilles (1985 [1983]) *Cinema 1: The Movement-Image*, trans. Hugh Tomlinson and Barbara Habberjam. Minneapolis: University of Minnesota Press.

____ (1989 [1985]) *Cinema 2: The Time-Image*, trans. Hugh Tomlinson and Robert Galeta. London: Athlone Press.

____ (1995a [1976]) 'Three Questions on *Six Times Two*', trans. Martin Joughin, in *Negotiations: 1972–1990*. New York: Columbia University Press.

____ (1995b [1983]) 'On *The Movement-Image*', trans. Martin Joughin, in *Negotiations: 1972–1990*. New York: Columbia University Press.

____ (1995c [1985]) 'On *The Time-Image*', trans. Martin Joughin, in *Negotiations: 1972–1990*. New York: Columbia University Press.

____ (1995d [1986]) 'Doubts About the Imaginary', trans. Martin Joughin, in *Negotiations: 1972–1990*. New York: Columbia University Press.

____ (1995e [1988]) 'On Philosophy', trans. Martin Joughin, in *Negotiations: 1972–1990*. New York: Columbia University Press.

____ (1998 [1989]) 'The Brain is the Screen: Interview with Gilles Deleuze on *The Time-Image*', trans. Melissa McMahon, in Réda Bensmaïa and Jalal Toufic (eds) *Gilles Deleuze: A Reason to Believe in this World*, special issue of *Discourse: Journal for Theoretical Studies in Media and Culture*, vol. 20, no. 3.

Deleuze, Gilles and Félix Guattari (1984) *What is Philosophy?*, trans. Graham Burchell and Hugh Tomlinson. London and New York: Verso.

Derrida, Jacques (1976) *Of Grammatology*. Baltimore: Johns Hopkins University Press.

____ (1982) *Margins of Philosophy*, trans. Alan Bass. Brighton: Harvester Press.

____ (1993) 'The Spatial Arts: An Interview', in Peter Brunette and David Wills (eds) *Deconstruction and the Spatial Arts: Art, Media, Architecture*. Cambridge: Cambridge University Press.

Dienst, Richard (1994) *Still Life in Real Time: Theory After Television*. Durham, NC: Duke University Press.

Douglass, Paul (1992) 'Deleuze's Bergson: Bergson Redux', in Frederick Burwick and Paul Douglass (eds) *The Crisis in Modernism*. Cambridge: Cambridge University Press.

Duhamel, Georges (1930) *Scènes de la vie future*. Paris: Mercure de France.

Dulac, Germaine (1978 [1925]) 'The Essence of Cinema: The Visual Idea', trans. Robert Lamberton, in P. Adams Sitney (ed.) *The Avant-Garde Film: A Reader of Theory and Criticism*. New York University Press.

____ (1988a [1924]) 'The Expressive Techniques of the Cinema', trans. Stuart Liebman, in Richard Abel (ed.) *French Film Theory and Criticism: A History/Anthology, 1907–1939, Volume I: 1907–1929*. Princeton, NJ: Princeton University Press.

____ (1988b [1926]) 'Aesthetics, Obstacles, Integral *Cinégraphie*', trans. Stuart Liebman, in Richard Abel (ed.) *French Film Theory and Criticism: A History/Anthology, 1907–1939, Volume I: 1907–1929*. Princeton, NJ: Princeton University Press.

Eisenstein, Sergei M. (1970 [1948]) 'Color Film', in *Notes of a Film Director*. New York: Dover.

____ (1987 [1964]) *Nonindifferent Nature: Film and the Structure of Things*, trans. Herbert Marshall. Cambridge: Cambridge University Press.

_____ (1988a [1929]) 'The Dramaturgy of Film Form', in *Selected Works, Volume 1: Writings, 1922–34*, ed. Richard Taylor. London: British Film Institute.

_____ (1988b [1929a]) 'The Fourth Dimension in Cinema', in *Selected Works, Volume 1: Writings, 1922–34*, ed. Richard Taylor. London: British Film Institute.

_____ (1988c [1929b] 'Perspectives', in *Selected Works, Volume 1: Writings, 1922–34*, ed. Richard Taylor. London: British Film Institute.

_____ (1988d [1932]) 'Help Yourself!', in *Selected Works, Volume 1: Writings, 1922–34*, ed. Richard Taylor. London: British Film Institute.

_____ (1988d [1933]) 'Pantagruel Will Be Born', in *Selected Works, Volume 1: Writings, 1922–34*, ed. Richard Taylor. London: British Film Institute.

_____ (1994a [1937]) 'Unity in the Image', in *Selected Works, Volume 2: Towards a Theory of Montage*, edited by Richard Taylor and Michael Glenny. London: British Film Institute.

_____ (1994b [1939]) 'Montage 1938', in *Selected Works, Volume 2: Towards a Theory of Montage*, edited by Richard Taylor and Michael Glenny. London: British Film Institute.

Elsaesser, Thomas and Warren Buckland (2002) *Studying Contemporary American Film: A Guide to Movie Analysis*. London: Arnold.

Epstein, Jean (1974) *Ecrits sur le cinéma, Volume I*. Paris: Seghers.

_____ (1975) *Ecrits sur le cinéma, Volume II*. Paris: Seghers.

_____ (1977) 'Magnification and Other Writings', trans. Stuart Liebman, *October*, 3, Spring.

_____ (1981) *'Bonjour cinéma* and Other Writings', trans. Tom Milne, *Afterimage*, 10, Autumn.

_____ (1978) 'For a New Avant Garde', trans. Stuart Liebman, in P. Adams Sitney (ed.) *The Avant-Garde Film: A Reader of Theory and Criticism*. New York: New York University Press.

Fleishman, Avrom (1992) *Narrated Films: Storytelling Situations in Cinema History*. Baltimore: Johns Hopkins University Press.

Fotiade, Ramona (1995) 'The Untamed Eye: Surrealism and Film Theory', *Screen*, vol. 36, no. 4.

Frampton, Daniel (1996) 'Filmosophy: Colour', in Colin MacCabe and Duncan Petrie (eds) *New Scholarship from BFI Research*. London: British Film Institute.

Freeland, Cynthia A. and Thomas E. Wartenberg (eds) (1995) *Philosophy and Film*. New York: Routledge.

Gaudreault, André (1987) 'Narration and Monstration in the Cinema', *Journal of Film and Video*, vol. 39, no. 1.

Gilbert-Lecomte, Roger (1991) 'The Alchemy of the Eye: Cinema as a Form of Mind', trans. Phil Powrie, *Quarterly Review of Film and Video*, vol. 12, no. 4.

Gorky, Maxim (1996) 'Nizhegorodski Listok', in C. Harding and S. Popple (eds) *In the Kingdom of Shadows: A Companion to Early Cinema*. London: Cygnus Arts Press.

Goudal, Jean (1988 [1925]) 'Surrealism and Cinema', in Richard Abel (ed.) *French Film Theory and Criticism: A History/Anthology, 1907–1939, Volume I: 1907–1929*. Princeton, NJ: Princeton University Press.

Grafton, Donald (1990) *Emile Cohl, Caricature, and Film*. Princeton, NJ: Princeton University Press.

Grodal, Torben (1997) *Moving Pictures: A New Theory of Film Genres, Feelings and Cognition*.

Oxford: Clarendon Press.

Guttenplan, Samuel (ed.) (1994) *A Companion to the Philosophy of Mind*. Oxford: Basil Blackwell.

Heidegger, Martin (1966) *Discourse on Thinking*, trans. John M. Anderson and E. Hans Freund. New York: Harper and Row.

____ (1971) 'The Origin of the Work of Art', in *Poetry, Language, Thought*, trans. Albert Hofstadter. New York: Harper and Row.

____ (1977) 'The Time of the World-Picture', in *The Question Concerning Technology and Other Essays*, trans. William Lovitt. New York: Harper and Row.

____ (1993) 'The End of Philosophy and the Task of Thinking', trans. Joan Stambaugh, in *Basic Writings*. London: Routledge.

Herwitz, Daniel (1995) 'Screening *The 'I' of the Camera'*, *Film and Philosophy*, vol. 2.

Roy Huss (1986) *The Mindscapes of Art: Dimensions of the Psyche in Fiction, Drama, and Film*. Rutherford, NJ: Fairleigh Dickinson University Press.

Inness, Julie (1995) 'Passing in *Europa, Europa'*, in Cynthia A. Freeland and Tho-mas E. Wartenberg (eds) *Philosophy and Film*. New York: Routledge.

Jarvie, Ian (1987) *Philosophy of the Film*. New York: Routledge.

Jones, R. E. (1941) *The Dramatic Imagination: Reflections and Speculations on the Art of the Theatre*. New York: Duell, Sloan and Pearce.

Kant, Immanuel (1987) *Critique of Judgment*, trans. W. S. Pluhar. Indianapolis: Hackett.

Kawin, Bruce (1978) *Mindscreen: Bergman, Godard, and the First-Person Film*. Princeton, NJ: Princeton University Press.

Kayser, William (1977) 'Qui raconte le roman?', in *Poétique du récit*. Paris: Seuil.

Krauss, Rosalind E. (1993) *The Optical Unconscious*. Cambridge, MA: MIT Press.

Kubrick, Stanley (2001) *Interviews*, ed. Gene D. Phillips. Jackson, MI: University of Mississippi Press.

Lakoff, George and Mark Johnson (1980) *Metaphors We Live By*. Chicago: University of Chicago Press.

____ (1999) *Philosophy in the Flesh: The Embodied Mind and its Challenge to Western Thought*. New York: Basic Books.

Langer, Susanne K. (1953) *Feeling and Form: A Theory of Art Developed from Philosophy in a New Key*. London: Routledge.

Le Clezio, J. M. G. (1971) 'The Extra-terrestrial', *L'Arc*, 45.

Levinson, Jerrold (1996) 'Film Music and Narrative Agency', in David Bordwell and Noël Carroll (eds) *Post-Theory: Reconstructing Film Studies*. Madison: University of Wisconsin Press.

L'Herbier, Marcel (1988a [1918]) 'Hermes and Silence', in Richard Abel (ed.) *French Film Theory and Criticism: A History/Anthology, 1907–1939, Volume I: 1907–1929*. Princeton, NJ: Princeton University Press.

Linden, George W. (1970) *Reflections on the Screen*. Belmont, CA: Wadsworth.

Lindsay, Vaschel (1970) *The Art of the Moving Picture*. New York: Liveright.

Lyotard, Jean-François (1991) 'Something Like: "Communication … without Communication"', in *The Inhuman: Reflections on Time*. Oxford: Polity Press.

MacCabe, Colin (1985) *Theoretical Essays: Film, Linguistics, Literature*. Manchester: Manchester University Press.

Manvell, Roger (1950) *Film*. Harmondsworth, Middlesex: Penguin.

Marks, John (1996) *Gilles Deleuze: Vitalism and Multiplicity*. London: Pluto Press.

Merleau-Ponty, Maurice (1964a) 'The Film and the New Psychology', in *Sense and Non-Sense*, trans. Hubert L. Dreyfus and Patricia Allen Dreyfus. Evanston, IL: Northwestern University Press.

____ (1964b) 'Eye and Mind', trans. Carleton Dallery, in *The Primacy of Perception*, ed. James Edie. Evanston, IL: Northwestern University Press.

____ (1968) *The Visible and the Invisible*, trans. Alphonso Lingus. Evanston, IL: Northwestern University Press.

____ (1981) *The Phenomenology of Perception*, trans. Colin Smith. London: Routledge and Kegan Paul.

Messaris, Paul (1994) *Visual 'Literacy': Image, Mind and Reality*. Boulder, CO: Westview Press.

Metz, Christian (1973) 'Current Problems of Film Theory', *Screen*, vol. 14, nos 1–2.

____ (1974) *Film Language: A Semiotics of the Cinema*, trans. Michael Taylor. New York: Oxford University Press.

Münsterberg, Hugo (1916) *The Photoplay: A Psychological Study*. New York: D. Appleton.

Nietzsche, Friedrich (1968) *The Will to Power*, trans. Walter Kaufman and R. J. Hollingdale, ed. Walter Kaufman. New York: Vintage Books.

____ (1972) *Beyond Good and Evil*, trans. R. J. Hollingdale. Harmondsworth, Middlesex: Penguin.

____ (1989) *On Rhetoric and Language*, ed. and trans. Sander L. Gilman, Carole Blair and David J. Parent. Oxford: Oxford University Press.

Nowell-Smith (1994) Geoffrey, 'Eisenstein on Montage', in Eisenstein, *Selected Works, Volume 2: Towards a Theory of Montage*, edited by Richard Taylor and Michael Glenny. London: British Film Institute.

Odin, Roger (1995) 'For a Semio-Pragmatics of Film', in Warren Buckland (ed.) *The Film Spectator: From Sign to Mind*. Amsterdam: Amsterdam University Press.

Perkins, V. F. (1972) *Film as Film*. Harmondsworth, Middlesex: Penguin.

Plantinga (1993) 'Film Theory and Aesthetics: Notes on a Schism', *Journal of Aesthetics and Art Criticism*, 51, 3.

Powrie, Phil (1991) 'Film-Form-Mind: The Hegelian Follies of Roger Gilbert-Lecomte', *Quarterly Review of Film and Video*, vol. 12, no. 4.

Prince, Stephen (1993) 'Contemporary Directions in Film Theory: An Introduction', *Post Script: Essays in Film and the Humanities*, vol. 13, no. 1.

Pudovkin, Vsevolod I. (1960) *Film Technique and Film Acting*. New York: Grove.

Ramain, Paul (1988 [1925]) 'The Influence of Dream on the Cinema', in Richard Abel (ed.) *French Film Theory and Criticism: A History/Anthology, 1907–1939, Volume I: 1907–1929*. Princeton, NJ: Princeton University Press.

Reisz, Karel and Gavin Millar (1968) *The Technique of Film Editing*. London: Focal Press.

Rimmon-Kenan, Shlomith (1983) *Narrative Fiction: Contemporary Poetics*. New York: Taylor and

Francis.

Robbe-Grillet, Alain (1965) *Snapshots, or Towards a New Novel*, trans. Barbara Wright. London: Calder and Boyars.

Rodowick, D. N. (1997) *Gilles Deleuze's Time-Machine*. Durham, NC: Duke University Press.

Romney, Jonathan (2000) 'An Audience with Uncle Jean-Luc', *Guardian* Friday Review, 11 February.

Rorty, Richard (1982) *Consequences of Pragmatism*. Brighton: Harvester Press.

____ (1984) 'Deconstruction and Circumvention', *Critical Inquiry*, 11, September.

____ (1991) *Essays on Heidegger and Others: Philosophical Papers, Volume 2*. Cambridge: Cambridge University Press.

____ (1992) 'The Pragmatist's Progress', in Stefan Collini (ed.) *Interpretation and Overinterpretation*. Cambridge: Cambridge University Press.

Rothman, William (1988) *The 'I' of the Camera*. Cambridge: Cambridge University Press.

Ruiz, Raúl (1995) *Poetics of Cinema 1: Miscellanies*, trans. Brian Holmes. Paris: Dis Voir.

Schefer, Jean Louis (1981) *L'Homme ordinaire du cinema*. Paris: Gallimard.

____ (1995) *The Enigmatic Body: Essays on the Arts*, ed. and trans. Paul Smith. Cambridge: Cambridge University Press.

Seton, Marie (1978) *Sergei M. Eisenstein: A Biography*. London: Dennis Dobson.

Sharits, Paul (1978) 'Cinema as Cognition', *Afterimage*, vol. 7, no. 7.

Shepard, Jim (1999) *Nosferatu in Love*. London: Faber and Faber.

Silverman, Kaja (1983) *The Subject of Semiotics*. Oxford: Oxford University Press.

Skoller, Donald (1972) 'Aspects of Cinematic Consciousness', *Film Comment*, 8, 3, September–October.

Small, Edward S. (1980) 'Cinevideo and Mental Images', *Journal of the University Film Association*, vol. 32, nos. 1–2.

Sobchack, Vivian (1990) 'The Active Eye: A Phenomenology of Cinematic Vision', *Quarterly Review of Film and Video*, vol. 12, no. 3.

____ (1992) *The Address of the Eye : A Phenomenology of Film Experience*. Princeton, NJ: Princeton University Press.

Sontag, Susan (1970) *Styles of Radical Will*. New York: Delta Books.

Spiegel, Alan (1976) *Fiction and the Camera Eye: Visual Consciousness in Film and the Modern Novel*. Charlottesville, VI: University Press of Virginia.

Stam, Robert (2000) *Film Theory: An Introduction*. Oxford: Blackwell.

Stam, Robert, Robert Burgoyne, and Sandy Flitterman-Lewis (1992), *New Vocabularies in Film Semiotics: Structuralism, Post-Structuralism – and Beyond*. New York: Routledge.

Stuber, Dorian (2001) 'Art Objects', *Film-Philosophy*, 5, 28, September 2001 <http://www.film-philosophy.com/vol5-2001/n28stuber>.

Tan, Ed S. (1996) *Emotion and the Structure of Narrative Film: Film as an Emotion Machine*. Mahwah, NJ: Lawrence Erlbaum.

Turvey, Malcolm (1997) 'Seeing Theory: On Perception and Emotional Response in Current Film Theory', in Richard Allen and Murray Smith (eds) *Film Theory and Philosophy*. Oxford: Clarendon Press.

Tyler, Parker (1972) *The Shadow of an Airplane Climbs the Empire State Building: A World Theory of Film*. Garden City, NY: Doubleday.

Vertov, Dziga (1967) 'Kinoks-Revolution', in Harry M. Geduld (ed.) *Film Makers on Film Making*. Harmondsworth, Middlesex: Penguin.

Viola, Bill (1995) *Reasons for Knocking at an Empty House, Writings 1973–1994*, ed. Robert Violette. London: Thames and Hudson.

Vuillermoz, Emile (1988a [1917]) 'Before the Screen: *Les Frères corses*', in Richard Abel (ed.) *French Film Theory and Criticism: A History/Anthology, 1907–1939, Volume I: 1907–1929*. Princeton, NJ: Princeton University Press.

_____ (1988b [1918a]) 'Before the Screen: *La Dixième Symphonie*', in Richard Abel (ed.) *French Film Theory and Criticism: A History/Anthology, 1907–1939, Volume I: 1907–1929*. Princeton, NJ: Princeton University Press.

_____ (1988c [1918b]) 'Before the Screen: Hermes and Silence', in Richard Abel (ed.) *French Film Theory and Criticism: A History/Anthology, 1907–1939, Volume I: 1907–1929*. Princeton, NJ: Princeton University Press.

_____ (1988d [1920]) 'Before the Screen: Aesthetic', in Richard Abel (ed.) *French Film Theory and Criticism: A History/Anthology, 1907–1939, Volume I: 1907–1929*. Princeton, NJ: Princeton University Press.

Walton, Kendal (1978) 'Fearing Fictions', *Journal of Philosophy*, vol. 75, no. 1.

Weigel, Sigrid (1996) *Body- and Image-Space: Re-Reading Walter Benjamin*. London: Routledge.

Wicclair, Mark R. (1978) 'Film Theory and Hugo Münsterberg's *The Film: A Psychological Study*', *Journal of Aesthetic Education*, vol. 12, no. 3.

Willemen, Paul (1994) *Looks and Frictions: Essays in Cultural Studies and Film Theory*. London: British Film Institute.

Wilson, George M. (1986) *Narration in Light: Studies in Cinematic Point of View*. Baltimore: Johns Hopkins University Press.

_____ (1997) '*Le Grand Imagier* Steps Out: The Primitive Basis of Film Narration', *Philosophical Topics*, vol. 25, no. 1.

Wittgenstein, Ludwig (1980) *Culture and Value*, trans. Peter Winch, ed. G. H. von Wright and H. Nyman. Chicago: University of Chicago Press.

Woolf, Virginia (1996 [1926]) 'On Cinema', in Michael O'Pray (ed.) *The British Avant-Garde Film, 1926–1995: An Anthology of Writings*. Luton: University of Luton Press/John Libbey Media.

Wurzer, Wilhelm S. (1990) *Filming and Judgment: Between Heidegger and Adorno*. Atlantic Highlands, NJ: Humanities Press International.

Yhcam, 'Cinematography' (1988 [1912]), in Richard Abel, *French Film Theory and Criticism: A History/Anthology, 1907–1939, Volume I: 1907–1929*. Princeton, NJ: Princeton University Press.

Zizek, Slavoj (2001) *The Fright of Real Tears: Krzysztof Kieslowski Between Theory and Post-Theory*. London: British Film Institute.

index